Read On . . . Fantasy Fiction

Recent Titles in
Libraries Unlimited Read On Series

Read On: Historial Fiction
Brad Hooper

Read On: Horror Fiction
June Michele Pulliam and Anthony J. Fonseca

Read On . . . Fantasy Fiction

Reading Lists for Every Taste

Neil Hollands

Read On Series
Barry Trott, Series Editor

A Member of the Greenwood Publishing Group

Westport, Connecticut • London

Library of Congress Cataloging-in-Publication Data

Hollands, Neil.

    Read on—fantasy fiction : reading lists for every taste / Neil Hollands.

        p. cm.—(Read on series)

    Includes index.

    ISBN-13: 978–1–59158–330–1 (alk. paper)

1. Fantasy fiction, American—Bibliography. 2. Fantasy fiction, English—Bibliography. 3. Fiction in libraries—United States. 4. Readers' advisory services—United States. 5. Public libraries—United States—Book lists. I. Title.

Z1231.F32H65   2007

[PS374.F27]

016.813'0876608—dc22   2007007841

British Library Cataloguing in Publication Data is available.

Library of Congress Catalog Card Number: 2007007841

ISBN: 978–1–59158–330–1

First published in 2007

Libraries Unlimited, 88 Post Road West, Westport, CT 06881

A Member of the Greenwood Publishing Group, Inc.

www.lu.com

Printed in the United States of America

The paper used in this book complies with the Permanent Paper Standard issued by the National Information Standards Organization (Z39.48–1984).

10 9 8 7 6 5 4 3 2 1

To the librarians at Williamsburg Regional Library and the members of the Williamsburg Science Fiction/Fantasy Book Group, whose support and friendship make this book and so much more possible.

Contents

Series Foreword

Welcome to Libraries Unlimited's Read On series of genre guides for readers' advisors and for readers. The Read On series introduces readers and those who work with them to new ways of looking at books, genres, and reading interests.

Over the past decade, readers' advisory services have become vital in public libraries. A quick glance at the schedule of any library conference at the state or national level will reveal a wealth of programs on various aspects of connecting readers to books they will enjoy. Working with unfamiliar genres or types of reading can be a challenge, particularly for those new to the field. Equally, readers may find it a bit overwhelming to look for books outside their favorite authors and preferred reading interests. The titles in the Read On series offer you a new way to approach reading:

- they introduce you to a broad sampling of the materials available in a given genre;
- they offer you new directions to explore in a genre—through appeal features and unconventional topics;
- they help readers' advisors better understand and navigate genres with which they are less familiar;
- and they provide reading lists that you can use to create quick displays, include on your library web sites and in the library newsletter, or to hand out to readers.

The lists in the Read On series are arranged in sections based on appeal characteristics—story, character, setting, and language (as described in Joyce Saricks' Reader's Advisory Services in the Public Library, 3d ed., ALA Editions, 2005), with a fifth section on mood. These appeal characteristics are the hidden elements of a book that attract readers. Remember that a book can have multiple appeal factors; and sometimes readers are drawn to a particular book for several factors, while other times for only one. In the Read On lists, titles are placed according to their primary appeal characteristics, and then put into a list that reflects common reading interests. So if you are working with a reader who loves fantasy that features quests for magical objects you will be able to find a list of titles whose main appeal centers around this search. Each list indicates a title that is an especially good starting place for readers, an exemplar of that appeal characteristic.

Story is perhaps the most basic appeal characteristic. It relates to the plot of the book—what are the elements of the tale? Is the emphasis more on the people or the situations? Is the story action focused or more interior? Is it funny? Scary?

Many readers are drawn to the books they love by the characters. The Character appeal reflects such aspects as whether there are lots of characters or only a single main character; are the characters easily recognizable types? Do the characters grow and change over the course of the story? What are the characters' occupations?

Setting covers a range of elements that might appeal to readers. What is the time period or geographic locale of the tale? How much does the author describe the surroundings of the story? Does the reader feel as though he or she is "there", when reading the book? Are there special features such as the monastic location of Ellis Peters' Brother Cadfael mysteries or the small town setting of Jan Karon's Mitford series?

Although not traditionally considered an appeal characteristic, mood is important to readers as well. It relates to how the author uses the tools of narrative—language, pacing, story, and character—to create a feeling for the work. Mood can be difficult to quantify because the reader brings his or her own feelings to the story as well. Mood really asks how does the book make the reader feel? Creepy? Refreshed? Joyful? Sad?

Finally, the language appeal brings together titles where the author's writing style draws the reader. This can be anything from a lyrical prose style with lots of flourishes to a spare use of language ala Hemingway. Humor, snappy dialog, word-play, recipes and other language elements all have the potential to attract readers.

Dig into these lists. Use them to find new titles and authors in a genre that you love, or as a guide to expand your knowledge of a new type of writing. Above all, read, enjoy, and remember—never apologize for your reading tastes!

Barry Trott
Series Editor

Introduction: Take Off Your Mask; It's OK to Like Fantasy

You know the stereotypes: Fantasy readers are men who live with their parents to save money to buy more comic books; they're overweight women with 10 cats they talk to more than any person; they're kids who wear costumes on every day *but* Halloween; they're Renaissance fair inquisitors who make everything they use by hand and evaluate every word for the heresy of historical inaccuracy. Charmingly, there is some truth to these stereotypes. We fantasy readers like to be anything but mundane. We like the road less traveled, even if it gets a little strange.

But the tired analysis that fantasy is a genre that people read to escape is too simplistic. Although escape is a legitimate motive for any reader, it's not very flattering. It implies that reading is a way to run from something we can't handle. This view of reading as escape leads many nonreaders to feel guilty when they pick up a book. Sadly, they feel they are wasting precious time on frivolous diversions. Reading, particularly in so-called escapist genres like fantasy and romance, is a guilty pleasure for many who indulge in it—something to hide from the neighbors.

The purpose of this book, of the whole <u>Read On</u> series, and of the readers' advisory movement afoot in libraries is to legitimize the fact that there are as many combinations of reasons to read as there are readers. Fantasy fiction is a big, complex body of work that contains treasures *and* trapdoors for readers of all descriptions. The book that appeals to you might appall me, but lean in close, let me whisper this in your ear: *neither of us need to be embarrassed.*

The trick is figuring out what appeals to you and then finding the books that scratch that itch. This book identifies more than one hundred of the itches from which fantasy readers suffer—the reasons why we might turn to fantasy—and prescribes lists of books that soothe those itches (or turns them into exciting tingles).

Fantasy Defined

For those attracted to this book, a definition of fantasy probably is not necessary. But in case you thought this book would help you explore your fetishes, a brief definition of fantasy as a literary concept is in order. Fantasy, in this context, refers to any work with elements that violate what we consider to be the rules of reality. This includes elements of magic or the supernatural. A more exact definition would be counterproductive: The intent of this book is to show you that fantasy is not a restrictive genre. It has broad scope and allows many approaches.

Fantasy can occur on this world or an imaginary world. Although often associated with medieval times, it can occur in any time period. It frequently includes elements of myth and folklore. Sword and sorcery and epic fantasy are so closely associated with the genre that works that include sword battles, court politics in medieval settings, or epic quests are considered fantasy even when little or no magic is present. Presence of traditional high-fantasy elements, however, is not an absolute requirement. As this book shows, contemporary fantasy is pushing traditional boundaries in every direction. Fantasy can feature any kind of character, can occur in any era, can be set against any physical backdrop, and can be written in any literary style.

A current trend is to blend fantasy with other genres, particularly three close neighbors: science fiction, historical fiction, and horror. Sometimes it is difficult to tell these genres apart. Fantasy varies from science fiction in that it deals more with magic than technology. Although often historical, it doesn't insist on plausible realism as historical fiction does and includes elements of magic. It differs in degree from horror fiction by focusing less on evil than on those battling against evil, and by emphasizing magic that is more secular than religious in nature.

A Brief History of Fantasy Fiction

Myth and legend were among the first topics approached when written language began. Our best-known early fiction works—*Gilgamesh, Beowulf, The Iliad,* and *The Odyssey*—all feature fantastic elements. Fantasy has a deeper classical history than any other genre. Dante, Shakespeare, Milton, and Swift—to name just a few—wrote fantasy works. Giants of early American literature—Irving, Hawthorne, Poe, and Twain—also contributed to the fantasy canon.

In the modern era, fantastic elements appear in much of literary fiction. Fantasy infiltrates other genres as well. Most romance publishers now market at least one fantasy romance line. The publishing phenomenon of *The Da Vinci Code* owes much to the fantastic appeal of the Knights Templar and mystic religion. Fantasy remains a mainstay of the children's and young adult markets. It isn't difficult to make a case for the place of fantasy in mainstream fiction, past and present. Perhaps a more relevant question for this book is when and how the fantasy genre developed.

The Scot George MacDonald's books are some of the first written as fantasies still readable as such today. *Phantastes* was published in 1858. MacDonald convinced his protégé, Charles Dodgson (known to us as Lewis Carroll), to publish *Alice's Adventures in Wonderland*. William Morris's *The Well at the World's End* (1892) was one of the first imaginary world fantasies. H. Rider Haggard's adventures like *King Solomon's Mines* and *She* popularized the lost-civilization tale. Ireland's Lord Dunsany published stories in the early 1900s and prototypical novels like 1924's *The King of Elfland's Daughter*.

Americans helped create the genre as well. L. Frank Baum published *The Wonderful Wizard of Oz* in 1900. The series was a powerhouse of U.S. publishing long after Baum's death in 1919. Other important early U.S. fantasists are Edgar Rice Burroughs (*Tarzan the Ape Man,* 1912) and James Branch Cabell (*Jurgen, a Comedy of Justice*, 1919).

The fantasy genre might still not have coalesced without pulp magazines. *Weird Tales,* the most influential, appeared in 1923. Often cited as founders of horror and science fiction, pulp writers also were critical to fantasy's growth. H. P. Lovecraft's tales of the Cthulhu mythos are touchstones of dark fantasy. Robert E. Howard is best known for the Conan stories of the 1930s. Fritz Leiber coined the term *sword and sorcery* and defined it with Fafhrd and the Gray Mouser stories that began in 1939. L. Sprague de Camp pioneered time travel and light fantasy with works like *Lest Darkness Fall* and *The Incomplete Enchanter*, both published in 1941.

A group of Oxford dons who called themselves the Inklings brought high fantasy to prominence. In particular, J.R.R. Tolkien and C. S. Lewis should be familiar to every reader. Both were first associated with children's books: Tolkien's *The Hobbit* (1937) and Lewis's The Chronicles of Narnia (1950–1956) made fantasy more important than ever as a genre for youth. Susan Cooper's The Dark Is Rising sequence and Lloyd Alexander's Chronicles of Prydain would appear in 1965. Ursula K. Le Guin's Earthsea books began in 1968. Fantasy has never faltered as a staple of young people's literature, with writers like Brian Jacques, Robin McKinley, Diana Wynne Jones, Philip Pullman, and Garth Nix leading the way.

The popularity of Tolkien's *Hobbit* led his publisher to request more. We know the results as his masterpiece, *The Lord of the Rings* (1954–1955). This work defined high fantasy and establish many of the tropes of the genre. Trilogies, elves, dwarves, double-edged magic, natural settings, epic quests, simple folk who make good, and struggles against absolute evil: Tolkien didn't originate them, but he forged them into the backbone of fantasy.

The 1965 U.S. edition of *The Lord of the Rings* pushed fantasy to the forefront of speculative fiction. Other fantasy writers who became known in the late 1960s and early 1970s include Andre Norton, Peter S. Beagle, Michael Moorcock, Katherine Kurtz, and Roger Zelazny. Tolkien's success led Ballantine's tremendous run as a fantasy publisher in the 1960s and 1970s. Other imprints like DAW and Ace appeared in the same era, with Del Rey following in 1977 and Tor arriving in 1980.

With so many publishers, fantasy was ready to hit the mass markets. Gary Gygax's role-playing game Dungeons & Dragons became a cultural phenomenon. By 1977, the time was ripe for a wave of fantasy best sellers. Three key series launched that year: Terry Brooks's Shannara, Stephen R. Donaldson's Thomas Covenant, and Piers Anthony's Xanth. These were followed in the 1980s by perennial best sellers like Marion Zimmer Bradley, David Eddings, Raymond Feist, Margaret Weis and Tracy Hickman, Guy Gavriel Kay, and R. A. Salvatore. Robert Jordan's Wheel of Time series was the epic fantasy publishing phenomenon of the 1990s.

Although epic fantasy remains central to the genre, new trends have emerged. Patricia A. McKillip reinvigorated the tradition of more lyrical, fablelike fantasy. Terry Pratchett's Discworld novels have been making us smirk knowingly since 1983. Charles de Lint led the charge to urban fantasy. Mercedes Lackey cast attention on outsider characters such as abuse victims and homosexuals. Harry Turtledove has made a long exploration of alternate history.

Two recent events pushed fantasy to even greater heights. J. K. Rowling's Harry Potter series began in 1997 and set all kinds of sales records, fostering a legion of fans whose wildness for Harry will boost the genre for years to come. Peter Jackson's Lord of the Rings films were of such high quality and popularity that they have sparked a wave of fantasy filmmaking.

Fantasy is more popular and influential today than ever. Writers like Robin Hobb, Lois McMaster Bujold, and George R. R. Martin are producing some of the best mainstream fantasy yet. Avant-garde writers such as Tim Powers, Jonathan Carroll, and China Miéville expand the genre. Fantasy is alive and very well. You (you lucky devil) get to use this book to explore it.

Insert Finger, Turn Pages: How to Use this Book

There are as many ways to use this book as there are ways to assemble a meal at a Las Vegas buffet (and as much sauciness and mystery meat contained within as well). You can read it in order, sample here and there, or pile your whole reading plate with the stuff in one container. Still, some general guidelines might help.

First and foremost, this book is neither exhaustive nor purely objective. Other thematic lists could have been included. More books could be highlighted in any given list. Taken as a whole, however, the book will give you a good overview of what the genre has to offer. Taken in parts, each list is an opinion-ated sampler, full of wit (or at least half-wit; you decide). Talking with fantasy fans over the years, I've learned we're an opinionated, often contrary bunch. If you disagree in part with the choice of books that follows, you're definitely one of the gang.

Unless otherwise noted, lists are sorted alphabetically by author. Citations contain the author, title, and, when applicable, the series title of each book. The original publication date of the material is listed. Publisher, International Standard Book Number (ISBN), and page count are for a current, in-print edition. In the rare circumstance in which an out-of-print book is listed, that is noted in the citation.

The loyal purchasing of fantasy readers is rewarded with books that stay in print for many years or are brought back into print by popular demand. Paperbacks, in particular, have a long shelf life, so paperback editions are listed in most cases (noting with the abbreviation *hbk.* when a hardcover is listed instead). If you prefer hardbacks, check your favorite purchasing source to find if one is still available, particularly for recent publications.

For the sake of space, annotations do not include a lengthy plot summary for most books. Instead, they focus on explaining why the book is included in the particular list. Annotations do provide the book's place in a series sequence when that sequence matters. Although later books in series are annotated when they fit a list best, reading series in order is recommended unless the annotation mentions otherwise. The series referenced in this book are listed in the index. The Web site *Fantastic Fiction* (http://www.fantasticfiction.co.uk) is a good source for series sequence: It's accurate and up-to-date in its coverage of novels in print.

Symbols Used in Annotations

⇨   Start Here: This book makes a fine entry point to the appeal factors covered by its particular list.

YA   This book is typically marketed to young adults (although the YA books selected for this volume should appeal to adult fantasy readers as well).

AW   This book won one of the five major awards for fantasy writing: a Nebula, Hugo, World Fantasy, Mythopoeic, or Locus Award.

Chapter One

Story

Fantasy readers have an ambiguous relationship with recurring themes. Some label them clichés: once-fertile ground reworked so many times that only a dust bowl remains. Those who espouse this view are quick to point out that a hallmark of fantasy is great imagination. Overdone themes become mundane and cease to spark the imagination.

More generous souls upgrade such patterns to "archetype", arguing that we revisit themes again and again because they matter to us in some deep and fundamental way. Quoting Carl Jung and Joseph Campbell, those of this view cite common threads running throughout mythology. Proponents of recurring themes also view them as the literary equivalent to comfort food, valuing the dependable joy of the tastiest genre conventions.

No matter which side of this debate you lean toward, this chapter can be helpful. If you hate clichés, jump to the more unusual or unfamiliar themes. If, however, you have favorite fantasy themes, use the lists to find more books that mine them for fresh gold.

Down the Rabbit Hole: The Way from Here to Fantasyland

As a youngster, I caught flak for trying to form a society of NBs: Narnian Believers. Now that I'm older and wiser, I might schedule new meetings. You are not a fantasy reader if you don't occasionally dream of finding a way into a magical realm. In creating a convincing portal from here to there—whether it be

Alice's rabbit hole, Dorothy's cyclone-borne house, or Lucy's wardrobe—the writer allows us to believe again in the possibility of magic.

Barker, Clive
⇨ *Weaveworld.* 1987. Pocket Books, ISBN: 0743417356, 672p.

Barker is best known as a horror writer, but many of his best efforts are fantasy novels (albeit dark fantasy). This imaginative entry is about the Fugue: a magical world woven into a carpet. When its protector dies, her ravenous sister Immacolata and the salesman Shadwell close in. Young Cal and Suzanna must defend the carpet from their greed.

De Lint, Charles
Moonheart. 1984. Orb, ISBN: 0312890044, 496p.

De Lint's world next door doesn't require a magic portal to visit, just expanded awareness: the ability to see what is always there. Humans in modern Ottawa discover a magical world overlapping their own that follows Celtic and Native American folklore. De Lint's breakout book is a good entry point to one of fantasy's best-loved authors.

Jones, Diana Wynne
Dark Lord of Derkholm. 1998. HarperTrophy, ISBN: 0064473368, 528p. **YA**, **AW**.

What if there was not only a magical world next door, but you also could visit it on a package tour? That's the premise of this funny book, in which one unlucky local must play Dark Lord and tour guide while others stage goofy magical charades for the tourists. As in many of her best books, Jones participates in genre traditions while also spoofing them.

Stasheff, Christopher
Her Majesty's Wizard. **Wizard in Rhyme.** 1986. Del Rey, ISBN: 0345274563, 352p.

As the beginning of a long-running series, this nicely executed formula fantasy makes good use of the old ploy of reading an ancient book or scroll to gain entry to another world. When career student Matt arrives in the alternate world, he discovers his rhymes work as spells. This reads like a traditional morality play reshaped as light fantasy.

Stross, Charles
The Family Trade. **The Merchant Princes.** 2004. Tor, ISBN: 0765348217, 320p.

Another way between worlds is via contact with magical objects. Staring at the pattern on a locket sends thoroughly modern Miriam to a medieval world where powerful families battle for control through pretechnical organized crime. Add touches of sarcasm and romance, and you get a popcorn-light new series with a jumpy, eccentric style.

Williams, Tad
The War of the Flowers. 2003. DAW, ISBN: 075640181X, 832p.

A bottom-dwelling rock musician is pulled into a dark urban fairyland by a foulmouthed faerie at the start of Williams's one-volume satire. The "flowers" of the title are rival fantasy gangs that represent a variety of belief systems, allowing the author to satirize a variety of current events in a fantasy setting.

Windling, Terri, and Sherman, Delia, eds.
The Essential Bordertown. 1998. Tor, ISBN: 0312867034, 384p.

This shared-world story collection finds several authors exploring what would happen on the streets of a border zone between the land of humans and faerie inhabited by criminals and teen runaways from both sides of the tracks. Emma Bull and Will Shetterly write novels in the same milieu.

Never Mind the Acne; I'm Here to Save the World: Coming-of-Age Stories

Fantasy is youth-obsessed. Farm boys with magical gifts and tomboy queens-to-be can be attributed to authors trying to please a core audience of young readers. And youth is the time for craving adventure and seeking glory. Young protagonists fit the tradition of untested, unexpected heroes. Their journey to maturity creates a nice story arc and allows us to root for an underdog (and against overconfident villains). For readers like me who find themselves twice the age of many lead characters, I have two recommendations: learn to relate to secondary characters and be grateful that your reading keeps you young! Here are 10 of the best coming-of-age fantasies.

Benjamin, Curt
The Prince of Dreams. <u>Seven Brothers</u>. 2002. DAW, ISBN: 0756401143, 512p.

In the Asian-flavored series opener, *Prince of Shadow,* Llesho's parents are killed and his six brothers scattered into slavery. Training as a kind of samurai, he begins a quest to find his brothers and reclaim his kingdom. This book finds a maturing Llesho coming to grips with the duplicitous world and the dream magic he must master to fulfill his destiny.

Feist, Raymond E.
Magician: Master. <u>The Riftwar Saga</u>. 1982. Bantam Spectra, ISBN: 0553564935, 544p.

Pug, Thomas, and company continue the maturation begun in *Magician: Apprentice.* In this book, the lead characters find adult roles, with Pug progressing from slave to master magician on the strange insectoid world of the

Tsurani Empire and Thomas donning armor that transforms him into a powerful warrior but begins to sap his free will.

Gardner, Sally
I, Coriander. 2005. Dial, ISBN: 0803730993, 288p. (hbk.) YA.
    Both daughter of a London merchant and princess from the land of fairy, Coriander travels both worlds as she tries to decide where she fits. An engaging lead and detailed English Revolution background make this historical fantasy successful.

Le Guin, Ursula K.
⇨ *The Wizard of Earthsea.* **Earthsea.** 1968. Bantam Spectra, ISBN: 0553383043, 183p. YA.
    In *Wizard,* Sparrowhawk leaves his homeland to find his magical potential but must first learn his limits. Le Guin's terse, mythic style highlights the universality of her story. There's nothing cute or light about this tale that appeals to serious, contemplative readers.

Le Guin, Ursula K.
The Tombs of Atuan. **Earthsea.** 1971. Simon Pulse, ISBN: 0689845367, 192p. YA.
    A counterpart for females is this follow-up to *Wizard of Earthsea,* featuring a young priestess who must decide whether to follow her instincts or support her religious order when she encounters Sparrowhawk (now called Ged) in the tombs she guards.

McKinley, Robin
The Blue Sword. **Damar.** 1982. Ace, ISBN: 0441068804, 248p. YA.
    Recently orphaned Harry Crewe feels isolated in her foreign outpost home (think of a Brit in the early twentieth-century Middle East). She catches the eye of the King of the Hillfolk who takes her hostage. Among his people she finds her place, becoming a warrior leader. As she comes to identify with her new people, she also finds unexpected romance.

Modesitt, L. E.
The Magic of Recluce. **Recluce.** 1991. Tor, ISBN: 0812505182, 512p.
    Lerris is a skeptic in a world where Order is the basis of a magic that fights to defeat Chaos. In this classic coming-of-age tale, a bored, rebellious youngster lacks maturity yet also has qualities critical to the survival of his world. Your reaction to this first book in this series will be a good indication of whether you will become a fan.

Nix, Garth
Sabriel. **The Abhorsen Trilogy.** 1995. Eos, ISBN: 0060575816, 320p. YA.
    Pulled from school by a desperate message from her necromancer father, Sabriel finds responsibility beyond her years in a land beyond her understanding.

She acquires allies (some willing, some not) in her battle with the dead and her search for her father. Great characters and a vivid mix of magic with early technology make a sparkling series start.

Rowling, J. K.
Harry Potter and the Half-Blood Prince. **Harry Potter series.** 2005. Scholastic, ISBN: 0439785960, 672p. YA.

In early books, Harry and friends are more concerned with magical treats, Quidditch, and classes than the large events in which they are fated to participate. Growing rapidly, their increasing sophistication is matched by deepening seriousness in the books. By this sixth book, they are fully on the path to adult destinies, and the stakes are high indeed.

Stevermer, Caroline
A College of Magics. 1994. Starscape, ISBN: 0765342456, 480p.

Edwardian comedy of manners meets coming of age in the tale of a duchess sent to a magical boarding school by a scheming uncle. Faris acquires an archenemy, and the two get in trouble for dueling with wild magic. The story culminates in a trip to the European continent where Faris and friends become embroiled in romance and political plots.

Magic 101: Memorable Systems of Magic

Magic without defined boundaries, without challenges and costs for its practitioners, makes for bad fantasy. It creates an arbitrary world where any random *deus ex machina* can decide the result in the final act. Original, deeply developed magical systems are hard to come by. Many books suffer from magic that is too familiar, reeks of phoniness, and never seems plausible to the reader. These books overcome this sizable challenge to create memorable systems of magic.

Duncan, Dave
The Gilded Chain. **The King's Blades.** 1998. Eos, ISBN: 0380791269, 432p.

Duncan's knights are magically bound to the king or other leaders. After binding, they are unable to harm their masters, defending them unceasingly until death or release. A knight faces a dilemma when bound to someone of poor qualities or if other interests vie for hisloyalty. This first book follows Durendal, one of the greatest of the Blades.

Farland, David
⇨*Brotherhood of the Wolf.* **The Runelords.** 1999. Tor, ISBN: 0812570693, 672p.

In Farland's series, attributes such as strength, memory, and vision can be endowed on wealthy heroes. Loss of the attributes cripples those who endow them, and the process is permanent, until the recipient dies (when the endowment returns to its source) or the donor dies (and the endowment is lost). This second book, in which former enemies must join forces, is as engaging as the first, *The Runelords*.

Lackey, Mercedes, and Mallory, James
The Outstretched Shadow. <u>The Obsidian Trilogy</u>. 2003. Tor, ISBN: 0765341417, 736p.

When Kellen tries forbidden Wild Magic and is caught, he must escape the Council of Mages headed by his father. Thus begins an adventure made notable by three competing systems of magic: strictly regimented High Magic, an earth-based Wild Magic that requires practitioners to bargain for their powers, and the evil Endarkened Magic.

Marks, Laurie J.
Fire Logic. <u>Elemental Logic</u>. 2002. Tor, ISBN: 081256653X, 384p.

Shaftal's elementals practice four kinds of magic: air, fire, water, and earth. Marks doesn't spoon-feed readers; it takes work to identify the skills and personality traits that accompany each of the four magics. If you can decipher the unusual gender relationships, complex politics, and cryptic magic, you will be rewarded with eventful, character-driven fantasy.

McGarry, Terry
Illumination. <u>Eiden Myr trilogy</u>. 2001. Tor, ISBN: 0812540034, 640p.

Magic in Eiden Myr requires teams, whose words, signing, and illuminating build a spell. When Liath's mage talent fails, she petitions the Ennead, a ruling caste of magicians, for help. They require her to draw a mage back into the fold, but when she finds him, he tells her things that turn her world upside down. This novel about threes begins a trilogy.

Modesitt, L. E.
The Death of Chaos. <u>Recluce</u>. 1995. Tor, ISBN: 0812548248, 640p.

Modesitt's exploration of the balance of order and chaos in magic is the best thing about his <u>Recluce</u> series. Strictly governed order rules Recluce and its magic. This fifth book returns to Lerris, the original protagonist, and creates one of the best books of the long-running series.

Rowling, J. K.
Harry Potter and the Sorcerer's Stone. <u>Harry Potter series</u>. 1997. Arthur A. Levine, ISBN: 043936213X, 400p. **YA**.

Rowling makes this list because she catalogs different magics so well. Following the Hogwarts crew through their classes—Defense against the Dark Arts, Potions, Care of Magical Creatures, Divination, Herbology, Transfiguration, and more—is a vivid education for readers in the many aspects of fantasy magic.

Sanderson, Brandon
Mistborn: The Final Empire. **Mistborn.** Tor, ISBN: 076531178X, 544p. (hbk.)
> Following his successful stand-alone, *Elantris,* Sanderson begins a new quartet. His inventive allomancy involves burning combinations of metals internally. This new breed of magic gives different, yet well-defined powers to each member of a team of characters. Add a creepy, burned-out world, and you have a fine series start.

Watt-Evans, Lawrence
The Wizard Lord. **Annals of the Chosen.** 2006. Tor, ISBN: 0765349019, 368p.
> Watt-Evans explores how magic interacts with a rational world. His latest book depicts elaborate checks and balances in a world where a Wizard Lord monitors wizards but in turn can be subject to the Chosen, eight heroes who can work collectively to control a rogue Lord. As this series open, they are reluctantly required to do exactly that.

Dizzy Spells: When Magic Goes Awry

There's no such thing as a free lunch, and if magic's involved, your lunch just might eat you. One of fantasy's great themes is the trickster nature of magic. If fantasy has one great lesson to teach, it is that great responsibility accompanies power. If you grab for the gold ring, it might grab back! Here are a few fine examples of magic gone awry.

Barker, Clive
Imajica. 1991. Harper, ISBN: 0060937262, 896p.
> In a universe of five dominions, Earth alone is not reconciled (aware of the others). The last attempt to reconcile Earth loosed demons. Into this setting come a sensual man, the woman he loves, and a strange assassin. The man and assassin circle each other with dark intent, until recognizing each other for what they are, they turn to a greater goal. Barker's sprawling dark fantasy is vivid, violent, sexually graphic, and otherworldly.

Britain, Kristen
First Rider's Call. **The Green Rider.** 2003. DAW, ISBN: 0756401933, 608p.
> Green Riders are a sort of magical Pony Express, but magic in their land has become erratic due to an influx of power through the breached wall that keeps out Blackveil Forest. The hauntings of the ghost of the first Rider reveal a key to the battle with ancient evil to heroine Kerigan. This book follows the series opening, *The Green Rider.*

Cook, Dawn
Forgotten Truth. **The Truth series.** 2003. Ace, ISBN: 0441011179, 384p.
> In the series, magicians channel beastly powers. In this third entry (which can be read independently from the first two), heroine Alissa has two problems.

First, a magical miscalculation has sent her back 400 years in time. Second, the beast of her power begins to emerge of its own will, threatening to take her over entirely.

Hale, Shannon
Enna Burning. <u>Bayern</u>. 2004. Bloomsbury, ISBN: 1582348898, 317p. `YA`.

When soccer hooligans set a new age singer on fire . . . oh wait, that's *Enya Burning.* In *Enna Burning,* a magical power to start fires has a dark side, as the wielder of the magic becomes increasingly possessed with an urge for arson. Enna sets off to solve her problem, even as her fire lust threatens to overwhelm her. A follow-up to *The Goose Girl.*

McKillip, Patricia A.
The Book of Atrix Wolfe. 1995. Ace, ISBN: 0441003613, 247p. (out of print.)

Stories of magic gone awry often demonstrate the harms of overreaching one's powers. That's the basis of one of McKillip's best, about a magician who goes into hiding after his attempt to stop an invasion created a terrible hunter who obliterates both armies. Here, a prince calls Atrix Wolfe from hiding to remedy his misdeed.

Pratchett, Terry
The Color of Magic. <u>Discworld</u>. 1983. HarperTorch, ISBN: 0061020710, 240p.
The Light Fantastic. <u>Discworld</u>. 1986. HarperTorch, ISBN: 0061020702, 272p.

It's rare when magic *doesn't* go wrong in <u>Discworld</u>. It definitely causes havoc in these openers of the long-running series. Though less cohesive than later titles, the satirical jokes in these books work, and characters and places are introduced that recur later. Both books feature the bumbling wizard Rince-wind blundering about with a cheerful but clueless tourist named Twoflower and some very persistent animated luggage.

Watt-Evans, Lawrence
⇨ *Night of Madness.* <u>Ethshar</u>. 2000. Tor, ISBN: 0812577949, 384p.

<u>Ethshar</u> books feature likable characters and swift-moving plots and don't need to be read in order. Magical snafus are a frequent plot device. This title is a good example: A night of mayhem has heavy consequences for a country run by carefully controlled magical rules. Try *The Misenchanted Sword* or *With a Single Spell* for similar fun.

Domestic Disputes: Fantasy's Fickle Family Values

Ah, the idyllic joy of fantasy family life! Father's away for the day (arranging your sale to the demon cult), but mother's here with a tall glass of something sweet (to hide the taste of the poison). Brother invites you to go hunting (accidents can happen on a hunt), and the little ones want you to play prisoner while they pretend to be keepers of the dungeon. It's a typical day of fantasy home life, in which no one knows their true parents, siblings nurse grudges and experiment with dark arts, and relatives count the corpses needed to clear their path to the throne.

Fallon, Jennifer
Medalon. <u>The Hythrun Chronicles</u>. 2000. Tor, ISBN: 0765348667, 512p.

    The Sisters of the Blade have systematically gained control of politics in Medalon by eradicating belief in magic and pagan gods. In this series opener, R'Shiel and her half brother Tarja begin to piece together the truth. They decide they must oppose their mother, the cold, domineering, and intolerant leader of the Sisterhood.

Farrell, S. L.
Mage of Clouds. <u>Cloudmages</u>. 2004. DAW, ISBN: 0756402557, 672p.

    Villainous Doyle promises to do no harm to his half sister Jenna in the first book of Ferrell's Celtic trilogy. But that won't stop him from going after niece Meriel if she stands between him and the powers of the magical Lamh Shabhala stone. Meanwhile, Meriel wants nothing of the family power, preferring to pursue the path of a healer.

King, Stephen
The Eyes of the Dragon. 1986. Signet, ISBN: 0451166582, 384p.

    The evil magician Flagg secretly murders old King Roland's young wife, Sasha. Now Flagg wants to move malleable Prince Thomas ahead of brother Peter in succession to the throne. King's version of fantasy is straightforward but fun and includes characters you may recognize from some of his better-known horror and dark fantasy works.

Martin, George R. R.
⇨ *A Storm of Swords*. <u>A Song of Ice and Fire</u>. 2003. Bantam Spectra, ISBN: 055357342X, 1216p. AW.

    The Lannisters have to be the most complex set of villains ever put on paper. Sometimes sympathetic, sometimes truly appalling, they are always scheming five steps ahead. In this third book of the series, patriarch Tywin, his incestuous, treacherous golden children Jaime and Cersei, dwarf little brother Tyrion, and hideously spoiled grandson King Joffrey turn on each other, and the results are spectacular.

Williams, Tad
The Dragonbone Chair. <u>Memory, Sorrow, and Thorn</u>. 1988. DAW, ISBN: 0886773849, 800p.

    The backstory of Williams's series is a classic clash between brothers. When King John dies, son Elias takes the throne, but Elias is the pawn of a black magician. When he moves to eliminate the threat of younger brother Josua, a clash for the realm commences. A simple kitchen boy named Simon will be the pivot upon which the balance turns.

Wurts, Janny
Warhost of Vastmark. <u>Wars of Light and Shadow</u>. 1995. Eos, ISBN: 0061056677, 512p.
    The curse-created enmity between two powerful brothers reaches a climax in this follow-up to *The Curse of the Mistwraith* and *The Ships of Merior.* Arithon can control the compulsion toward hatred somewhat and so chooses to live on the run, but brother Lysaer has him cornered, and a ruinous confrontation seems unavoidable.

End-Djinn Trouble:
When Magic Meets Technology

The clash of magic and technology is a common theme in fantasy, because it is evocative of so many essential conflicts: the past versus the future, humanity versus machine, belief versus proof, art versus science, and the fading of magic from the world. If you, too, yearn for a little more magic and a little less logic in your life, try these books.

Anthony, Piers
Split Infinity. <u>Apprentice Adept</u>. 1980. Del Rey, ISBN: 0345354915, 368p.
    This series opener follows Stile, a serf from technological Proton, where he is a master of the Games, a competitive entertainment that tests all kinds of skills. His facility makes him the target of assassins, and in trying to escape he crosses to the alternate reality of Phaze, which is dominated by magic. This series is light fun, particularly the first three books.

Coe, David B.
Eagle-Sage. <u>Lon-Tobyn Chronicles</u>. 2000. Tor, ISBN: 0812566866, 640p.
    The sylvan Tobyn-Ser is a pastoral paradise led by magicians who bond with birds. Across the border, magicless Lon-Ser rapidly develops industry and technology. The resulting conflict is the subject of Coe's series, which concludes with this volume.

Freer, Dave
A Mankind Witch. <u>Heirs of Alexandria</u>. 2005. Baen, ISBN: 1416521151, 400p.
    An inventive corsair, skeptical of all things unscientific, is captured and enslaved by a Norse society full of myth and magical creatures. Although part of the *Alexandria* series, this book is shorter, different in style and setting, and can be read independently.

Harrison, Harry
One King's Way. <u>The Hammer and the Cross</u>. 1994. Tor, ISBN: 0812536452, 480p.

A fledgling ruler, Shef Sigvarthsson, tests new inventions while combating two powerful brothers and the Holy Roman Empire. A veteran science fiction writer, Harrison also produced this rich alternate history in medieval Viking settings. This middle volume features a blend of Norse mythology and religion at the dawn of technology.

Kirstein, Rosemary
⇨ *The Steerswoman's Road.* <u>Steerswoman series</u>. 2003. Del Rey, ISBN: 0345461053, 668p.

Steerswomen keep and expand knowledge. When asked a question, they must answer truthfully; in turn, they compel others to answer questions honestly. When they meet wizards (who actually keep technology from the masses), they discover truths that put them in danger and their world in a spin. If you believe the truth will set you free, you'll find this series both thought-provoking and entertaining.

Norton, Andre
The Gates to Witch World. <u>Witch World</u>. 1963–1965. Orb, ISBN: 0765300516, 464p.

The science fantasies of Norton's <u>Witch World</u> often explore the theme of magic combating invasive technologies. This omnibus of the first three novels is a great entry into the long-running series.

Zicree, Marc Scott, and Hambly, Barbara
Magic Time. <u>Magic Time series</u>. 2001. Eos, ISBN: 0061059579, 448p.

When fantasy has a contemporary setting, technology often gives way to magic instead of the other way around. *Magic Time* is a good example, in which a secret government experiment reintroduces magic into the world, wiping out most technology, and imbuing some people with supernatural powers. This is the first of a fast-paced trilogy.

Fabulous: The Best Fantasy Derived from Familiar Fables

Although they are thought of primarily as entertainment (and warnings) for children, the great fables are more than scary fun. At their core are truths that can be used to teach young people societal norms for behavior, but these dark morals also make fables fantastic fodder for recycling, recasting, and reimagining. The resulting books will provoke thought in readers of all ages, not just children. Here are some highlights from this major subgenre of fantasy.

Card, Orson Scott
Enchantment. 1999. Del Rey, ISBN: 0345416880, 432p.

Little Ivan Smetski sees a woman asleep in a Russian wood, but a sense of foreboding sends him fleeing. His family immigrates to America, but years later he returns, unable to quell his curiosity about whether what he saw was real. Interweaving Sleeping Beauty and myths of the witch Baba Yaga, Card balances cultural content with romance and humor.

Jones, Diana Wynne
Fire and Hemlock. 1984. HarperTrophy, ISBN: 006447352X, 432p. `YA`.

The Celtic ballads *Thomas the Rhymer* and *Tam Lin* are a touchstone for fantasy writers. In this version, teen Polly tries to save Tom Lynn, a man who seems caught in the fringes of her memory. Jones moves the traditional tale to 1980s England in a book that is darker and subtler than her usual, confusing in spots, but ultimately captivating.

Kerr, Peg
The Wild Swans. 1999. Aspect, ISBN: 0446608475, 464p. (out of print).

In Hans Christian Andersen's tale, 11 brothers turn into swans each night and only their sister can save them. Kerr alternates between retelling this story in a seventeenth-century setting and a parallel story of a young gay man in the twentieth century. For another successful take on the Andersen story, try Juliet Marillier's *Daughter of the Forest.*

Lackey, Mercedes
The Fairy Godmother. **Five Hundred Kingdoms.** 2004. Luna, ISBN: 0373802455, 496p.

A cruel twist gives Elena Klovis a prince in diapers, so instead of finding perfect romance, she becomes a fairy godmother in training. But she's young for the work, and fate might bring love her way yet. Light fantasy for those after something sweet and airy. Harlequin launched their Luna romantic fantasy line with this retelling of *Cinderella.*

Lynn, Tracy
Snow. **Once upon a Time series.** 2003. Simon Pulse, ISBN: 1416905189, 224p. `YA`.

Send Snow White running to London's streets instead of the woods, have her find a gang of five animal-like people instead of seven dwarves, and you have *Snow.* This is a good example of <u>Once upon a Time</u>, a series written with young and youngish adults in mind.

McKiernan, Dennis
Once upon a Winter's Night. **Once upon a ... series.** 2001. Roc, ISBN: 0451458540, 432p.

With this book, McKiernan left his Tolkien-derivative <u>Mithgar</u> behind and began a series that retells fairy tales. Here, he moves *East of the Sun, West of the Moon*—a Norse tale about a polar bear that takes a young girl away to the land of Faery—to France and pumps it up with action and romance. Edith Pattou also retells this tale successfully in *East.*

McKinley, Robin
Beauty. 1978. Eos, ISBN: 0060753102, 336p. **YA**.
⇨ *Rose Daughter.* 1997. Ace, ISBN: 0441005837, 304p. **YA**.

McKinley's fans split over which of her two versions of "Beauty and the Beast" are better: *Beauty,* written for a younger audience, or the darker, more mystical *Rose Daughter,* published almost twenty years later and appropriate for older young adults. Books like these, *Spindle's End,* and *Deerskin* have made McKinley the queen of the retold tale.

Miéville, China
King Rat. 1998. Tor, ISBN: 0312890729, 320p.

Before his Bas-Lag novels made him a star, Miéville turned out this kinetic take on the Pied Piper of Hamelin, reset against a background of Cockney rhyming slang and the drum-and-bass jungle music scene in modern London. Another successful retelling of this fable is Adam and Keith McCune's *The Rats of Hamelin: A Piper's Tale.*

Napoli, Donna Jo
Zel. 1996. Puffin, ISBN: 0141301163, 240p. **YA**.

Napoli takes Rapunzel to medieval Switzerland and focuses on the dark, possessive side of love. She finds the emotional core of the fable in a book about relationships. Also recommended are the author's *Crazy Jack* (from "Jack and the Beanstalk"), *The Magic Circle* ("Hansel and Gretel"), *Beast* ("Beauty and the Beast"), and *Sirena.*

Pratchett, Terry
Witches Abroad. **Discworld, Witches series.** 1991. HarperTorch, ISBN: 0061020613, 384p.

Pratchett's witches travel to Genua to stop Emberella from going to the ball. A hearty dose of "Cinderella," dollops of "Little Red Riding Hood," "Sleeping Beauty," and the "Three Little Pigs," wickedly funny witches, and the dwarf lothario Casanunda are just a few of the wacky ingredients in one of Pratchett's funniest, weirdest books.

Holy Grail, Batman! Amazing Quests for Magical Objects

Frodo's ring? Bo-ring. Dorothy's slippers? Tacky. There are more remarkable gewgaws. Imagine a mall where scattered among thingamajigs and doohickeys are red-tag specials: great stuff with magical powers. Such goods motivate fantasy's supershoppers on a crazed spree to find *the* one-of-a-kind object in fantasy worlds as big as the Mall of America. In *Batman,* Jack Nicholson's Joker asks, "Where does he get those wonderful toys?" You'll have to go farther than the Bat Belt to find fantasy's best. Try these books.

Anthony, Piers
Swell Foop. <u>Xanth series</u>. 2001. Tor, ISBN: 0812574745, 384p.

> Six characters must find six magic rings. In turn, those will lead to the Foop, which can control a demon who can prevent Xanth from losing gravity. The quest road is paved with Anthony's usual puns and naughty-boy humor. Almost any <u>Xanth</u> novel fits this category, as Anthony frequently sends his characters questing for the goods.

Baird, Alison
The Stone of the Stars. <u>Dragon Throne</u>. 2004. Aspect, ISBN: 0446690988, 384p.

> A tyrant threatens the world of Mera, and only one prophesied to wield the Stone of Stars can stop him. Four people—a bookish girl, a priest whose faith is threatened by the possibility of the old magic, a runaway soldier/slave, and a young woman who may be the chosen one—begin a quest to find the Stone in this series starter.

Farrell, S. L.
Holder of Lightning. <u>Cloudmages trilogy</u>. 2003. DAW, ISBN: 0756401526, 624p.

> A herder in this Celtic-flavored series starter finds (drum roll, please): a rock! She can tell it's magical because . . . it feels good in her hand. Hang on, the rock is the Lamh Shabhala, a spell stone that controls all others. As it turns out, *it* has chosen Jenna. It holds the spirits of all who previously used it. Can Jenna put it to better use than they did?

Hemingway, Amanda
The Greenstone Grail. <u>Sangreal trilogy</u>. 2005. Del Rey, ISBN: 0345460790, 384p.
The Sword of Straw. <u>Sangreal trilogy</u>. 2005. Del Rey, ISBN: 0345460804, 336p.

> Nathan, an English boy who can dream himself into other worlds; his protective mother, Annie; and Bartlemy, an ancient albino, are the central characters in Hemingway's update of the Grail legend. The second book of the trilogy sends Nathan and company to the realm of a cursed king after more grail relics.

Jones, J. V.
The Barbed Coil. 1997. Warner, ISBN: 0446606235, 704p.

> When Tessa finds a ring, it pricks her finger and transports her to the world of King Izgard, an insane warmonger whose crown is a large version of the

ring. Both objects are ephemera: They fall in and out of time bearing power but also nasty side effects. Helped by a handsome rebel, Tessa must release Izgard's coil before he destroys everyone.

Rowling, J. K.
⇨ *Harry Potter and the Goblet of Fire.* **Harry Potter series.** 2000. Arthur A. Levine, ISBN: 0439139597, 734p. (hbk.) YA, AW.

The Harry Potter series brims with imaginative objects: the Sorting Hat; Quidditch brooms, bludgers, quaffles, and snitches; howlers; and the prank items devised by the Weasley twins. Many of the best appear in this fourth book, such as the Marauder's Map, which shows both the corridors of Hogwarts and the people moving through them, and the title Goblet, which magically selects participants for the Triwizard Tournament.

Stackpole, Michael A.
When Dragons Rage. **DragonCrown War.** 2002. Spectra, ISBN: 0553379208, 480p.
The Grand Crusade. **DragonCrown War.** 2002. Spectra, ISBN: 0553379216, 480p.

An evil empress and her minions search for pieces of the DragonCrown, which will allow her to commune with dragons and complete her world conquest. Racing against her are a young thief who is the subject of prophecy, a charismatic princess, and their motley crew of friends. These volumes finish a twist-filled trilogy that starts with *Fortress Draconis.*

Steiber, Ellen
A Rumor of Gems. 2005. Tor, ISBN: 0312858795, 464p. (hbk.)

Arcato, a weird and squalid port city, teems with gods, mythical creatures, and pathways into coexisting periods of time. Sentient gems with magical powers begin to appear around the town, and chaos ensues. Watch out for a jade dragon in particular.

There and Back Again: Fantasy in Which the Journey Is the Story

A popular bumper sticker among fantasy fans is Tolkien's quote, "Not All Who Wander Are Lost." Because we have day jobs, most of us wander vicariously through favorite characters. Adventures rarely come knocking like a gang of dwarves on a hobbit's round door, so fantasy requires road stories that send heroes to the action. The best writers make you feel the sun's warmth on your face, taste the ocean spray, smell the crackling campfire, or ache with saddle soreness, all while sitting in your favorite armchair. Here are some of fantasy's great road trips.

Britain, Kristen
The Green Rider. <u>The Green Rider trilogy</u>. 1998. DAW, ISBN: 0886778581, 480p.
    On the run from trouble at school, Karigan stumbles across a Green Rider (a cross-country messenger for the king) who has been ambushed and is dying. She agrees to carry the message herself, beginning a long and perilous journey. Although not original, this book gallops along quickly: a book about a journey that makes a good vacation read.

Dart-Thornton, Cecilia
The Ill-Made Mute. <u>Bitterbynde trilogy</u>. 2001. Aspect, ISBN: 0446610801, 576p.
    A scarred and mute amnesiac journeys on an air-sailing windship in search of an elusive past. Befriended by a trader turned pirate, the amnesiac travels a world full of creatures from Celtic folklore. Dart-Thornton brings a poetic style to this debut.

Erikson, Steven
Deadhouse Gates. <u>Malazan Book of the Fallen</u>. 2000. Tor, ISBN: 0765314290, 608p.
    Following an army and refugees retreating across a continent, this second book in the series can be read before the first, although elements from both merge in later volumes. Erikson is *not* for everybody. His style is gritty, grim, and cryptic. Readers who like complexity and aren't squeamish are enormous fans of this series.

Foster, Alan Dean
Carnivores of Light and Darkness. <u>Journeys of the Catechist</u>. 1998. Aspect, ISBN: 0446606979, 368p.
    A resourceful herdsman who can talk to animals takes a jaunty trip across his world in a quest to save a kidnapped woman. Along the way he attracts companions (a treasure-hunting swordsman and a majestic big cat) and foes (sentient tornadoes and sand dunes, a race of tiny warriors). Foster is not a complex writer, but he always tells a good story.

Johnson, Kij
Fudoki. 2003. Tor, ISBN: 0765303914, 320p.
    A cat whose home, family, and fudoki (collective clan history) have been destroyed by a fire in the imperial capital sets out on a wandering trek across twelfth-century Japan. Encountering a god of the roads, she is turned into a human warrior. Johnson's vivid, fluent style makes this mix of fantasy and historical novel sing.

Moers, Walter
The 13 1/2 Lives of Captain Bluebear. 2005. Overlook, ISBN: 1585678449, 704p. `YA`.
    An azure bear takes a path of picaresque adventure through multiple lives. Captain Bluebear is a notorious liar, but you'll devour his convincing yarns

about the challenges he overcomes in each of the titular lifetimes. This zany German children's story may be an even better read for adults with a love of sarcasm, parody, and irony.

Stackpole, Michael
The Dark Glory War. 2000. Bantam Spectra, ISBN: 0553578073, 416p.

In a prequel to his DragonCrown War, Stackpole sends three young men through a survival ordeal and then in pursuit of enemies in this better-than-average hack 'n' slash. Their journeys across the fictional landscape introduce the cultures and politics of Stackpole's fictional world while telling the back-story of series hero Tarrant Hawkins.

Tolkien, J.R.R.
⇨ *The Fellowship of the Ring.* **The Lord of the Rings.** 1954. Houghton Mifflin, ISBN: 0618574948, 506p.

When the hobbits finally hit the road, The Lord of the Rings takes flight. An aspect of the books that the films can't capture is Tolkien's sense of extended travel across the countryside. These are real journeys: you'll feel miles accumulate as you turn the pages.

Games of Thrones: Fantasy's Most Devious Royal Intrigues

Yet another reason to love fantasy: the complex political intrigues captured in its pages. More thrilling than thrillers, with the realism of a good historical novel, political fantasy captures the devious contest that underlies the pageantry of royal courts. Heroes of this arena rise and conquer through subtlety in snake pits where mere survival is a tall order. If you enjoy the chess game of scheming, backstabbing, and outmaneuvering, give these titles a try.

Coe, David B.
Rules of Ascension. **The Winds of the Forelands.** 2002. Tor, ISBN: 081258984X, 672p.

As Coe's series opens, Tavin, son of the new king, is jailed for murdering his girlfriend. His only hope rests in the Qirsi, a race of seers, magicians, and political advisors whose power is controversial because of a long-past attempt at revolution. Coe smartly interweaves murder mystery with political intrigue in this character-driven epic.

Duncan, Dave
Children of Chaos. 2006. Tor, ISBN: 0765353814, 432p.

When war-loving Werists attack Florengia, Duke Piero saves his city by giving his children up as hostages. The four are raised separately in Vigaelia.

Now the Duke is dying. One of the four must take his place as puppet leader, and the others must die. But when the children rediscover their siblings, they sense weakness in the overextended Werists, leading them to formulate a new plot.

Elliott, Kate
King's Dragon. Crown of Stars. 1997. DAW, ISBN: 0886777712, 640p.

Wendar faces two big problems: invading barbarians with huge dogs and a civil war waged between the king and his half sister. Two young narrators, Alain and Liath, are drawn into the struggle. Elliott's sprawling, seven-book series starts strongly here.

Fallon, Jennifer
⇨ *Wolfblade.* Wolfblade trilogy. 2004. Tor, ISBN: 0765348691, 640p.

Marla, the High Prince's sister, rises from whining pawn in a political marriage to power in her own right, even though women are not valued in her patriarchal society. Fallon showed facility for political intrigue in her first *Hythrun* trilogy. Now she starts a promising new trilogy set a generation earlier in the same world.

Feist, Raymond, and Wurts, Janny
Servant of the Empire. Riftwar: The Other Side. 1989. Bantam Spectra, ISBN: 0553292455, 704p.

Set (sympathetically) in the world of the opposing side in Feist's Riftwar, *Daughter of the Empire* surprised fans. The trilogy continues with this book, in which Mara contends with the progeny of her earlier political foe. What makes this series different is the Asia-like society in which heavy social stratification and complex protocols give the political intrigue and romance a different flavor than medieval fantasy.

Gilligan, ElizaBeth
Magic's Silken Snare. 2003. DAW, ISBN: 0756401275, 560p.

Luciana, a young Romani duchessa in an alternate Sicily, must find her murdered sister's body before it becomes a demon. Her sister's killing was part of a political plot, and Luciana's search involves her in a struggle against powerful and dangerous opponents.

Martin, George R. R.
A Game of Thrones. A Song of Ice and Fire. 1996. Bantam Spectra, ISBN: 0553573403, 864p. `AW`.

When northern Lord Eddard Stark is appointed as King's Hand, his family is drawn south to King's Landing, where they begin a series of epic clashes with the devious Lannisters. Martin sets the benchmark for royal intrigues with this book and those that follow.

Sanderson, Brandon
Elantris. 2005. Tor, ISBN: 0765350378, 608p.
  Political intrigue in one volume is a rarity, but newcomer Sanderson shows how it is done in this tale of a charismatic prince and princess separated just before their wedding by his "death." Each unaware of the other's proximity, Raoden and Sarene maneuver in two neighboring societies, building to a shared confrontation with powerful religious enemies.

Snyder, Maria V.
Poison Study. 2005. Luna, ISBN: 0373802579, 392p.
  Yelena is given the choice between a death sentence and testing the Ixian Commander's food for poison. General Brazell, whose son she was convicted of killing, still wants her dead. This entry in the new Luna line from Harlequin blends fantasy with romance.

Wander Lust: The Great Love Affairs and Romantic Pursuits of Fantasy

Something about a backdrop of great consequence makes a couple's battle to keep love alive even more romantic. Readers swoon to suffering, heroics, and perseverance. With fantasy, even men secretly satisfy amorous urges, provided that the cover doesn't embarrass them by broadcasting the book's romantic tendencies. Here are stellar examples of impassioned struggle in fantasy settings.

Bantock, Nick
⇨ *Griffin & Sabine*. 1991. Chronicle Books, ISBN: 0877017883, 48p. (hbk.)
  This unusual book reveals a budding romance through letters between the lovers. Sabine finds Griffin on the other side of the world because she shares his sight. Bantock's exotic art covers the book's cards and letters with symbolic, often jarring images that elevate the mystery of the story. Several sequels follow.

Beagle, Peter S.
The Innkeeper's Song. 1993. Roc, ISBN: 0451454146, 352p. (out of print) AW.
  Tikat views the drowning and resurrection of his love Lukassa before she disappears. Thus begins his quest to reunite with her, a quest involved in a wider story of two powerful women, two battling wizards, an innkeeper, and his beleaguered assistant. Examining what happens when love tries to cheat death, this exquisite book may be the best of Beagle's small, wonderful oeuvre; let's hope it finds reissue soon.

Bishop, Anne

Sebastian. 2006. Roc, ISBN: 0451460960, 464p.

Ephemera is broken into lands, each uniquely shaped by a Landscaper. Sebastian, an incubus in the land of a darkly erotic Landscaper, falls for a girl who calls to him from a pristine land. The exotic relationship holds double-edged danger for both, but worse is the threat from the Eater of the World, escaped from the land where he was sequestered.

Carey, Jacqueline

Kushiel's Avatar. **Kushiel trilogy.** 2003. Tor, ISBN: 0765347539, 768p.

Carey's series is full of emotion-charged relationships. Her masochistic courtesan Phèdre has aged gracefully but carries one regret: the sacrifice that left a friend forever isolated. With love and protector Joscelin, Phèdre tries to free Hyacinthe, but the quest sends them through a hell that threatens body, heart, and soul. A fine finish to a great trilogy.

Goldman, William

The Princess Bride. 1973. Ballantine, ISBN: 0345418263, 480p.

The enduring love of Buttercup and Wesley is the exemplary fantasy romance. Goldman isn't shy about this fact: He breaks into his story repeatedly to tell you how archetypal their love is. This witty, wonderful classic is a must read for lovers of fantasy, romance, adventure, or humor.

King, Stephen

Wizard & Glass. **The Dark Tower.** 1997. Plume, ISBN: 0452284724, 720p.

Trapped on a runaway train, hero Roland spends this middle novel of seven relating his history: the tragic tale of his doomed first love. Fans who navigate the perplexing first book and slow revelations of the next two are rewarded here with a clear look at Roland's motivations.

Marillier, Juliet

Son of the Shadows. **Sevenwaters trilogy.** 2001. Tor, ISBN: 0765343266, 608p.

Outlaws kidnap Liaden to heal their leader. She falls for him, which is trouble: He's an enemy to the man she expects to marry. After she returns to her family, events conspire to force a choice between them and her secret love. Add meddling from the Fair Folk and you have the makings of this follow-up to *Daughter of the Forest.*

Miles, Rosalind

Isolde, Queen of the Western Isle. **Tristan and Isolde trilogy.** 2002. Three Rivers, ISBN: 1400047862, 368p.

The author of the historical fantasy Guinevere trilogy returns to similar romantic ground with this version of Tristan and Isolde. The historical romance is imbued with modern spiritual and psychological philosophies—a style not for everybody but very satisfying to certain readers.

Zettel, Sarah
Usurper's Crown. <u>Isavalta.</u> 2002. Tor, ISBN: 0812565185, 544p.
> The empress of Isavalta exiles her mentor to Wisconsin for opposing her marriage. Her chosen husband usurps the throne and starts a war with a powerful neighbor. When mentor Avanasy returns to save Isavalta, his Wisconsin-born lover Ingrid follows to play a key role. This tragic romance blends exotic myths of Russia, China, and India.

Why Does This Baby Have a Tattoo? Prophecy and Fate in Fantasy

Birthmark bearers rejoice! If you've read enough fantasy, you know that any kid with a birthmark, tattoo, piercing, or funny-but-unexplained nickname is most likely the so-called chosen one. If not that, then at least a king or queen, foreordained to return at the time of need. Stories of fate and prophecy are appealing, especially if you like to indulge daydreams of great deeds for which you might be destined. I've got this funny triangle of moles on my chest. I wonder . . .

Eddings, David
⇨ *Guardians of the West.* <u>The Malloreon.</u> 1985. Del Rey, ISBN: 0345352661, 448p.
> Conflicting prophecies figure strongly in the 10 books of Eddings's first two series, which follow a common set of characters. *Guardians* opens the second series. When his child is stolen, King Garion and company begin combat with a new dark foe. All but the newest fantasy readers will find these books familiar, but they are fun and easy exemplars of the best fantasy traditions.

Gemmell, David
Lion of Macedon. 1990. Del Rey, ISBN: 0345485351, 528p.
> This turbulent historical fantasy follows a half-Spartan, half-Macedonian soldier of fortune connected by prophecy to the chaotic rise of a dark god. Parmenion, a warrior in the world of Philip of Macedon, Alexander the Great, and Aristotle, fulfills his fate by waging battle across the ancient Greek world and into Hades. Followed by *Dark Prince.*

Howard, Madeline
The Hidden Stars. <u>The Rune of Unmaking.</u> 2004. Eos, ISBN: 0060575875, 432p.
> Years ago, a wizard spirited away a baby princess. When evil Empress Ouriána, whom prophecy says the princess will overthrow, thinks she has finally located the girl in the far north, forces of good and evil race to aid or destroy the princess. This is Howard's debut.

Le Guin, Ursula K.
The Farthest Shore. <u>Earthsea.</u> 1972. Simon Pulse, ISBN: 0689845340, 272p. YA.
Le Guin's mythic style makes <u>Earthsea</u> read like ancient prophecy. Hundreds of years ago, the last king foretold that no one would succeed him until one appeared who had crossed the farthest shore. Aging Ged and a young prince take the journey into decay, hallucination, and death in an attempt to stop magic from draining out of the world.

McKiernan, Dennis
Silver Wolf, Black Falcon. <u>Mithgar.</u> 2000. Roc, ISBN: 0451458036, 560p.
The Tolkien-derived <u>Mithgar</u> series closes with this tale of not one but two babies, born under miraculous circumstances and destined to lead the sides of light and dark. Who will win, good or evil? OK, maybe you know the answer, but this is still epic fun.

Resnick, Laura
The White Dragon. <u>In Fire Forged.</u> 2003. Tor, ISBN: 0812555481, 672p.
Josarian is thought to be the Firebringer, whom prophecy says will lead his people to freedom. But in Resnick's spin on the theme, former allies treacherously leave him to be slain by an ice dragon. On their island world of Sileria, full of deities and magic, Josarian's second in command and a prophetess are left to pick up the pieces.

Stackpole, Michael A.
Fortress Draconis. <u>DragonCrown War Cycle.</u> 2001. Bantam Spectra, ISBN: 0553379194, 513p.
Legend foretells that Will, an orphaned thief, will defeat tyrannical empress Chytrine. Joined by a Vorquelf and a soldier who is the last surviving hero of the previous generation, the young hero begins his fight in this first military fantasy of Stackpole's <u>DragonCrown War Cycle</u>.

Yolen, Jane
Sister Light, Sister Dark. <u>Great Alta trilogy.</u> 1998. Tor, ISBN: 0765343576, 256p. YA.
Here's a welcome reissue: Yolen's trilogy begins with this story of a girl who is the Anna: a white-haired child orphaned three times who will change the world. Backed by a sect of religious women who train to call up their magical dark sisters, young Jenna is brought reluctantly toward her destiny in this successful feminist fantasy series.

"You Killed My Father, Prepare to Die!" The Fantasy of Revenge

The catchphrase of swordsman Inigo Montoya, often repeated in *The Princess Bride,* captures one of fantasy's great motivations. Given the unfairness we encounter in everyday life, it's no surprise that readers empathize strongly with the desire of fantasy heroes to right past wrongs. But leave balancing the scales of justice to the professionals. Before you indulge your "duel personality" and pull that sword from the scabbard, try these books instead.

Bujold, Lois McMaster
⇨ *The Curse of Chalion.* **Chalion.** 2001. HarperTorch, ISBN: 0380818604, 512p. AW.

    A jealous rival sold noble Cazaril into slavery. Barely alive, he returns to his homeland four years later, hoping for no more than a quiet life. Instead, the swell of events lands him back in the thick of politics, in danger from the same rivals. Through wisdom, honor, and self-sacrifice, Cazaril may find a way to turn the tables in this superb fantasy.

Card, Orson Scott
Hart's Hope. 1982. Orb, ISBN: 0765306786, 304p.

    Consider the many guises of revenge. Palicrovol deposes a tyrant by killing him in front of his daughter. He publicly rapes her, sarcastically dubbing her Beauty, then sends her into exile. Years later, Beauty, full of ugly vengeance, exacts it not only on Palicrovol but also on innocents. Most of the book concerns choices that Orem, Palicrovol's son, makes in pursuit of his own revenge.

David, Peter
Sir Apropos of Nothing. **Apropos of Nothing.** 2001. Pocket, ISBN: 0743412346, 672p.

    Deliberately vile and darkly comic, in David's novel a boy conceived through rape by a gang of knights grows up lame, bitter, and cynical about chivalry and heroes. So begins his quest for revenge and antiheroic rise to knighthood: a story of adventure, sarcasm, and bad puns. Despite his best intentions, Apropos can't seem to do the wrong thing.

Feist, Raymond E.
Talon of the Silver Hawk. **Conclave of Shadows.** 2002. Eos, ISBN: 0380803240, 400p.

    The Conclave trains a young boy, sole survivor of his mountain tribe's massacre, in a variety of skills. Ultimately, he passes as noble Talon to pursue revenge. Set in Midkemia like many Feist novels, this picks up where Serpent War ends, beginning a new trilogy.

Hearn, Lian
The Brilliance of the Moon. **Tales of the Otori.** 2004. Riverhead, ISBN: 1594480869, 368p.

    The first two novels in this medieval Japanese series left Takeo Otori with conflicting loyalties (to a religious group called the Hidden, the Otori clan, and the ninjalike Tribe) and a long list of revenge motives. His love, Kaede, has lists of enemies almost as long. *Brilliance* closes their saga while hinting at adventures for the next generation.

Marco, John
   The Grand Design. <u>Tyrants and Kings</u>. 2000. Spectra, ISBN: 0553580299, 800p.
      Richius Vantran is exiled to the country. His former ally, Count Biagio, has betrayed him to gain control of Nar's Black Renaissance. Richius wavers between pursuing revenge and keeping his family hidden. Meanwhile, the fanatical followers of the God of Light revolt, threatening all of Nar. This military fantasy follows *The Jackal of Nar.*

Watt-Evans, Lawrence
   Dragon Weather. <u>The Obsidian Chronicles</u>. 1999. Tor, ISBN: 0812589556, 560p.
      Dragons destroy Arlian's village and enslave him. He escapes to a brothel, but Lord Dragon captures that, too. As Arlian grows, he is torn between seeking justice and his fascination and identification with the dragons. This is *The Count of Monte Cristo* with big leathery lizards: With a swift pace and a great ending, it starts the series strongly.

It's Not Nice to Fool with Mother Nature: Ecological Fantasy

Although urban fantasy is spreading like urban sprawl, the great majority of fantasy is set in preindustrial worlds. Nature lovers fancy fantasy, as its characters spend more time in the sun than those of any other genre. From forests to mountains to oceans to deserts, every environment is represented. Nature isn't just used as pretty scenery either; magic and herb lore nourish wholesome powers that stand against destructive foes. So to shrug off the oppressiveness of strip malls, hazy skies, and a shortage of green plants and clear water, try these.

Adams, Richard
   ⇨ *Watership Down*. 1972. Scribner, ISBN: 068483605X, 448p. (hbk.)
      It's not a rewrite of *Titanic* but a heroic quest of a small band to find a green place they can call home. It's a testament to Adams's writing skill that a novel about talking rabbits is not cartoonish but has real emotional resonance for young readers and adults alike.

Barron, T. A.
   The Ancient One. 1992. Ace, ISBN: 0441010326, 320p. YA.
      Seeking to defend a virgin forest of Oregon redwood on Native American holy land, Kate is transported to the past, where she helps the Halami Indians

save the same homeland from an evil volcanic creature named Gashra. Plenty of action keeps this story hopping.

Coe, David B.
The Outlanders. Lon-Tobyn Chronicles. 1998. Tor, ISBN: 0812571134, 640p.

In this sequel to *The Children of Amarid,* Coe depicts a rural, magic-based nation (Tobyn-Ser) defending itself against its mundane but technologically powerful neighbor (Lon-Ser). When attacks against Tobyn-Ser are linked to the Overlord of Lon-Ser, the mage Orris must undertake a quest to save his homeland.

Donaldson, Stephen R.
The Wounded Land. The Second Chronicles of Thomas Covenant. 1980. Del Rey, ISBN: 0345348680, 512p.

One reason for the success of Thomas Covenant is the author's radiant depiction of a natural world called simply The Land. In this opener to the Second Chronicles, Lord Foul's Sunbane has wasted The Land and sapped the power from its people. Covenant and Linden Avery must confront their own weaknesses to try to heal it.

Duane, Diane
Deep Wizardry. Young Wizards. 1985. Magic Carpet, ISBN: 0152162577, 384p. **YA**.

Think "deep" as in deep ecology and ocean deeps in this novel about two aspiring young wizards called by dolphins to defense of the oceans. Duane trades her usual humor for a weightier approach here, but the book still works. Watch for Master-Shark, a character who steals the book from the teen wizard/ whale protagonists.

McKiernan, Dennis
The Eye of the Hunter. Mithgar. 1992. Roc, ISBN: 0451452682, 592p.

Appearance of the title comet in the sky means it's time for five warrows, elves, and men to fulfill their destiny, crossing environments from glaciers to deserts in pursuit of the rotten Baron Stoke. Those unmoved by environmental causes may find this preachy, but McKiernan gives granolas and greens plenty to cheer as he probes the harms of pollution.

Stevenson, Jennifer
Trash Sex Magic. 2004. Small Beer, ISBN: 1931520127, 292p.

Forget hugging trees and petting animals, the women of this erotic contemporary fable go all the way in Stevenson's story of trailer-dwelling folk who try to maintain their um . . . nature-loving way of life from developers on the banks of the Fox River.

Tolkien, J.R.R.
The Two Towers. <u>The Lord of the Rings</u>. 1954. Houghton Mifflin, ISBN: 0618574956, 924p.

Deep attachment to the natural world runs throughout Tolkien's work but is nowhere more evident than here. Contrasts between beauty and blight abound as characters cross all kinds of terrain. The ancient tree-herding Ents are literature's finest personification of nature. Their rally against the industrial blight of Isengard is truly moving.

Poor, Poor Powerful Me: Accepting One's Power and Otherness

Deep down, we are torn by ambivalence. We want to be exceptional, but we want to fit in. We want to make a difference, but power to make a difference brings responsibility, and increased accountability takes away from freedom. Fantasy characters offer a forum to explore this internal dilemma. Their one-of-a-kind powers also can leave them feeling loneliness, self-pity, or crushing responsibility. One minute they're singing about being off to see the wizard, and the next, there's no place like home. Here are some fantasies that explore this theme.

Ash, Sarah
Lord of Snow and Shadows. <u>Tears of Artamon</u>. 2003. Bantam Spectra, ISBN: 0553586211, 608p.

Gavril Andar wants to be an artist, but two things have been kept from him. First, he is heir to the throne of a grim northern kingdom (modeled after Russia). Second, he has terrible powers that will drain his humanity more each time he uses them. How he copes with these discoveries is at the center of this series starter.

Clemens, James
Wit'ch Fire. <u>The Banned and the Banished</u>. 1998. Del Rey, ISBN: 0345417062, 448p.

In a world beleaguered by evil, three powerful mages sacrifice themselves to create a Blood Diary, a magical tool to fight for good in the future. As Elena becomes a woman, she has strong flashes of power. She learns to focus her magic, unhappily preparing to accept the legacy of the Blood Diary while assembling some unlikely allies in Clemens's cracking series opener.

Cook, Dawn
First Truth. <u>Truth series</u>. 2002. Ace, ISBN: 044100945X, 352p.

Alissa's father disappears when she is five. She grows up self-dependent and practical, resenting his legacy, but when Alissa's magical talent appears, her mother sends her after her father to be trained at The Hold. Alissa follows her destiny with anger and reluctance. When she and Strell, a newly orphaned musician, reach The Hold, they discover their troubles have only begun. The beginning of a series.

Hobb, Robin

⇨ *Fool's Errand.* <u>The Tawny Man</u>. 2001. Bantam Spectra, ISBN: 0553582445, 688p.

FitzChivalry Farseer has reason to face destiny with reluctance. He's already survived Hobb's <u>Farseer trilogy</u>, in which he gave up many of his dreams to save his kingdom. As <u>The Tawny Man</u> opens, he is dragged out of the reclusive life he has made, back into the thick of adventures. Altogether, these six books form one of fantasy's great epics.

Hoffman, Nina Kiriki

A Fistful of Sky. 2002. Ace, ISBN: 0441011772, 368p. `YA`.

Growing up in a powerful magical family in sunny So. Cal. should be great, but Gypsum has two problems. First, she's late to undergo the transition, and to assume magical powers at her age may kill her. Second, the magic she's destined to wield has a dark side: Gypsum can only curse others. Though this may sound like the pilot for a hip teen TV show, it's actually a successful fantasy novel.

Jordan, Robert

The Dragon Reborn. <u>The Wheel of Time</u>. 1991. Tor, ISBN: 0812513711, 704p.

<u>Wheel of Time</u> is all about reluctance to accept your magic. Every character seems to balk at destiny. In early books, such as *The Dragon Reborn,* in which the dragging of magical feet is highly prevalent, one can still see why the young heroes would fear their unwieldy powers, and the series works.

Larbalestier, Justine

Magic or Madness. 2005. Razorbill, ISBN: 1595140700, 304p. `YA`.

Adolescence and reluctance go together like fire and smoke, like Liz Taylor and her next husband, like Itchy and Scratchy. So it's no surprise that many YA novels fit this list. In *Magic,* Reason (whose name tells you how Mom felt about magic) must move in with seemingly crazy grandma Esmerelda. You can probably guess what grandma really is.

Le Guin, Ursula K.

Gifts. 2004. Harcourt, ISBN: 0152051244, 300p. `YA`.

Orrec's magic is so dangerously uncontrollable that he's blindfolded and isolated. His friend Gry won't use her power to call animals because it leads them to death. In her compact, poetic style, Le Guin explores how they learn to believe in themselves and relate to others. The cost of power is a theme running throughout Le Guin's fantasy.

Westerfeld, Scott
  The Secret Hour. <u>The Midnighters</u>. 2004. Eos, ISBN: 0060519533, 400p. YA.
    The Midnighters are teens with fantastic powers who live an extra hour at
  night when the rest of the world freezes. These new friends excite Jessica, just
  arrived in town, but when she discovers that her gifts make her a target of evil
  in the 25th hour, she begins to have second thoughts.

Barbarians at the Gate:
Invasion Fantasy

You've had those days. Credit card bills are mounting. The principal called
about Johnny. Your boss is on a micromanaging streak. A monster headache is
coming on. And what's that on the horizon? Oh great, another invading horde.
Pull up the drawbridge, heat the boiling oil, and hope you don't run out of
arrows and fresh water again. And somebody, please, try to sober up the wizard.
Invasion fantasy is for any reader feeling the stress of keeping life's barbarians
at bay day after day. It also should appeal to fans of military fiction or anyone,
for that matter, who likes an action story.

Bell, Hilari
  Fall of a Kingdom. <u>Farsala trilogy</u>. 2003. Simon Pulse, ISBN: 0689854145,
    448p. YA.
    Given the title, I'm not giving much away if I tell you the defense doesn't
  go well. Bell starts a trilogy with parallels to ancient Persia and the mighty at-
  tacking Hrum (you know them as the Hromans, er . . . Romans). Three young
  people—Jiaan, Soraya, and Kavi—emerge from the struggle as leaders of a
  future resistance.

Butcher, Jim
  Furies of Calderon. <u>Codex Alera</u>. 2004. Ace, ISBN: 044101268X, 512p.
    The furies of the title are elemental spirits used by the Aleran people to
  defend their land. Tavi, a mountain boy whose magical gifts are late to bloom,
  and Amara, a female spy, are in the thick of attempts to prevent assassination
  and invasion. Butcher takes time out from his fantasy mystery series to begin
  an equally successful epic trilogy.

De Lint, Charles
  Forests of the Heart. <u>Newford</u>. 2000. Tor, ISBN: 0312875681, 400p.
    Violent spirits called Gentry come to Canada with Irish immigrants and
  try to wrest control from local manitou spirits in this Newford-set fantasy. To
  aid their invasion, they want to waken an ancient Green Man. The residents
  of an art colony, some of whom have their own mystic powers, form the heart
  of the defense in this intriguing mix of Celtic, Native American, and Mexican
  myths.

Donaldson, Stephen R.
The Power that Preserves. **The First Chronicles of Thomas Covenant.** 1977. Del Rey, ISBN: 0345348672, 512p.

The First Chronicles culminate in siege of majestic Revelstone, the giant-carved fortress that is the last bastion of hope against the armies of Lord Foul. Will the battle end in despair or triumph? With most authors, the answer to that question would be obvious, but with the dour Donaldson, you won't know the answer until the end.

Gemmell, David
➪ *Legend.* **Drenai.** 1984. Del Rey, ISBN: 0345379063, 345p.

Druss is a legend, but he's fat, arthritic, and retired to the mountains to await death. When his country has only one point of defense against suddenly invading hordes, Druss takes command of an overwhelmed amateur army and prepares his last stand. Gemmell gets to the action quickly in the stirring first book of his long-running series.

Rawn, Melanie
Stronghold. **Dragon Star trilogy.** 1990. DAW, ISBN: 0886774829, 592p.

Rohan, High Prince of Stronghold, is trying to accustom his people to rule by law instead of pure might. But now a foreign invasion will put his leadership to the test. Rawn juggles several characters successfully in this trilogy opener. If you want to start at the beginning (you don't have to), read the Dragon Prince series first.

Spencer, Wen
Wolf Who Rules. 2006. Baen, ISBN: 1416520554, 368p. (hbk.)

Spencer follows *Tinker* with this novel set in that exotic fantasy realm of . . . Pittsburgh. An elven noble tries to maintain his realm against dragon invaders and their half-human children. Spencer's quirky urban style is influenced by manga comics.

Wells, Martha
The Gate of Gods. **The Fall of Ile-Rien.** 2005. Eos, ISBN: 0380808005, 496p.

This finishes a trilogy begun with *The Wizard Hunters.* Running out of time, the defenders of Ile-Rien risk the use of sorcerous World Gates to travel in search of stronger magic. It's their only hope to stop the Gardier, an ominous force invading in magical black airships. Wells writes one winning fantasy after another.

Armageddon Out of Here: Fantasy's Furious Final Battles

Fantasy writers, cruel souls that they are, enjoy teasing and torturing readers for hundreds of pages that lead inexorably into the valley of destruction at the end of the book. If the big finish does its job—takes your breath away and leaves you emotionally spent—you will happily forgive the hours spent meandering through subplots to get there. Here are fantasies guaranteed to leave you singing the R.E.M. lyrics, "It's the end of the world as we know it, and I feel fine." Note: Most of the books in this list finish series that should be read in their entirety.

Brown, Simon
Sovereign. <u>Keys of Power trilogy</u>. 2003. DAW, ISBN: 075640200X, 432p.
> If you like battles, this is for you: It's almost all fighting from start to finish. Brown includes plenty of plot twists and a strong final showdown. Characters are surprisingly complex, mixing good and bad qualities. Did I mention there were battles?

Feist, Raymond
A Darkness at Sethanon. <u>Riftwar Saga</u>. 1985. Bantam Spectra, ISBN: 0553263285, 464p.
> With the two parts of *Magician* and then *Silverthorn,* Feist got <u>Riftwar</u> off to a strong start. The payoff doesn't let the reader down. On the home world of Midkemia, Prince Arutha and Jimmy the Hand engage in military battles, and Pug and Tomas quest across space to find the man who can prepare them to do magical battle with the Enemy. Rousing stuff!

Jordan, Robert
⇨ *The Great Hunt.* <u>The Wheel of Time</u>. 1990. Tor, ISBN: 0812517725, 736p.
> Disparate paths converge as the second <u>Wheel of Time</u> epic ends, with the women escaping magical slavery while the men fight the fanatical Whitecloaks and Ba'alzamon. Though faults that undermine the series begin in this book, Jordan writes a slam-bang finish. You may not choose to finish the series, but it's certainly worth reading this far.

King, Stephen
The Dark Tower. <u>The Dark Tower</u>. 2004. Scribner, ISBN: 0743254562, 864p.
> King caps the seven-book <u>Tower</u> series with this novel and also provides denouements for characters from many of his other books. Thousands of fans love the way this series ends, and an equal number hate it. No matter which side of the controversy you choose, you'll find the end thought provoking and different than others you have encountered.

Lewis. C. S.
The Last Battle. <u>The Chronicles of Narnia</u>. 1956. HarperTrophy, ISBN: 006447108X, 240p. **YA**.
> Lewis resolves all of the series characters and explains the cosmic purpose of the land of Narnia. <u>The Chronicles</u> are episodic. Each book is self-contained, so the final volume in these classics for children of all ages is not as climactic as some series finishers.

Russell, Sean
The Shadow Roads. The Swans' War. 2004. Eos, ISBN: 038079229X, 464p.

    The last book of The Swans' War features both mortal and immortal battles as dark knight Hafydd tries to release Death into the world while skirmishes between two powerful houses blaze into total war. Russell's strong prose brings this series to an emotionally powerful end.

Williams, Tad
To Green Angel Tower. Memory, Sorrow, and Thorn. 1993. DAW, ISBN: 0756402980, 1104p.

    While one group of heroes crosses many terrains for final battle with the Storm King, another set struggles to unravel the riddle of how this unslayable foe can be defeated. With a scant 1104 pages, Williams must rush to draw his series to a close. OK, just kidding. Williams does weave a fine cloth from the series' multiple plot threads.

Sailing into the West: Dying Lands and Races

    Heroism is the core stuff of fantasy, and to have heroism, there must be a credible threat. Readers like it when the stakes are high, when there is no doubt of the motivation to battle on in the face of terrible ordeals. It's no surprise then that a common theme in fantasy is the threatened extinction of a people, land, or world. The dying race motif makes heart-wrenching reading for those with a strong sense of the tragic.

Bishop, Anne
The Pillars of the World. 2001. Roc, ISBN: 0451458508, 432p.

    Someone or something is destroying the bridges between the Fae and human worlds. When the bridges go, pieces of the Fae world disappear with them. In the human world, inquisitors hunt witches, who guard paths between the realms. At the center of danger is Ari, a witch whose love for one of the Fae makes her suspect to both sides.

Donaldson, Stephen R.
⇨ *The Illearth War*. The First Chronicles of Thomas Covenant. 1977. Del Rey, ISBN: 0345348664, 544p.

    Whether you like antihero Thomas Covenant or not, if you respond to tragedy you will be moved when Lord Foul and his Ravers threaten the beautiful Land with extinction. Even jaded fantasy veterans might shed a tear at the plight of the giants or the gallant stand of a small army defending its world against overwhelming force.

Kay, Guy Gavriel
   Tigana. 1990. Roc, ISBN: 0451457765, 688p.
     When Tigana's army kills the son of an invading sorcerer, he wreaks a horrid revenge: a spell that erases all memories of conquered Tigana, even ability to hear its name, from everyone but those born there. Afflicting his heroes with various forms of loss of identity, Kay creates a compelling background for one of fantasy's best stand-alone novels.

Marks, Laurie J.
   Earth Logic. <u>Elemental Logic</u>. 2004. Tor, ISBN: 0765348381, 448p.
     In Shaftal, the Sainnite invasion persists, and plague and violence ravage the land. Karis survived the initial attack, but she and the people she leads remain in hiding. If you don't like same-sex relationships, you may not enjoy <u>Elemental Logic</u>, but too bad for you: One of fantasy's best new series comes from a writer with a truly unique voice.

McKillip, Patricia A.
   Ombria in Shadow. 2002. Ace, ISBN: 0441010164, 304p. `AW`.
     Trouble's brewing in Ombria, as the prince has died. His evil regent, Domina Pearl, lets the kingdom waste away. Mag, a girl who doesn't know if she belongs above or below, must play a key role in untangling the dark magic that slowly suffocates the city.

Palmatier, Joshua
   The Skewed Throne. <u>Throne series</u>. 2006. DAW, ISBN: 0756403820, 384p.
     In the wake of the White Fire, the city of Amenkor descends into insanity, famine, and disease. In this gritty first novel, a streetwise girl who perceives a red aura around those who intend harm becomes an assassin. But Varis must develop new moral sophistication to see through the treacherous plots that threaten the city.

Tolkien, J.R.R.
   The Return of the King. <u>The Lord of the Rings</u>. 1956. Houghton Mifflin, ISBN: 0618574972, 500p.
     Would this list be complete without Tolkien's elves? They aren't dying but taking a one-way retirement cruise to the West, leaving Middle Earth to the humans. For those who long for magic in the world, Tolkien crafts the ultimate sad metaphor for the dimming light of a mythic past.

Once upon a Time: Fantasy's Love Affair with Books and Storytelling

One of my favorite physical exercises involves stretching around to pat myself on the back for carrying on the important tradition of reading. Other readers who share this vanity have dozens of great books awaiting them on the fantasy bookshelf. In these books, reading or storytelling take on magical power or become a conduit into a magical world. For those who love reading and long for some magic in our world, what could be better than that?

Ende, Michael
The Neverending Story. 1976. Dutton. ISBN: 0525457585, 384p. (hbk.) YA.

> Titled *Die Unendliche Geschichte* (say that five times fast) in its original German, Ende's book is a good choice for readers of all ages. Although the book contains more of Bastian Balthazar Box's adventures than the 1984 film, it won't seem neverending to readers accustomed to modern fantasy's huge books.

Fforde, Jasper
The Eyre Affair. Thursday Next series. 2001. Penguin, ISBN: 0142001805, 384p.
Lost in a Good Book. Thursday Next series. 2002. Penguin, ISBN: 0142004030, 416p.

> An adult take on "entering the book" can be found in Fforde's series. Full of zany, reference- and wordplay-laden humor, these books follow the Literature Division of Special Operations. In *Eyre Affair,* an archvillain kidnaps characters from the great works. Read *Lost in a Good Book,* so that you will know Jack Schitt. If you enjoy these, by all means continue the series. Technically science fiction or mystery, this appeals to fantasy readers as well.

Funke, Cornelia
Inkheart. 2003. Scholastic, ISBN: 0439709105, 560p. YA.
Inkspell. 2005. Chicken House, ISBN: 1904442838, 688p. YA.

> These are truly for bibliophiles, with loving passages about binding, collecting, and reading books aloud mixed into exciting adventures. In *Inkheart,* characters from books are sometimes read into our real world. In *Inkspell,* roles are reversed, and characters from the real world enter books.

⇨ Goldman, William
The Princess Bride. 1973. Ballantine, ISBN: 0345418263, 480p.

> "Fencing. Fighting. Torture. Poison. True love. Hate. Revenge. Giants. Hunters. Bad men. Good men. Beautifulest ladies. Snakes. Spiders. Beasts of all natures and descriptions. Pain. Death. Brave men. Coward men. Strongest men. Chases. Escapes. Lies. Truths. Passion. Miracles." In a charming frame to the story, Goldman explains that when he was a boy, his father read him S. Morgenstern's Florinese history, abridging as he went and dropping asides about the parts he cut.

McKillip, Patricia A.
Alphabet of Thorn. 2004. Ace, ISBN: 0441012434, 304p.

> A foundling child raised by librarians (our work is never done) has a gift for translation. Only she can decipher a work written in a script that looks like

thorns (it must be terrible in Braille). The exotic script soon begins to exert an obsessive power over both the translator and the queen.

Nix, Garth
Lirael. <u>Abhorsen trilogy</u>. 2001. Eos, ISBN: 0060590165, 480p. YA.

Young Lirael, depressed over her inability to develop the magical sight, is assigned to work as a third assistant librarian. Exploring the back corners of the immense library with her companion, the Disreputable Dog, Lirael finds amazing and frightening things. For a truly memorable visit to the library, try this follow-up to *Sabriel.*

Odom, Mel
The Rover. 2001. Tor, ISBN: 0765341948, 512p.
The Destruction of the Books. 2004. Tor, ISBN: 0765346494, 432p.
The Lord of the Libraries. 2005. Tor, ISBN: 0765345608, 384p.

This series of Tolkienesque epic fantasies features librarians and books prominently. In *The Rover,* we meet Wick, a "lowly" librarian kidnapped into slavery who escapes through book knowledge and the help of others. In later books, Wick mentors another young librarian, Juhg.

Pratchett, Terry
The Light Fantastic. <u>Discworld</u>. 2000. HarperCollins, ISBN: 0061020702, 272p.

Pterry's library and book references are some of his best bits. They start in this second book, with a powerful grimoire of black magic called the Octavo and the origins of The Librarian, a wizard turned orangutan who expresses delicate shades of meaning with a one-word vocabulary: OOK!? In other <u>Discworld books</u>, watch for a magical readers' advisory in *Guards! Guards!* and a wonderful instance of bedtime reading in *Thud!*

Dangerous Minds: Marvelous Mental Powers

Have you seen the ancient fantasy book that will make your head explode if you try to read it? Well of course you haven't, or you wouldn't be reading this. I won't put it in the list that follows, as most of you are just perverse enough to try it. The mind is powerful and mysterious enough that good writers can make us believe that new magical capacities can be tapped through its use. Try, for instance, these mental magic missives.

Hobb, Robin
⇨ *Royal Assassin.* <u>Farseer Trilogy</u>. 1996. Bantam Spectra, ISBN: 0553573411, 675p.

Hero Fitz has two powers: Skill, which allows long-distance mental communication and placement of suggestions in others minds, and Wit, the ability to meld minds with animals. Add the forging of the enemy, which turns their captives into zombies, and you have enough mind games to power this middle book to the top of the fantasy heap.

Hoffman, Nina Kiriki
A Red Heart of Memories. 1999. Ace, ISBN: 0441007686, 329p. (out of print) **YA**.

Matt (short for Matilda) can talk to inanimate objects (so can you, but hers talk back) and see the working of others' minds. When she connects with a witch named Edmund and his friend Susan, the three begin exploring their loneliness and unlocking traumatic memories. Powerful magic is a coping mechanism in Hoffman's raw-hearted fantasy.

Lackey, Mercedes
Arrows of the Queen. **Heralds of Valdemar.** 1987. DAW, ISBN: 0886773784, 320p.

Talia, a self-conscious, abused girl, is discovered by one of the Companions (which appear as white horses; fantasy girls *love* horses). She enters training as a Herald, a magical guard and counselor to royals. Talia is a powerful empath: she can sense and sometimes affect the feelings of others. This starts one trilogy in the larger *Valdemar* series. Simpler than later efforts, this is still a good introduction to the author.

Lindskold, Jane
Wolf Hunting. **Firekeeper.** 2006. Tor, ISBN: 0765351439, 624p.

In the fifth volume of the series, Firekeeper, the girl heroine who mentally communes with wolves, comes to the aid of a jaguar named Truth, who is a soothsayer. Truth's problem is that lately she has been hearing someone else's voice making predictions inside of her head instead of her own. (Now that's when you know you're crazy!)

Norton, Andre
Lost Lands of Witch World. **Witch World.** 1965–1968. Tor, ISBN: 0765300524, 448p. (hbk.)

Writing from the 1940s until her death in 2005, Norton was best known in fantasy circles for her Witch World series, which recently have been collected in omnibus editions. The novels collected in this omnibus form a trilogy about triplets with telepathic powers.

Pierce, Tamora
The Will of the Empress. **The Circle Reforged.** 2005. Scholastic, ISBN: 0439441722, 560p. **YA**.

As four youths enter adulthood, they begin to wonder if they want to remain open to the telepathic circle they use to enrich the power of their magical gifts. When kidnapping and forced marriage threaten one of their number, they must decide where their loyalties lie. This postscript to the *Circle of Magic* and *Circle Opens* series also can stand alone.

Speak Softly and Carry a Big Sword: Fantasy's Memorable Weapons

A fantasy hero just isn't fully dressed without a magic weapon of some kind. These books are for the fantasy reader who likes plenty of action. Here's an armory-full of the best books featuring these double-edged weapons.

Gemmell, David
The Swords of Night and Day. **Drenai.** 2004. Del Rey, ISBN: 0345458346, 512p.

> Typical of David Gemmell's long-running saga, this volume (the 11th) features Skilgannon, an ancient hero returned to life with the science-fantasy weapons of the title to fight his ancient enemy and lover, the Empress Eternal.

Moorcock, Michael
Elric of Melniboné. 1972. Ace, ISBN: 0441203981, 192p. (out of print.)
Elric: Song of the Black Sword. 1997. White Wolf, ISBN: 156504195X, 504p. (out of print).

> Elric is a superpowerful albino warrior empowered by and dependent on his Black Sword. This series, starting with *Elric of Melniboné* or the omnibus *Elric: Song of the Black Sword,* is recommended for fans of old-fashioned, blood-and-guts, pulp fantasy.

Pullman, Philip
The Subtle Knife. **His Dark Materials.** 1997. Yearling, ISBN: 044041833X, 326p. YA.

> Subtle, indeed. The title knife is not for anything vulgar like hacking up enemies. It can cut pathways that allow travel between dimensions, but is there a hidden cost to its use? To find out, read Pullman's excellent trilogy, and progress to this, the second book.

Saberhagen, Fred.
The First Swords. **Book of Swords series.** 1983–1984. Tor, ISBN: 0312869169, 480p.

> This list wouldn't be complete without Saberhagen's series, in which Vulcan forges 12 magical swords, each with a different power, and scatters them around earth. *First Swords* is an omnibus containing the first three books, which are also the best.

Salvatore, R. A.
Spearwielder's Tale. 1993–1995. Ace, ISBN: 0441011942, 662p.
　　　Salvatore's work is full of magical weapons in barbaric worlds. For an example, try this omnibus of a trilogy of tales about Gary Leger, who wanders into the world of Faerie and takes up the telepathic weapon of its lost hero.

Turtledove, Harry
⇨ *The Misplaced Legion.* **Videssos Cycle.** 1987. Del Rey, ISBN: 0345330676, 336p.
　　　When a Roman with a spell-scribed sword faces off against a Celtic chieftain with a similar weapon, they are transported, with an entire Roman legion, to the world of Videssos. *The Misplaced Legion* begins this four-volume, character-driven saga of war and cultural politics.

Watt-Evans, Lawrence
The Misenchanted Sword. **Ethshar.** 1985. Wildside, ISBN: 1587152827, 228p.
　　　The title blade Wirikidor comes with troublesome rules: Its bearer must use it to kill 100 people, sheathing the sword between each killing. The bearer is unbeatable, but the sword will turn on him and kill him after 100 uses. He ages normally during his time with the killing sword but cannot die until he becomes the 101st kill.

Riddle Me This: Fantasy's Fascination with Brainteasers

This thing all things devours: birds, beasts, trees, flowers; gnaws iron, bites steel; grinds hard stones to meal; slays king, ruins town, beats high mountain down. If you are quick to recognize that the answer to this riddle is not Spam or Microsoft but is actually time, then you probably read *The Hobbit.* Riddles in fantasy go back much farther than Tolkien, to the earliest stories and myths. Fantasies that feature riddles are a great choice for young readers or those who like puzzles or quick-thinking characters. Here are a few of fantasy's best uses of riddles.

De Lint, Charles
Into the Green. 1993. Orb, ISBN: 0765300222, 256p.
　　　A mysterious puzzle box has the power to destroy the fey world's Middle Kingdom. To defeat it, tinker witch Angharad and her allies must wage battle against their own weaknesses. Forgoing his usual urban fantasy, de Lint explores the time before magic went underground.

Hobb, Robin
Assassin's Apprentice. **Farseer Trilogy.** 1995. Bantam Spectra, ISBN: 055357339X, 464p.
Fool's Errand. **The Tawny Man.** 2001. Bantam Spectra, ISBN: 0553582445, 688p.

Riddle lovers will enjoy deciphering the wordplay of the Fool, fantasy's most enigmatic jester. He lives in two trilogies by Robin Hobb, The Farseer Trilogy, which begins with *Assassin's Apprentice,* and The Tawny Man, starting with *Fool's Errand.*

Kelso, Sylvia
Everran's Bane. 2006. Five Star, ISBN: 1410402568, 227p.

A riddle is the key to ending a dragon's reign of terror in Kelso's first novel, but the answer to that riddle may pose an even bigger dilemma for its possessor, Harran the Harper.

King, Stephen
The Waste Lands. The Dark Tower. 1991. Viking, ISBN: 0452284716, 448p.

King's entire Dark Tower sequence is a riddle within a riddle, but in this third volume, *The Waste Lands* a book of riddles and a sentient monorail that likes riddles play prominent roles.

Kushner, Ellen
Thomas the Rhymer. 1990. Bantam Spectra, ISBN: 0553586971, 304p. **AW**.

As adapted from the ancient ballad, Thomas is a seductive minstrel abducted by the Queen of Elfland for seven years. A riddling game played by the Lords of Elfland is central to the plot, as are the riddlelike prophecies that Thomas makes when he is allowed to return, on condition that he speaks only truth, to his regular existence.

McKillip, Patricia A.
⇨ *Riddle-Master: The Complete Trilogy.* 1976–1979. Ace, ISBN: 0441005969, 592p. **AW**.

In this trilogy, riddles are historical stories with complex morals best interpreted by the masters, whose skill is highly valued. Lushly descriptive, dreamlike prose, and well-defined characters distinguish this series.

Schmidt, Gary D.
Straw into Gold. 2001. Clarion, ISBN: 0618056017, 176p. (hbk.) **YA**.

The starting point for *Straw* is *Rumpelstiltskin,* but in this case the queen fails to guess the little man's name, so he takes the baby prince. In this twisty retelling, a boy in pursuit of a riddle's answer finds himself grappling with the kingdom's deep mysteries.

Tolkien, J.R.R.
The Hobbit. 1937. Houghton Mifflin, ISBN: 061815082X, 320p. **YA**.

Bilbo's riddle battle in the dark with Gollum is one of fiction's truly memorable moments and also the most critical scene in the book for those who will go on to read The Lord of the Rings.

To Hell and Back: Necromancy and the Afterworld in Fantasy

Ain't death grand? OK, not really, but it's certainly a fascination. No one knows for sure what comes next after our candle sputters out (at least I'm not privy to the information), but speculative fiction is the genre best equipped to explore the topic. And explore it does, with books about afterworlds ranging from the truly heavenly to the deeply hellish. Fantasy authors devise many flavors of necromantic magic to communicate with and try to manipulate their great beyonds. So if you're ready, follow me toward the book light . . .

Beagle, Peter S.
A Fine and Private Place. 1960. Tachyon, ISBN: 1892391469, 296p.
> A new edition is due of Beagle's lovely study of the meaning of life and death. A pharmacist lives a hidden life in a cemetery, emotionally unable to reenter the real world. He speaks to the newly dead, becoming involved in both the romance of a young dead couple and his own relationship with a widow who visits her husband's grave.

Bujold, Lois McMaster
Paladin of Souls. <u>Chalion</u>. 2003. HarperTorch, ISBN: 0380818612, 496p. **AW**.
> In her forties, Ista has spent adulthood trapped in a castle by a family curse and grief-induced madness. But Ista is a survivor. Her first short excursion into the world becomes an adventure when two dashing brothers who harbor a deep secret rescue her from kidnapping. About reentering life (in many ways), this deservedly won the Nebula Award.

Butcher, Jim
Dead Beat. <u>Dresden Files</u>. 2005. Roc, ISBN: 045146091X, 448p.
> Wizard/detective Harry Dresden must find a lost artifact or vampires will frame his policewoman friend for murder. As usual, Hardback Harry has less raw power than his foes (this time the disciples of a nasty necromancer), but he muddles through. Martial arts action and quirky secondary characters continue to enliven this series in its seventh entry.

Lisle, Holly
Memory of Fire. <u>World Gates trilogy</u>. 2002. Eos, ISBN: 038081837X, 384p.
The Wreck of Heaven. <u>World Gates trilogy</u>. 2003. Eos, ISBN: 0380818388, 352p.
Gods Old and Dark. <u>World Gates trilogy</u>. 2004. Eos, ISBN: 0380818396, 336p.
> In the first two books of this trilogy, two sisters visit North Carolina, Oria (a world next door), and heaven before returning to Earth. Mixing with gods, sentinels (keepers of the ways between worlds), and an officious heavenly administrator, the sisters pass through plot twists and turns as they ramp up for the colossal final battles of the final book.

Nix, Garth
⇨ *Sabriel.* <u>**Abhorsen trilogy**</u>. 1995. Eos, ISBN: 0064471837, 496p. YA.

> Young Sabriel is plunged into necromancy as she searches for her missing father, the Abhorsen, whose job is to send restless spirits back to the after-world. Exotic rituals with magic bells provide this series with one of the most interesting depictions ever of the practice of magic.

Pratchett, Terry
Mort. <u>**Discworld, Death series**</u>. 1987. HarperTorch, ISBN: 0061020680, 272p.

> Although Death is ever-present in <u>Discworld</u>, this fourth book is his first showcase. Seeking to understand human emotion, Death takes a holiday, leaving the work to his awkward apprentice, Mort. The results are, as Death would say, HILARIOUS. For more of Death, try *Reaper Man, Soul Music,* or *Hogfather.*

Pullman, Philip
The Amber Spyglass. <u>**His Dark Materials**</u>. 1999. Yearling, ISBN: 0440418569, 544p. YA.

> <u>His Dark Materials</u> climaxes with protagonists Lyra and Will traveling into the harrowing world of the dead to retrieve a friend. The decisions they make there will overturn the cosmic order. You'll want to start at the beginning with *The Golden Compass.*

Lyres and Lutes and Fiddles and Flutes: Music in Fantasy

Interest in certain kinds of traditional music and an interest in fantasy harmonize beautifully, as a quick survey of fantasy titles proves. Musicians make convenient fantasy characters: They are often storytellers, have an excuse to wander about the countryside, and mix with social classes high and low. Whether you sing in the shower or on the stage, if you enjoy music check out these titles, which will certainly pluck your strings.

Bull, Emma
⇨ *War for the Oaks.* 1987. Orb, ISBN: 0765300346, 336p.

> Updating from the countryside to urban Minneapolis, Minnesota, and from the folk music that usually accompanies fantasy to rock and roll, Bull creates a believable modern setting for the traditional story of humans drawn into the affairs of the Seelie Court. Music lovers will feel the exhilaration of performance every time singer Eddi takes the stage.

De Lint, Charles
Jack of Kinrowan. 1990. Tor, ISBN: 0312869592, 384p.

> Music and the other arts are integral to de Lint's tales, such as the second novella in *Jack of Kinrowan, Drink Down the Moon,* in which a young Ottawa

fiddler discovers that his musical gifts carry magical power in the world of Faerie next door.

Isaak, Elaine
The Singer's Crown. 2005. Eos, ISBN: 0060782536, 480p.

When his uncle usurps the throne, Kattanan is spared death but castrated so he cannot produce threatening heirs. He becomes a singer, often traded to new masters. But when he begins a secret love with Princess Melisande, Kattanan finds himself in the midst of a plot to reclaim the throne. A series is forthcoming.

Jones, Diana Wynne
Cart and Cwidder. **The Dalemark Quartet.** 1975. HarperTrophy, ISBN: 0064473139, 240p. **YA**.

Moril is the youngest of a family of traveling musicians. When tragedy strikes, breaking up his family, he must learn the powers of a magical, lutelike cwidder to save himself and reunite his country. First of the loosely connected Dalemark Quartet.

Kay, Guy Gavriel
A Song for Arbonne. 1992. Roc, ISBN: 0451458974, 512p.

Intrigues and power struggles of two neighboring nations—one patriarchal, sun-worshipping, and militaristic, the other ruled by moon-worshipping women and steeped in poetry and song—are described in this historical fantasy based on troubadour culture in early medieval France. Kay's lyrical style and masterful feel for emotions are again on display.

Modesitt, L. E.
The Soprano Sorceress. **The Spellsong Cycle.** 1997. Tor, ISBN: 0812545591, 672p.

An Iowa music teacher is thrown into a world where musical skills make her a powerful sorceress. Modesitt broke away from his long-running Recluce series with this book to start the shorter Spellsong Cycle.

Pratchett, Terry
Soul Music. **Discworld, Death series.** 1994. HarperTorch, ISBN: 0061054895, 384p.

Soul Music mixes Death and his cohorts with Cut-Me-Own-Throat Dibbler, who takes a sojourn from selling mysterious sausages into the role of rock-and-roll impresario. He manages a band featuring a dwarf and troll rhythm section, the orangutan Librarian on keyboards, and some guy whose name translates as "Bud y Holly."

Pratchett, Terry
Maskerade. **Discworld, Witches series.** 1995. HarperTorch, ISBN: 006105691X, 368p.

If musical theater is more your style, try *Maskerade,* in which Granny and Nanny try to convince the proverbial fat lady to try witching instead of opera.

Of course, the point is to parody *The Phantom of the Opera* and many other classics.

Curses (Foiled Again): The Making and Breaking of Fantasy's Worst Curses

I curse you with a compelling need to finish every one of the fifteen thousand pages of that awful fantasy series just because you read the first book. The only way to escape my curse is to read the rest of my book very carefully. That's the best that I could come up with, but the genre has worse curses than that. For instance . . .

Bujold, Lois McMaster
The Curse of Chalion. Chalion. 2001. HarperTorch, ISBN: 0380818604, 512p. AW.

The royal family of Chalion has been cursed ever since its questionable rise to power, a curse that slowly destroys both family and country. It falls to Cazaril, an ex-noble, now tutor to Royesse Iselle, to break the curse, while at the same time facing old enemies who betrayed him into slavery. The solution he finds may force him into the highest sacrifice.

García y Robertson, R.
Firebird. 2006. Tor, ISBN: 0765313561, 320p. (hbk.)

In Markovy (a land with a medieval Russian feel), orphan Aria heals the injured Sir Roye. She joins him on his quest to return the Firebird's Egg to its nest, which will lift the curse that plagues the land. This is an old-fashioned adventure yarn supercharged with erotic energy and grim thrills.

Greenwood, Ed
The Silent House. 2004. Tor, ISBN: 0765347261, 480p.

A sentient house protects the fortunes of the family that lives within. The Silvertrees becomes a dynasty, dominating their land for generations. But success has a price: release of a curse that forever entraps the souls sheltered by the house as part of its sentient force.

Hoffman, Nina Kiriki
A Fistful of Sky. 2002. Ace, ISBN: 0441011772, 368p. YA.

Young Gyp, late coming to magic, has a difficult talent to use: the ability to cast curses. Deciding how to use such a power creates a series of interesting dilemmas. Hoffman mines the ground between the teen problem novel and fantasy effectively. If you don't mind a sensitive approach to the genre, you will enjoy her work.

McKillip, Patricia A.
In the Forests of Serre. 2003. Ace, ISBN: 0441011578, 295p.
> Prince Ronan, blinded by grief for his lost wife and child, accidentally rides over a chicken owned by the witch Brume. Her responding curse will have lasting repercussions for Ronan and those around him in a mysterious, lyrical offering that explores what it means to lose heart.

Sanderson, Brandon
⇨ *Elantris.* 2005. Tor, ISBN: 0765350378, 656p.
> A curse brings a powerful city to ruin and turns its wise inhabitants into living dead: people who feel every wound as if it's fresh but only can go insane from the pain, not die. When Prince Raoden is caught up in the curse, he'll have to find a solution soon or degenerate into the insanity of his comrades.

Wurts, Janny
The Curse of the Mistwraith. <u>Wars of Light and Shadow</u>. 1993. HarperCollins, ISBN: 0586210695, 841p.
> Two half brothers, raised in feuding lands, begin to forge a bond when transported to the world of Alera, where they must fight the ancient curse of a sentient fog that has brought the land to ruin. Both brothers' magic is needed to combat the wraith, but it fights back by turning the two against each other. Thus begins an elaborate series.

At an All-You-Can-Eat Buffet, Don't Eat All that You Can: Great Books in So-So Series

Fantasy writing is dominated by series. For every stand-alone fantasy on the bookstore shelf, there are dozens of series entries. Many reasons contribute to this: tradition, publishing economics, and the number of pages required for epic storytelling, to name a few. A problem with series is that you can struggle through a thousand pages before it becomes clear that the author isn't going to pull it off. It's like eating your way to the bottom of a jumbo-size box of cereal in search of a prize that isn't there, growing ever more tired of the flavor. To help you avoid the nauseating aftertaste of a good series gone bad, I present some delicious single servings. Bon appétit!

Anthony, Piers
On a Pale Horse. <u>Incarnations of Immortality</u>. 1983. Del Rey, ISBN: 0345338588, 336p.
For Love of Evil. <u>Incarnations of Immortality</u>. 1988. Eos, ISBN: 0380752859, 336p.

Anthony is full of creative ideas, as in this series in which mythical entities such as Death, Time, and Nature are offices held by a succession of humans. These two entries about Death and Evil are well done, but later books suffer from formulaic writing, juvenile humor, and shallow female characters.

Farland, David
The Runelords: The Sum of All Men. <u>Runelords</u>. 1998. Tor, ISBN: 0812541626, 624p.

At the core of this series is an interesting idea: Vassals can endow lords with their personal attributes such as strength, sight, or intelligence. This creates a social system with some superbeings and many weakened dedicators. This idea is strong enough to power a great first book, but the series becomes increasingly confusing and clumsy.

Furey, Maggie
Aurian. <u>Artifacts of Power</u>. 1994. Bantam Spectra, ISBN: 0553565257, 608p.

Here's an example of a common problem: a series that just can't close the deal. Furey begins well. Her strong female lead character is particularly praiseworthy. The three books that follow take a slow path downhill with repetitive plot elements and long, slow stretches leading to a rushed, unsatisfying ending.

Jordan, Robert
⇨ *The Eye of the World.* <u>The Wheel of Time</u>. 1990. Tor, ISBN: 0312850093, 688p.

My friend calls this the "big but" series: Everyone likes it, *but* . . . Fans spend hours debating when the <u>Wheel</u> went spinning out of control, but almost all agree that by book four or five, complications come more quickly than plot advancements. That said, there's a reason why everyone started this series. The world and mythos that Jordan creates in this first volume are among the most vivid fantasy has ever seen.

Lindskold, Jane
Wolf Captured. <u>Firekeeper</u>. 2004. Tor, ISBN: 0765348233, 768p.

Including this book is a little unfair. Lindskold's series—about a girl raised by wolves who later calls on her connection to them—is far better than so-so. But the third book, *The Dragon of Despair,* lived up to its title: The plot was draggin' and readers despaired. There's a happy ending: Lindskold came roaring back with book four, *Wolf Captured.*

McKiernan, Dennis
Dragondoom. <u>Mithgar</u>. 1990. Roc, ISBN: 0451458818, 544p.

Readers who complain that McKiernan is derivative pay him a backhanded compliment: <u>Mithgar</u> was intended as a sequel to <u>Lord of the Rings</u>, but rights were denied and the material reworked. The similarities are intentional. But McKiernan is no Tolkien. Still, his best books are loads of fun. Try this one about two civilizations, dwarf and human, that war over a treasure hoard but must combine forces against an evil dragon.

Peake, Mervyn
The Gormenghast Novels. 1946–1959. Overlook, ISBN: 0879516283, 1168p.

Sixty years after publication, Peake's trilogy is still like no other reading experience. <u>Gormenghast</u> takes patience. Plot isn't the point. Enjoy the characters and ornate imagery. Wallow in the complexities. The last book, *Titus Alone,* was written after illness made writing difficult for Peake. It doesn't fit thematically or achieve the same quality.

Stackpole, Michael
Fortress Draconis. **DragonCrown War Cycle.** 2001. Bantam Spectra, ISBN: 0553379194, 513p.

This first book gets Stackpole's series off to a strong start, with compelling, fast-moving action. The second book, *When Dragons Rage,* is good, too, but something surprising happens at the end of that book, and though it's original, it doesn't work. Most fans agree that book three, *The Grand Crusade,* just doesn't recover from the mistake.

Down the Generations: Epic Family Sagas of Fantasy

If you only can be satisfied by "happily ever after" when every detail of ever after is described, then family sagas are for you. Some authors have made a specialty of checking in with their favorite fantasy families in every generation. When done well, the family saga creates real depth of characterization and lets greedy readers trust that they always can come back for another helping. Family characters have the unique ability to satisfy both those who want to revisit familiar traits and those who prefer new protagonists.

Brooks, Terry
⇨ *The Scions of Shannara.* **The Heritage of Shannara.** 1990. Del Rey, ISBN: 0345370740, 432p.

Three hundred years after the events of the first *Shannara* trilogy, the evil Federation has conquered the Four Lands. Just as their ancestors were called upon in the first series, the current Ohmsford scions are summoned to save civilization. Brooks turns in another solid effort.

Carey, Jacqueline
Kushiel's Scion. **Kushiel's Legacy.** 2006. Warner Aspect, ISBN: 044661002X, 976p.

Carey begins a new trilogy featuring Imriel, the adopted son of Phèdre and Joscelin in the world of Terre d'Ange. She continues her exploration of masochism based in religion (which works better than you'd suspect). Fans were excited by Carey's return to her signature setting.

Donaldson, Stephen R.
The Runes of Earth. <u>The Last Chronicles of Thomas Covenant</u>. 2004. Ace, ISBN: 044101304X, 560p.

Ten years of earth time in the series, more than 300 years in the Land (where heroine Linden Avery returns), and 21 years after the last books were written, Donaldson returns to the <u>Chronicles</u>. It's good to see new readers exposed to one of the best writers of the 1980s and appropriate that many of the characters are descended from those in earlier volumes.

Farrell, S. L.
Heir of Stone. <u>Cloudmages</u>. 2005. DAW, ISBN: 0756403219, 656p.

The first book in this series deals with Jenna and her spellstone. The second focuses on daughter Meriel. This third entry follows the grandchildren: twins Sevei, a cloudmage in training, and brother Kayne, who is on a military campaign. Farrell shows signs of becoming one of the genre's best writers, particularly of Celtic-themed fantasy.

Greenwood, Ed
The Silent House. 2004. Tor, ISBN: 0765347261, 480p.

In this book, related to his <u>Band of Four</u> quartet, Greenwood explores the roots of the Silvertree clan, in particular their ancestral home, The Silent House, which is not only a stronghold but a living force. This surprisingly complex book examines the cost of magical prowess.

Hobb, Robin
Ship of Destiny. <u>The Liveship Traders</u>. 2000. Bantam Spectra, ISBN: 0553575651, 816p.

You'll be swept up by the trilogy this book concludes. It's about three generations of the seagoing Vestrit family and their attempts to protect the harbor city, Bingtown, and their magical sentient liveships. This is stirring stuff, of the top echelon of high fantasy.

Marillier, Juliet
Child of the Prophecy. <u>Sevenwaters trilogy</u>. 2002. Tor, ISBN: 0312870361, 528p.

Romance, family loyalty, and Celtic mythology are the ingredients of the trilogy that this book concludes. Three entries feature heroines from three generations, guardians of the forest at Sevenwaters. The stakes rise in each book, and as such, this book is darker and less romantic than the first two, but it brings the trilogy to a thoughtful conclusion.

Pierce, Tamora

Trickster's Choice. <u>**Daughter of the Lioness**</u>. 2003. Random House, ISBN: 0375828796, 448p. ██.

Pierce returns to the girl-power themes of her Tortall adventures, this time tracking Alianne, daughter of <u>Lioness Quartet</u> heroine Alanna. Aly finds it difficult to follow the living legend of her mother. Attempting to strike out on her own, Aly's adventures begin when she is kidnapped and sold into the service of a foreign royal family.

Stackpole, Michael

Cartomancy. <u>**The Age of Discovery**</u>. 2006. Bantam Spectra, ISBN: 0553382381, 448p.

<u>The Age of Discovery</u> features map magic in a setting close to our sixteenth- and seventeenth-century world. The first book, *A Secret Atlas*, followed the adventures of grandmaster cartographer Qiro Anturasi, but this second volume focuses on his grandchildren.

Chapter Two

Character

Some readers wish to identify and empathize with characters. If you're of this type, you want introspective characters into whose situation you can project yourself with minimum fuss. Conversely, you might desire vicarious excitement, in which case you may prefer characters whose lives are as different from your own as possible. In their shoes, you can walk (albeit quite safely) on the proverbial wild side. If you are tired of traveling in the same circle, you may value character interactions most, treating a cast of characters almost like a new set of friends.

Fantasy has more than its share of stock types: classes of characters that appear again and again. For fantasy writers and readers, the goal is not usually a completely new character type, but a fresh or particularly convincing implementation of a familiar character type. For the most part, lists in this chapter reinforce common character classifications, but they also break down each class into more subtle genus and species divisions.

Of course if you know the kind of characters you respond to, the lists that follow will lead you to more of them. If you are tired of certain character types, find some new types to explore or turn to some of the quirkier lists. Either way, you're reading in a genre that is full of vivid, fleshed-out folk; you won't run out of good characters anytime soon.

The Fellowship Is the Thing: Companions on a Quest

Was I the only one who gasped aloud when the Fellowship of the Ring walked in slow motion past the camera in Peter Jackson's film as they began their quest? For readers who love characterization, one of the great genre traditions is the collection of companions—with different strengths and weaknesses, bonds and arguments, and individual goals—who unite in pursuit of a common good. Reading about such groups is a reminder of why we take on the risks and burdens of relationships in our lives. These fantasies capture the fellowship ethic.

Anthony, Piers
Harpy Thyme. **Xanth series.** 1993. Tor, ISBN: 0812534840, 352p.

> In this 17th entry, Gloha, the goblin-harpy half-breed, goes in search of a mate, meeting a magician, a demoness, a skeleton, and a giant along the way. After 30 (!) <u>Xanth</u> novels, Anthony has sent every possible combination of fantasy characters on a quest, but new young readers and established fans keep gulping down the wacky candy of this series.

Eddings, David
Queen of Sorcery. **The Belgariad.** 1982. Del Rey, ISBN: 0345335651, 336p.

> In his classic series, Eddings slowly assembles a large and motley band of characters. By the end of this second book, the group is so large that they must make quite a clatter coming down the road, but Eddings knows the fantasy archetypes well, and the assured way he blends these personalities is what makes this series really cook.

Furey, Maggie
The Heart of Myrial. **Shadowleague.** 1998. Bantam Spectra, ISBN: 055357938X, 469p.

> Members of the Shadowleague—humans, dragons, centaurs, and sprites—maintain walls that protect their world from interspecies strife, but the walls are collapsing. As lines of communication break, horrible weather and disastrous battles plague the landscape. Against this backdrop, the mysterious Shadowleague struggles to stave off destruction.

Golden, Christopher, and Sniegoski, Thomas E.
The Nimble Man. **The Menagerie.** 2004. Ace, ISBN: 0441012159, 352p.

> The Menagerie, a band of heroes, protects the world from evil. Arthur Conan Doyle (a sorcerer) leads a faerie princess, a hobgoblin manservant, an ancient shape-shifter, the bible's Eve (cast as a vampire), an adventurer ghost, and a teenage demon. This fast-paced adventure promises an exciting dark fantasy series to come.

Shinn, Sharon
   ⇨ *Mystic and Rider*. <u>Twelve Houses</u>. 2005. Ace, ISBN: 0441013031, 432p.
  The Thirteenth House. <u>Twelve Houses</u>. 2006. Ace, ISBN: 0441014143, 432p.

     In *Mystic and Rider,* King Baryn sends five riders south to check into growing unrest in Gillengaria. Group dynamics between the fire mystic, healer, shape-shifter, warrior, and urchin-turned-soldier make the book click. *The Thirteenth House* brings the companions together again for more political intrigue.

Snyder, Midori
  The Innamorati. 1998. Tor, ISBN: 031286924X, 381p. (out of print). **AW**.

     A mask maker, a failed poet, a Siren, a thief, a stuttering actor, a priest, and a mercenary swordsman are among those who travel to a labyrinth that could either solve the problems that afflict them or swallow them up forever. Relationships between the pilgrims create a complex and entertaining allegory set against a rich Renaissance backdrop.

Bosom Buddies, Odd Couples, and Dynamic Duos

If Rob had left Fab, where would Milli Vanilli be today? Without Butthead, would anyone appreciate Beavis's comic stylings? And who mentions Tom Hanks without bosom buddy Peter Scolari immediately jumping to mind? OK, those aren't good examples, but sometimes in fantasy, partnership really does work better. Here are some of the great fantasy twosomes.

Jones, J. V.
  A Fortress of Grey Ice. <u>Sword of Shadows</u>. 2000. Tor, ISBN: 0765345498, 624p.

     The first volume of <u>Sword of Shadows</u>, *A Cavern of Black Ice,* told the story of Ash, a female warrior, and Raif, a huntsman expelled from his clan. In this volume, the pair split to pursue different ends—Ash tries to get rid of her world endangering powers, and Raif tries to find the title Fortress and defends its Blindwall—but the impact of the story derives from their desire to reunite.

Kellogg, Marjorie
  The Dragon Quartet, Vol. 1. 1995–1997. DAW, ISBN: 0756403278, 688p.
  The Dragon Quartet, Vol. 2. 2000–2003. DAW, ISBN: 0756403324, 904p.

     In four novels, four elemental dragons, each with a human guide as partner, are revived to fulfill an ecological mission. Time settings vary from medieval Europe to the distant future. The series is now available in two omnibus editions.

Lackey, Mercedes
The Oathbound. <u>Valdemar Vows and Honor.</u> 1988. DAW, ISBN: 0886774144, 304p.

Think of a buddy cop story, but change the cops into a sword fighter and a wizard. Now throw out gender stereotypes, because both of the leads are women. That's the essence of this book, first of a trilogy about Kethry, Tarma, and their shared quest for justice.

Leiber, Fritz
⇨ *Swords in the Mist: Fafhrd and the Grey Mouser.* <u>Lankhmar.</u> 1968. ibooks, ISBN: 1596872721, 432p.

Fafhrd, a barbarian warrior with surprising depth, and the Grey Mouser, a clever (sometimes overly so) thief, appeared in many <u>Lankhmar</u> tales. Fantasy's original odd couple inhabits stories that combine pulp-fiction action with a more literary style. Leiber's work was the first identified as sword and sorcery. This omnibus collects the third and fourth books in the series. Graphic novel fans should watch for Dark Horse's adaptation, due in 2007.

Monette, Sarah
Mélusine. <u>Felix and Mildmay.</u> 2005. Ace, ISBN: 0441014178, 496p.
The Virtu. <u>Felix and Mildmay.</u> 2006. Ace, ISBN: 0441014046, 448p. (hbk.)

In the title city of Mélusine, a haughty, overconfident wizard and a rough-edged, pessimistic thief form an unlikely alliance when fate throws them together. Felix and Mildmay are an odd couple, but they need each other. In alternating between Felix and Mildmay as narrators, Monette created one of the best-received debuts of 2005 and then followed with *The Virtu* a year later. Two more novels will follow.

Moore, Moira J.
Resenting the Hero. 2006. Ace, ISBN: 0441013880, 304p.

Moore brings us a world in which pairs bonded as Source and Shield diffuse the energy of the natural disasters that beset the land. You don't need an oracle to guess from the title that the Source and Shield leads of this book, Lee and Taro, mix as well as pickles and peanut butter. It may be predictable, but it's fun, romantic fantasy. A sequel follows.

Roberson, Jennifer
The Novels of Tiger and Del, Vol. 1. <u>Tiger and Del series.</u> 1986–1988. DAW, ISBN: 0756403197, 640p.

Tiger is a charming rogue, the best sword dancer in the South. When he finds himself challenged by Del, who is northern and, worse still, a woman, a battle of the sexes begins. From what could easily become stereotypical, Roberson creates an interesting, well-told story that grows even more complex as the series progresses.

Tolkien, J.R.R.
The Two Towers. <u>The Lord of the Rings</u>. 1954. Houghton Mifflin, ISBN: 0618574956, 924p.

> The underestimated Merry and Pippin rally the Ents. Frodo and Sam press forward into Mordor. Gimli and Legolas find mutual admiration through competition despite a racial rift. The development of these three diverse and inspiring friendships saves *Towers* from the middle-book syndrome that slows many fantasy trilogies.

Chivalry in Flower: Fantasy's Most Noble Knights

In real life, you probably wouldn't hang out with knights. They're too earnest, the glamour boys and teacher's pets of the fantasy realm. But in that realm of good and evil, they seem to fit. Tales of knights explore the extent to which we are bound by duty and honor. For readers with an urge to question morality, indulge in medieval romance, or feel the charge of single combat, these novels will sparkle as brightly as newly polished armor.

Duncan, Dave
⇨ *The Gilded Chain*. <u>King's Blades series</u>. 1998. Eos, ISBN: 0380791269, 432p.

> Duncan's knights are magically bound to the men they serve, unable to do anything but their duty. The mix of derring-do and moral dilemma creates superb storytelling, exploring every corner of knightliness. <u>King's Blades</u> is the holy grail of knight fantasy, especially in this first trilogy (including *Lord of the Fire Lands* and *Sky of Swords*).

Martin, George R. R.
The Hedge Knight. 2004. Dabel Brothers, ISBN: 097640110X, 164p.

> Duncan, a young knight, tries to gain recognition for himself at a tournament but discovers some of the cruelty underlying the shining armor. As a writer, Martin explores aspects of knighthood, from the mercenary to the noble and duty-bound. If you're not sure you want to commit to his excellent but long <u>Song of Ice and Fire</u> series, try this short novel set in the same world, available in this illustrated edition.

McKenzie, Nancy
Grail Prince. 2002. Del Rey, ISBN: 0345456483, 510p.

> Explore the interior world of the noblest knight, Sir Galahad. Alternating between youth and maturity, the book follows him from early quests for absolute purity through later years in which his goal is to become more human and well-rounded. Arthurian touchstones are here, but this fresh take on the legend is served with a hearty dollop of romance.

Micklem, Sarah
   Firethorn. 2004. Bantam Spectra, ISBN: 055338340X, 400p.
       A realistic look at the life of knights and their supporters in a feudal system. The title character, seduced by Sire Galan, becomes his sheath (a camp follower). The tough, young heroine maintains her place, though most sheaths are eventually discarded. Galan has realistic depth, and you'll be unsure until the end about the quality of his character. A gritty book that does not romanticize feudal life.

Morris, Gerald
   The Squire's Tale. <u>Squire's Tales</u>. 1998. Laurel Leaf, ISBN: 0440228239, 224p. YA.
       Morris repackages Arthurian legends from the perspective of the knights' squires. In this series opener, Terence serves Gawain as he strives to join the Round Table and then pursues his own destiny as a knight and seer. The <u>Tales</u> are fresh, funny, unafraid of emotional moments, and intelligent enough that adults can read them without embarrassment.

Zindell, David
   The Lightstone. 2001. Tor, ISBN: 0765349930, 464p.
       Tolkien meets the Grail legend in this first volume of a saga. The golden cup of heaven (the title Lightstone) will enable the dark angel Morjin to rule forever if he claims it. The king of Alonia sponsors a knightly quest to find it first. Valashu, a knight and the seventh son of a royal family, brings his companion Brother Maram to join the hunt.

Developing Damsels, Not Distressed: Feisty Princesses and Tomboy Treasures

There is probably no character in fantasy's company of stock types more familiar than the tomboy princess whose feisty nature gets her in trouble in the first act but leads her to save the day later in the book. These characters appeal not only to young female readers but to anyone who feels underestimated, unwilling to behave as expected, or reluctant to back down from beliefs, even when the cause is hopeless. Because these young women are similar to the heroines of romance novels, these books also make a fine entry point to fantasy for readers of that genre.

Eddings, David
   The Magician's Gambit. <u>The Belgariad</u>. 1981. Del Rey, ISBN: 0345335457, 320p.
       Ce'Nedra is the prototypical princess, a scene-stealer who upstages hero Garion in every scene the two share. In this middle book of five, Ce'Nedra

develops beyond the tantrum-thrower of the second book into a young woman with romantic feelings for the hero who has plenty to contribute to the quest herself.

Fallon, Jennifer
Treason Keep. **Demon Child trilogy.** 2000. Tor, ISBN: 0765348675, 536p.

It's not easy to introduce a character midtrilogy, yet Fallon not only brings in Princess Adrina but also writes her so vividly that she nearly steals the show. Adrina's father arranges her marriage, but her headstrong ways turn his political intent inside out. The main plot of the Demon Child also advances as Fallon steps forward from series opener *Medalon.*

Hale, Shannon
The Goose Girl. **Bayern.** 2003. Bloomsbury, ISBN: 1582349908, 400p. **YA**.

Princess Ani is betrayed by Selia, her evil lady-in-waiting, and forced into hiding as the title goose girl. Ani can talk to animals, but the story is not as cutesy as that sounds. Ani's real success is driven by her strength and cleverness. Fleshing out a Brothers Grimm tale, Hale finds success.

Huff, Tanya
Sing the Four Quarters. **Quarters series.** 1994. DAW, ISBN: 0886776287, 410p.

No, it's not a drinking game. It's about Bards using spells (singing) to summon spirits of the four elements (the quarters.) Annice, sister to the king, is pregnant. That's dangerous, as she agreed not to bear children as a condition to her rejection of marriage and pursuit of the life of a Bard. To protect her child, the one-night-stand father, and her long-term lover (a woman), Annice must use magic, leadership, and gumption.

Keyes, J. Gregory
The Blackgod. **Children of the Changeling.** 1997. Del Rey, ISBN: 0345418808, 512p.

In a polytheistic society, Princess Hezhi is daughter to the river god and thus destined to rejoin him (drown). To escape her fate, Hezhi goes on the run into wastes inhabited by a jumble of gods, demons, and warring tribes. A reanimated assassin trails a few steps behind. Strong character growth is a highlight of this follow-up to *The Waterborn.*

McKinley, Robin
Spindle's End. 2000. Ace, ISBN: 0441008658, 368p. **YA**.

In McKinley's retelling of "Sleeping Beauty," the princess is considerably less prissy. To avoid the curse of sleep, she is spirited away and raised as a common country village girl. But fate will have its way, and Rosie cannot escape the pricked finger, the eternal sleep, and the rescue with a kiss. It just may not happen in the way that you expect . . .

Siegel, Jan
  Prospero's Children. <u>Fern Capel</u>. 1999. Del Rey, ISBN: 0345441435, 352p.
      Left with little brother Will in an old Yorkshire house, teen Fern encounters some shady characters and a key into another world: Atlantis. The switch from a pastoral, gothic setting to Atlantis feels a bit disjointed, but the journey Fern takes from a priggish, somewhat bossy teen to young womanhood is believably depicted.

Wrede, Patricia C.
  ⇨ *Dealing with Dragons*. <u>Enchanted Forest Chronicles</u>. 1990. Magic Carpet, ISBN: 015204566X, 240p. **YA**.
      An archetypal tomboy, Cimorene decides that instead of being trapped in a pampered life on a princess's pedestal with a dim prince, she'd rather be captured by a dragon. If she can just dodge the rescuing princes, she might be happy. Wrede uses modern teen language in a fantasy setting to good results in this fun fantasy.

Damsels Who Deal Distress: Women Warriors

Equality is a common theme in fantasy, so it's no surprise that those teen tomboys grow into women who do *not* need to be rescued, thank you very much! The only dress these women want is full battle dress, and don't expect them to pick up a needle unless it's to sew up a gaping wound. If you're still mourning the cancellation of Xena's hammy TV theatrics, try reading about these women warriors instead.

Caine, Rachel
  Chill Factor. <u>Weather Warden</u>. 2005. Roc, ISBN: 0451460103, 352p.
      Think of Joanne Baldwin as a woman warrior for a contemporary era. She likes fast cars, fashion, and men, but her job (and magical skill) is controlling the weather. In this third book in the fast-paced series, Joanne battles a troublesome djinn in Las Vegas.

Cherryh, C. J.
  The Morgaine Saga. 1976–1979. DAW, ISBN: 0886778778, 720p.
      Morgaine, a warrior out of legend, the last of her kind, travels the universe using her gate sword Changeling to close time gates and stop the time continuum from unraveling. With sidekick Vanye, she's constantly on the run, struggling in the dirt and the grit. Three original novels are collected in this omnibus edition of first-rate science fantasy.

Friesner, Esther, ed.
Turn the Other Chick. <u>Chicks in Chain Mail</u>. 2004. Baen, ISBN: 1416520538, 400p.

In her fifth anthology of female warrior stories, Friesner collects Harry Turtledove, Jodi Lynn Nye, Eric Flint, Wen Spencer, and others. The series makes it into hardback for the first time here. Like most story collections, these volumes are a mixed bag, but where else can riot grrrl readers find hearty helpings of Amazons with a sense of humor?

Martin, George R. R.
A Feast for Crows. <u>A Song of Ice and Fire</u>. 2005. Bantam Spectra, ISBN: 055358202X, 1088p.

This fourth book in <u>Ice and Fire</u> tested fan patience, both because it was slow to arrive and because the book, pushing size limits, was split in two parts. *Feast* covers only half of the series characters but was worth the wait. Female characters are particularly strong, especially Brienne, the homely warrior who is the purest of Martin's enormous cast.

Moon, Elizabeth
⇨ *The Deed of Paksenarrion*. 1988. Baen, ISBN: 0671721046, 1040p.

In three books, Moon follows heroine Paks from her origins as a sheep-farmer's daughter, through life as a soldier, and on to the exalted rank of paladin. Now, the books are available in one omnibus. Deep in military description and featuring a completely believable heroine, this is a highlight of the fantasy canon.

Pierce, Tamora
Alanna: The First Adventure. <u>The Song of the Lioness</u>. 1983. Simon Pulse, ISBN: 0689878559, 240p. YA.

Destined for the convent, Alanna disguises herself as her brother and begins training as a page. Budding female warriors will love the quartet this book starts, and their brothers and parents will want to join the fun. Cataloging the value of drive and perseverance, this fast-moving book hasn't aged a day since it appeared more than twenty years ago.

Scott, Manda
Dreaming the Eagle. <u>Boudica</u>. 2003. Bantam Spectra, ISBN: 0385337736, 496p.

The Celtic warrior queen who fought Roman invasion in the first century is brought to life. *Eagle* only scores a par, but Scott starts her trilogy solidly, bringing plenty of passion to the historical fantasy.

Walton, Jo
The King's Peace. <u>Tir Tanagiri</u>. 2000. Tor, ISBN: 0765343274, 544p.

Looking back at her long life, Sulien recalls how she survived (barely) a Jarnish raid at the age of 16 and thereafter dedicated herself to their destruction.

Her soldiering and smarts bring her to the attention of King Urdo, whose right hand she becomes. Think of this as a retelling of Arthurian myths with a woman in the part of Lancelot.

Conans for Librarians: Fantasy's Strongest Barbarian Warriors

With simple ethics, complex muscle definition, and a mind that's naive but quick to learn, the barbarian warrior makes an appealing hero, particularly for those who believe that choosing right and wrong doesn't have to be as complicated as some people make it. The barbarian wades easily into any fray knowing who he will hit first. He emerges covered in his enemy's blood, without having broken a sweat. Here are a few of fantasy's finest examples.

Gemmell, David
⇨ *Legend*. <u>Drenai</u>. 1984. Del Rey, ISBN: 0345379063, 345p.
    OK, Gemmell's heroes aren't barbarians. They usually fight with barbarians, but they have a barbarian ethic: simple men caught in big events who sort out the complexity one swing of the axe at a time. The <u>Drenai</u> series kicks off with this book, in which an over-the-hill hero and his ragtag troops must hold a fortress against a force 25 times larger.

Howard, Robert E.
The Coming of Conan the Cimmerian. 1932–1934. Del Rey, ISBN: 0345461517, 496p.
    Howard's brief Depression-era career produced the standard against which all barbarians are compared. Conan wanders his world in search of power and treasure, using brawn and a surprising brain to survive against all odds. Three Del Rey volumes return the original stories, enhanced by illustrations and excellent appendixes, to print after a long absence. Follow this with *The Bloody Crown of Conan* and *The Conquering Sword of Conan*.

Jordan, Robert
The Conan Chronicles. 1995. Tor, ISBN: 0312859295, 512p.
    Before he began his epic <u>Wheel of Time</u> series, Jordan made his name as a modern interpreter of Howard's Conan character. This volume collects three of his best efforts, *Conan the Invincible*, *Conan the Defender*, and *Conan the Unconquered*.

Marillier, Juliet
Wolfskin. <u>Children of the Light Isles</u>. 2003. Tor, ISBN: 0765345900, 544p.
    Viking Eyvind and his companion Somerled only want to be Wolfskins: berserker warriors who fight hard and die young. But when Eyvind is sent to

a beautiful foreign land and finds the love of a young seer, he starts to see his life in a different way.

Moorcock, Michael
Eternal Champion series. 1961–2003. (out of print.)
For fiber-rich, pulpy goodness, add Moorcock's books to your barbarian banquet. After writing for a few years, Moorcock linked several of his heroes with the story of The Eternal Champion, a warrior battling across space and time in different incarnations. Elric books are the best (and most barbaric) followed by tales of Von Bek and Jerry Cornelius.

Wagner, Karl Edward
Conan: The Road of Kings. 1979. Tor, ISBN: 0765340208, 224p.
Dozens of writers have attempted Conan pastiches, including luminaries Poul Anderson and L. Sprague de Camp. Opinion varies, but Wagner and Robert Jordan are judged successful most often. Roy Thomas and Kurt Busiek graphic novels are also worthy of attention.

Weber, David
The War God's Own. War God series. 1998. Baen, ISBN: 0671577921, 400p.
When Dave Weber isn't writing Honor Harrington space operas, he's often engaged with Bahzell Bahnakson. Bahzell is hradani: a giant humanoid with foxlike ears and a Sean Connery brogue. He's been made extra tough by his low position on the social ladder, but that doesn't restrain his spirit in entertaining adventures (this follows *Oath of Swords*).

Wizards and Warlocks: The Wise, the Wily, and the Wacky

Before relying on a wizard, you might rethink. We should learn this lesson young from the Wizard of Oz, but we persist in thinking wizards helpful. Count the times Dumbledore keeps critical knowledge from his young charges or turns to them at a perilous moment and says "Well it's been nice. I'll leave this one to you." Gandalf is forever dashing off or falling down a Balrog hole. Bilbo and Frodo would have it easy if their grey "friend" would stay put for more than fifteen minutes at a time. So unless you enjoy scanning the skyline for eagles at the end, hoping old what's-his-staff shambles by, take a little care. Need more proof? Consider these fellows.

Barron, T. A.
A T. A. Barron Collection. The Lost Years of Merlin. 1996–1998. Philomel, ISBN: 0399237348, 928p. (hbk.) YA.
Opening with Merlin suffering amnesia on the Welsh coast, this story tracks his development on the magical island of Fincayra. Barron's young

Merlin is likable but has a temper and cockiness that get him in trouble. This three-book omnibus is a great choice for Potter fans, who can compare Harry's youth to that of the most famous wizard of all.

Butcher, Jim
Blood Rites. Dresden Files. 2004. Roc, ISBN: 0451459873, 372p.

Harry Dresden is a modern Chicago detective and professional wizard. Full of witty banter, last-minute escapes, and Harry's flubs, the series has garnered a growing army of fans. This sixth book, an investigation of entropy curses hitting the associates of a sleazy producer, adds depth to secondary characters and gives insight into Harry's history.

Jones, Diana Wynne
The Chronicles of Chrestomanci, Vol. 1. 1977–1978. Eos, ISBN: 006447268X, 608p. YA.
The Chronicles of Chrestomanci, Vol. 2. 1980–1982. Eos, ISBN: 0064472698, 560p. YA.

Follow young Christopher Chant to his adulthood as Chrestomanci, a dapper Englishman with nine lives who is in charge of magic on many parallel worlds. Jones writes for an audience similar to that of J. K. Rowling, but her compact style may appeal to those who aren't sure they have time for the thick Potter books.

Kirstein, Rosemary
The Language of Power. Steerswomen series. 2004. Del Rey, ISBN: 034546835X, 400p.

In the fourth book in this series, Rowan's job is to collect and share information as she travels. She becomes involved in the investigation of a wizard and the followers she suspects had a role in both his death and those of many planetary settlers. With twisty plots and an unusual blend of science and magic, this series is building to a strong conclusion.

Le Guin, Ursula K.
⇨ *A Wizard of Earthsea*. Earthsea. 1968. Bantam Spectra, ISBN: 0553383043, 192p. YA.

The graceful life arc of wizard Ged begins in Le Guin's first Earthsea book. Progressing from overeager youth into more contemplative adulthood, Ged learns the power of true names. This classic shuns fireworks and jokiness, instead telling a meditative tale of tragedy and triumph. Thinking readers remember this quiet book long after they finish.

Pratchett, Terry
Sourcery. Discworld, Rincewind series. 1988. HarperTorch, ISBN: 0061020672, 288p.

From the sublime to the sublimely ridiculous: A classic bumbler like most of his absent-minded colleagues at Unseen University, Rincewind must stop a 10-year-old "sourceror" who has real magical power. With only the orangutan Librarian, a hairdressing warrior princess, and skinny Nijel the Destroyer to help, Discworld may be in trouble.

Stewart, Mary
Mary Stewart's Merlin Trilogy. 1970–1979. Eos, ISBN: 0688003478, 928p. (hbk.)
For a different take on the Merlin legend, here's a classic omnibus. Stewart's Merlin, who serves as first-person narrator, is a humble man who uses wisdom as much as magic to mentor Arthur through his rise and fall in fifth-century Britain. More historical than most of its competitors, this is the series that many Arthurian fiction fans rank first.

Witches: The Good, the Bad, and the Ugly among Fantasy's Women of Magic

Whether called witch, sorceress, or something more exotic, magic's women are every bit as mysterious as their male counterparts. They have tough exteriors, but you'll love them (or at least like them), warts and all. Underneath lies a nurturing side, often connected to nature. Don't underestimate their power: They show real strength, too. But put your stereotypes aside, there's an exception for every rule in this fascinating collection of magical women.

Clemens, James
Wit'ch Fire. **The Banned and the Banished.** 1998. Del Rey, ISBN: 0345417062, 448p.
You may have seen this plot before: A girl discovers she is the subject of prophecy and must marshal magical talents and allies before the Dark Lord overruns everything. But Clemens gets the story moving quickly and keeps a brisk pace. Elena, the reincarnated "wit'ch of spirit and stone" is engaging, and she's supported by an able cast of players. Get o'ver the distra'cting apostrop'hes. Hiding behind them is fine fantasy.

Hambly, Barbara
Dragonsbane. **Winterlands.** 1985. Del Rey, ISBN: 0345349393, 352p.
Jenny Waynest is a fantasy character with a real-world woman's dilemma. She is a mediocre mage who would like to study and learn more but can't because husband John and her children take too much of her time. When Jenny follows John to defend their capital city from a dragon, she finds herself in a test of her true strength.

Marcellas, Diana
Mother Ocean, Daughter Sea. <u>Witch of Two Suns.</u> 2001. Tor, ISBN: 0812561775, 448p.

> Brierley believes herself to be the last of a race of exterminated witches. She lives quietly, hiding in a cave until the day she is called to perform a healing. When her powers become known, she should flee, but instead she forestalls her escape because she discovers another young witch. Brierley risks her life to protect the girl and explore the history of her people.

Norton, Andre
<u>*The Gates to Witch World*.</u> 1963–1965. Orb, ISBN: 0765300516, 464p.

> The witches of Estcarp team with off-world strangers to defend themselves or their land against invasion or violation in these science fantasies. Norton wrote genre classics from the 1940s until her death in 2005, but her longest series was <u>Witch World</u>. This omnibus collects the first three books, written in the 1960s but still popular with readers.

Pratchett, Terry
Equal Rites. <u>Discworld Witches series</u>. 1987. HarperTorch, ISBN: 0061020699, 240p.

> The books in Pratchett's <u>Discworld</u> that feature the witches are some of the best. These are great if you like women of magic, because they explore and satirize all the clichés about them. The quick, funny *Equal Rites* deals with only one of the four recurring witches, but it provides a nice primer to Granny Weatherwax's oddly logical "headology."

Pratchett, Terry
⇨ *Wyrd Sisters.* <u>Discworld Witches series</u>. 1988. HarperTorch, ISBN: 0061020664, 288p.

> *Wyrd Sisters* is a standout that adds bawdy, sodden, grandmotherly Nanny Ogg and the new-age sensibilities of young but prim Magrat Garlick to the mix. This is Pratchett's grand spoof of Shakespeare, particularly Macbeth and Hamlet. Later books featuring the witches include *Witches Abroad, Lords and Ladies, Maskerade,* and *Carpe Jugulum.*

Reimann, Katya
Wind from a Foreign Sky. <u>Tielmaran</u>. 1996. Tor, ISBN: 0812549333, 384p.

> Gaultry, a huntress and hedgewitch, must master her powers and self-doubt to rescue her twin sister and her country. The story features sophisticated political and religious intrigue and an atypical female/male relationship at the novel's center. First of a series.

Absolutely the Worst: Fantasy's Most Detestable Villains

Are any genre's villains worse than those in fantasy? Sure, mysteries and thrillers have killers, and the realistic baddies in literary or historical fiction are scary, but fantasy has villains who commit genocide with a laugh and want to turn everyone to the dark side. In a real world in which evil comes in shades of gray, many readers enjoy rooting against fantasy villains who are absolutely rotten; here's a selection of the genre's most detestable.

Brooks, Terry
The Elfstones of Shannara. <u>**Shannara**</u>. 1982. Del Rey, ISBN: 0345285549, 576p.

Brooks's books may not win critical awards, but they'll be in print long after most that do. Many call this the best of his long <u>Shannara</u> series. It certainly has the scariest baddies, particularly the Reaper, a demon who leaves a trail of bodies behind in his pursuit of Amberle—the last who can regrow the Ellcrys tree—and her protector Will Ohmsford.

Lebbon, Tim
Dusk. 2006. Bantam Spectra, ISBN: 0553383647, 416p.

The Mages are *Dusk*'s main bad guys: a group that carefully controls the use of magic. The *truly* scary villains, however, are the Red Monks, minions of the Mages sent after people with magical ability. Many of the best scenes, nightmarish bits of action in Lebbon's mix of fantasy and horror, are those told from the Red Monks' point of view.

Lisle, Holly
The Diplomacy of Wolves. <u>**The Secret Texts**</u>. 1998. Aspect, ISBN: 0446607460, 416p.

If you shudder appreciatively at evil villains as they revel in hatred and egomania, then you'll enjoy the Wolves of Lisle's series starter (especially the odious Crispin Sabir). These dark magicians channel power from cruel sacrifices, absorbing a magical backlash that disfigures them. If you can't get past brutality, stay away.

McIntosh, Fiona
Myrren's Gift. <u>**The Quickening**</u>. 2005. Eos, ISBN: 0060747560, 576p.

How much does duty require of us? Young Wyl Thirsk inherits a generalship, but with that goes the duty to protect Prince Celimus, whose depravity seems to have no bounds. Taking pity on one of Celimus's victims, Wyl is gifted with powers that earn him permanent enmity from a nasty customer in this series opener.

Park, Paul
A Princess of Roumania. <u>**White Tyger series**</u>. 2005. Tor, ISBN: 0765349507, 480p.

In Park's alternate history series opener, Miranda, heir to the Roman Empire, escapes to a parallel world (our Massachusetts) to avoid evil Baroness Ceaucescu, whose dark magic soon unlocks her hiding place. The Baroness is crazy in a scary way, committing evil, crying about it, and then obliterating her tears with anger and more bad deeds.

Snicket, Lemony
⇨ *The Bad Beginning.* A Series of Unfortunate Events. 1999. HarperCollins, ISBN: 0064407667, 162p. (hbk.) YA.

Pity the Baudelaires. The sibling trio is put through a maze of miseries for the pleasure of readers. The awfulness emanates from Count Olaf, the greedy master of disguise who follows them through 13 books like a bad penny, merrily perpetrating evil against children. These books for young readers please anyone with a heart dressed in black.

Yarbro, Chelsea Quinn
Hotel Transylvania. Saint-Germain. 1978. Stealth, ISBN: 1588810097, 277p. (hbk.)

Whether or not you like Anne Rice, try Yarbro's vampire series, 18 books and counting. These are dark historical fantasies about a good-guy vampire's adventures throughout history. This first book (chronologically the latest) also has a deliciously evil enemy: Saint-Sebastien, head of a satanic cult and bane to both his friends and his foes.

Rogues' Gallery: Thieves, Assassins, and Other Charismatic Scoundrels

In the tradition of Robin Hood, fantasy thieves and assassins undermine crooked leaders, redistribute the wealth of the greedy, and deliver witty bons mots, all without breaking a sweat. These characters get the best names: something that sounds suave when whispered by a beautiful woman *or* when used as a curse by a corrupt official. These books will be a great pleasure to anyone who has a rebellious streak or who likes fantasy with dashes of derring-do and humor.

Brust, Steven
The Book of Jhereg. Vlad Taltos. 1983–1987. Ace, ISBN: 0441006159, 480p.

A stylish assassin and witch, Vlad Taltos works the gritty streets of Andrilankha. Whether busy with murder, love, or something between, he covers his inner turmoil with roguish panache. Brust's long-running series is distinguished by its wry humor and witty repartee. This edition is an omnibus of the first three novels of the series.

Colfer, Eoin
Artemis Fowl. Artemis Fowl series. 2001. Miramax, ISBN: 0786817070, 304p. YA.

A 12-year-old criminal mastermind antihero, Artemis uses both magic and technology. Aided by Butler, his appropriately named manservant, he perpetrates creative comic capers. Although kids might find better role models, adults looking to rediscover a preteen sense of humor will have a ball. Several sequels and prequels have followed.

Feist, Raymond E.
Silverthorn. __Riftwar Saga.__ 1985. Bantam Spectra, ISBN: 0553270540, 368p.
   Jimmy the Hand, a thief, is a secondary character in earlier books in Feist's series, but here he steals so many scenes that he becomes the best thing about this story of a prince's quest to find an antidote for the poisoning of his wife-to-be.

Flewelling, Lynn
Luck in the Shadows. __Nightrunner.__ 1996. Bantam Spectra, ISBN: 0553575422, 496p.
   When young Alec is imprisoned for a crime he didn't commit, his cell mate—the spy, thief, and rogue Seregil—becomes his mentor. If you ever wondered if Batman and Robin had something going on beyond crime fighting, this book, which explores the two men's relationship, may be for you. The first of a trilogy.

Funke, Cornelia
The Thief Lord. 2002. Chicken House, ISBN: 043942089X, 376p. `YA`.
   Mysterious Venetian settings and colorful characters enliven Funke's tale of Victor, an unusual detective hired to track Prosper and Bo, two orphaned brothers involved with an Oliver Twist-like gang of child thieves led by the cocky and oh-so-elusive title character, a young rascal named Scipio.

Gemmell, David
Waylander. __Drenai.__ 1986. Del Rey, ISBN: 0345379071, 320p.
   Against his better judgment, master assassin Waylander takes a contract and kills the king of Drenai, only to discover he was set up. On the run, in pursuit of redemption, he quests for magic armor that, if worn by the right general, will save his land from invasion.

McKenna, Juliet E.
The Thief's Gamble. __Tales of Einarinn.__ 1999. Eos, ISBN: 0061020362, 512p.
   A female thief and gambler, sudden attacks from strange, short, blonde men, mysterious forms of magic, and ever-rising stakes: sounds like Internet dating! But no, these are elements in McKenna's debut novel. First of the Tales of Einarinn.

Pratchett, Terry
Pyramids. __Discworld.__ 1989. HarperTorch, ISBN: 0061020656, 352p.
⇨ *Going Postal.* __Discworld.__ 2004. HarperTorch, ISBN: 0060502932, 416p.
   Almost everyone in Discworld is a con artist of some sort, but two excellent entries feature criminal leads. In *Pyramids,* an assassin is surprised to find

himself king of his Egypt-like homeland, which promptly goes missing from the space-time continuum. In *Postal,* master thief Moist von Lipwig avoids hanging by accepting the position of Postmaster General in Ankh-Morpork's decrepit post office. Of course, in both books, irreverent humor is the star (and the sun and the moon).

Reichert, Mickey Zucker
The Legend of Nightfall. <u>Nightfall series</u>. 1993. DAW, ISBN: 0886775876, 496p.
　　Nightfall, a thief and master of disguise, is forced to take on the mentoring of a naive young prince. His greatest challenge is coming to grips with his own history and the legend that surrounds his name. This is followed by *The Return of Nightfall.*

Turner, Megan Whalen
The Thief. <u>The Queen's Thief</u>. 1996. Puffin, ISBN: 0140388346, 219p. YA.
　　In Turner's treasure, Gen, a brash, undisciplined, but likable young thief, progresses from braggadocio to wisdom as he hunts a gemstone in ancient Greece. Gen is in over his head and must mature quickly if he is to survive. This opens a trilogy.

Life in the Hood: Monks and Other Religious Figures in Fantasy

　　In fantasy, religion can be good or evil but is almost always practiced vigorously. Those committed to the faith (whatever faith that may be) don't wait meekly for God (or the gods) to deliver miracles, they make miracles of their own with strong arms, swift wits, and faith-based magic. Others pursue intolerance fervidly to an unnatural and evil conclusion. No matter what your personal beliefs, fantasy has interpretations of religion that should be of interest. Here are books with interesting religious characters to help you start your search.

Canavan, Trudi
Priestess of the White. <u>Age of Five</u>. 2006. Eos, ISBN: 0060815701, 608p.
　　In this series opener, Auraya saves a village from invaders, becoming one of five White Guardians. But her mentor and love interest is of the Dreamweavers, a competing sect that believes the Whites' five gods are evil, not good. If that wasn't enough, a third sect, the Pentadrians, who promote new gods, are rapidly gaining power.

Carey, Jacqueline
Kushiel's Dart. <u>Kushiel trilogy</u>. 2001. Tor, ISBN: 0765342987, 816p.
　　He's a monk; he's a warrior; he's a guardian! He's heroine Phèdre's love interest, even though he's about the only male in the book that doesn't sleep

with her. He's Joscelin: the surly Cassiline brother and secondary character extraordinaire, whose role only grows as the <u>Kushiel</u> trilogy advances.

Douglass, Sara
The Nameless Day. <u>**The Crucible**</u>. 2000. Tor, ISBN: 0765342820, 576p.
    In an alternate fourteenth century, Brother Wynken guards the gates of hell. He dies, releasing demons into the world. Archangel Michael selects Thomas Neville as his successor: a hypocritical, ornery ex-soldier who became a Dominican to atone for his role in a woman's murder/suicide. If moral complexity appeals to you, choose this series opener.

Keyes, Greg
⇨ *The Briar King*. <u>**Kingdoms of Thorn and Bone**</u>. 2004. Del Rey, ISBN: 0345440706, 608p.
    Young know-it-all Stephen Darige wants the life of a cloistered scholar but instead finds that evil has infected the monastery. Keyes creates a world in which religious devotion can lead a monk to special powers. Stephen is one of many sympathetic protagonists—a gruff woodsman, a feisty princess, and an idealistic knight—in <u>Thorn and Bone</u>.

Pratchett, Terry
Small Gods. <u>**Discworld**</u>. 1992. HarperTorch, ISBN: 0061092177, 384p.
    When Pratchett takes on religious hypocrisy, beliefs will tremble and fall from the trees faster than anyone can rake them up. Skewering religion, philosophy, government, and science, *Small Gods* is the story of Brutha, a novitiate with a photographic memory but a bulb so dim that his mental slide show is fuzzy and out of sequence. He's the only follower of Om who accepts that the great god is trapped in the body of a turtle.

Pratchett, Terry
Thief of Time. <u>**Discworld, Death**</u>. 2001. HarperTorch, ISBN: 0061031321, 384p.
    Bureaucratic Auditors take on Death, tricking obsessive Jeremy into building a clock so perfect it will stop time. History Monk Lu-Tze and his apprentice Lobsang must find him before he can do it. Meanwhile, Death reassembles the Five Horsemen (one had split because of creative differences) for an apocalyptic ride. Like a Zen riddle, but sillier.

Tarr, Judith
The Hound and the Falcon. 1985–1986. Orb, ISBN: 0312853033, 688p.
    Alfred has been a monk for seventy years, but he realizes that he isn't aging, which means he is an elf, one of the fair folk. Unsure how to continue his life, he leaves his monastery and gets swept up in political events centering on Richard the Lionheart and the Crusades. This omnibus holds a trilogy of historical fantasist Tarr's best work.

Wells, Martha
Wheel of the Infinite. 2000. Eos, ISBN: 0380788152, 400p.

Maskelle was once the Voice of the Adversary, a sort of oracle passing judgment on evil and injustice in the Celestial Empire. But a false judgment led to the murder of an innocent, and she was exiled. When a critical rite is threatened by a black storm and the folk who sent it, Maskelle is called back into service in a dangerous quest for redemption.

Finding Courage: Fantasy Heroes Look Deep Within

Liver? Check. Pancreas? Check. Spleen? Check? Big Heart? Cast-Iron Stomach? Check. Check. And what's that? When fantasy heroes are up against it, they look deep inside and find something extra, a source of courage in the face of impossible odds. We all hope to find grace under pressure when we need it. Its depiction in fantasy is one reason why so many love the genre. Prepare for your own gut check by reading these books.

Dickson, Gordon R.
The Dragon and the George. **Dragon Knight series.** 1976. Del Rey, ISBN: 0345350502, 288p.

There's much to like in this classic: fast pace, humor, and believable, sympathetic characters. In the end, what makes the book special is heart. Each main character—Jim, a man turned into a dragon; a very English wolf; Dafydd the archer; and even Secoh, a cowardly magician—exhibits bravery and courage when it counts most.

Hobb, Robin
⇨ *The Golden Fool.* **Tawny Man.** 2002. Bantam Spectra, ISBN: 0553582453, 736p.

Hobb plays God to FitzChivalry's Job, putting him through a slew of trials. He's at his nadir in this middle book, with friends dead, dying, or estranged, his son gone astray, and a plague of political problems. Worse, he has contributed to his own unraveling. Fitz stays true to core beliefs while battling weakness, making him the best kind of hero.

Le Guin, Ursula K.
The Farthest Shore. **Earthsea.** 1972. Simon Pulse, ISBN: 0689845340, 272p.

When a wizard casts a spell that denies death, he puts Earthsea out of balance: Life and magic also have been denied. Archmage Ged and young Arren must sail for the farthest shore of the title and face the ultimate test (you can't take it with a number two pencil, if you know what I mean) to reestablish balance.

Lewis, C. S.
The Voyage of the Dawn Treader. <u>Chronicles of Narnia</u>. 1952. HarperTrophy, ISBN: 0064409465, 256p. YA.

Sometimes looking within is not just a matter of courage but of finding capacity to change. This personal growth is one charm of Lewis's young heroes. In *Dawn Treader,* obnoxious cousin Eustace torments Lucy and Edmund (who made his own improvements in the first <u>Narnia</u> book). But Eustace matures, becoming a help, not a hindrance, in a sea quest to find seven missing lords.

Nix, Garth
Grim Tuesday. <u>Keys to the Kingdom</u>. 2003. Scholastic, ISBN: 0439436559, 336p. YA.

Nix puts little Arthur Penhaligon up against a really bad week: Each day is a villain who represents one of the seven deadly sins. With each encounter, the future of Earth is in the balance. Clear of Monday, Arthur finds himself in the pits—greedy Grim Tuesday's Pit of Nothing, to be specific. He must escape and claim the second of the series' seven *Keys*.

Tolkien, J.R.R.
The Return of the King. <u>Lord of the Rings</u>. 1955. Houghton Mifflin, ISBN: 0618002243, 464p.

Frodo Baggins, the lovable hobbit hero of the <u>Lord of the Rings</u>, goes to the edge of the abyss: both the physical abyss of the Crack of Doom and the abyss at the center of his own character as he tries to cast off the ultimate power and burden of the One Ring.

Animal Attractions: Fantasy Characters to Bring Out Your Wild Side

Talking animals inhabit three worlds: Disney cartoons, bar jokes, and fantasy novels. It's no accident that a disproportionate percentage of fantasy fans are animal lovers: No other genre so vividly features their favorite creatures. Speaking of favorite creatures, I've been reading my book to my best editor: my cat Beelzebub. He likes it, but he'd probably prefer these novels.

Adams, Richard
➪ *Watership Down.* 1972. Scribner, ISBN: 0743277708, 496p.

One of the great novels is about talking rabbits with names like Dandelion and Bigwig. Those over 12 might feel childish reading such material in public, but it's for all ages. Fiver, a runt with sixth sense, foresees his warren's destruction. His brother Hazel, a natural leader, takes a small band of distinctive rabbits in search of a new home. Of Adams's other animal books, *Shardik,* about a bear god, is a good second choice.

Clement-Davies, David
Fire Bringer. 1999. Firebird, ISBN: 0142300608, 512p. **YA**.
The Sight. 2002. Puffin, ISBN: 014250047X, 480p. **YA**.
    Born on the day his father dies, Rannoch is destined by prophecy to depose a tyrant. His adventures lead him to a showdown with a fascist leader. Did I mention that Rannoch is a deer? If you wish you could read *Watership Down* again for the first time, *Fire Bringer* is a good substitute. *The Sight,* about a Transylvanian wolf pack, is just as compelling.

Duane, Diane
The Book of Night with Moon. 1997. Aspect, ISBN: 0446606332, 464p. **YA**.
    Duane's cats have their own society and history. They speak a secret language, protect the world from invaders, and guard transit gates. Despite these similarities to real cats, this is fiction. The feline characters here are each drawn as convincing individuals, and Duane maintains a sense of humor without sinking to the preciousness that hurts many anthropomorphic stories.

Jacques, Brian
Redwall. **Redwall series**. 1986. Philomel, ISBN: 0399214240, 352p. (hbk.) **YA**.
    With 18 books to date, the Redwall series is long, but quality has never flagged. This book started it. Mice who battle rats are the central characters, but a menagerie of other animals is mixed in. With charming characters and plots that mix heroics, tragedy, and humor, Jacques overcomes cynicism (both the youthful and the world-weary kinds) by involving readers deeply in his rattling good stories.

Johnson, Kij
The Fox Woman. 1999. Tor, ISBN: 0312875592, 384p.
    Expanding a Japanese folk tale, Johnson weaves the story of two families, one of humans and one of foxes, whose fates entwine at an isolated country estate. The foxes can don human form. In such a guise, young Kitsune falls in love with the human husband Yoshifuji. A poetic, meditative style gives this fantasy unusual depth.

Lindskold, Jane
Through Wolf's Eyes. **Firekeeper series**. 2001. Tor, ISBN: 0812575482, 608p.
    Raised by magic-enhanced wolves, Firekeeper returns to civilization, where she finds herself in a kingdom with no heir, surrounded by political intrigue. Using lessons and behaviors learned from the pack, she survives and succeeds in the complex human world.

Pierce, Tamora
Wild Magic. **The Immortals series**. 1992. Simon Pulse, ISBN: 1416903437, 384p. YA.

Opening a new saga, Pierce introduces Daine, a mountain girl who helps the Queen's Horse Keeper collect ponies while learning to focus wild magic: an ability to heal and communicate with animals. In the crowded stable of books about magical girls who love horses, this will put a canter in your step and make you whinny in delight.

Pullman, Philip
The Golden Compass. **His Dark Materials**. 1995. Laurel Leaf, ISBN: 0440238145, 304p. YA.

Each human character in *Compass* has an animal "daemon": a familiar that represents his or her soul. In young children (such as spirited heroine Lyra), the daemon shifts shape until a form is found that is the perfect fit. The opening volume also gets four hairy thumbs up for the magnificent showdown between two majestic, armored polar bears.

Williams, Tad
Tailchaser's Song. 1985. DAW, ISBN: 0886779537, 400p.

When his friend Hushpad goes missing, Tailchaser, a ginger tom, begins adventures in a world of cats in trouble. The story would work with human protagonists, but with felines, it's purr-fect. Before he began writing doorstop series, Williams captivated readers with this entry in the cat-alog of feline fantasy.

The Care and Feeding of Magical Creatures: A Fantastic Menagerie

Wait a minute, plain old animals? Hold your horses! In fact, hold all the horses! I will not wolf down another un-bear-able animal book. They're for the birds. Is that old zoo the best you can do? How about some imagination? There must be more interesting creatures than talking animals caged up inside those pages. Don't worry; if you're tired of reigning cats and dogs, there are indeed more fantastic beasties available for your fantasy reading pleasure.

Beagle, Peter S.
The Last Unicorn. 1968. Roc, ISBN: 0451450523, 224p.

Wondering if she is the last of her kind, a unicorn leaves her beloved forest to find the truth. If you saw the animated film and assume the book was for kids, give this classic another look. With lyrical language and vivid secondary characters, Beagle fully satisfies adult readers. The mythic qualities of the unicorn, the Red Bull, a horrible harpy, and other creatures will linger long after you finish this quick read.

Borchardt, Alice
The Silver Wolf. <u>Legends of the Wolves</u>. 1998. Ballantine, ISBN: 0345423615, 480p.

Regeane, a female werewolf, gets caught in a struggle between the Pope, Charlemagne, and the Lombards in the eighth century. With its wolf-suckling, womb-mate founders, where better to find werewolves than Rome? Borchardt blends history, romance, and horror in a satisfying fantasy. If you like this, *Night of the Wolf* and *The Wolf King* follow.

Hobb, Robin
Mad Ship. <u>Liveship Traders</u>. 1999. Bantam Spectra, ISBN: 0553575643, 864p.

How are sea serpents, dragons, and living ships related? This isn't a riddle from pirate school, it's the question at the core of this middle book of a trilogy. Of course, you'll want to read *Ship of Magic* before this and *Ship of Destiny* afterward. And by the way, the human characters are superlative here as well.

McKillip, Patricia A.
The Forgotten Beasts of Eld. 1974. Magic Carpet, ISBN: 0152055363, 352p. **AW**.

Having grown up with beasts, sorceress Sybel is drawn into the human world when Coren, a nobleman she comes to love, brings her a child. Coren's father the king betrays her, and Sybel must decide how far to take revenge. Readers won't forget the seven beasts, especially a bloodthirsty falcon, a riddle-posing boar, and the shadowy Blammor.

Pullman, Philip
The Amber Spyglass. <u>His Dark Materials</u>. 1999. Yearling, ISBN: 0440418569, 544p. **YA**.

The climactic volume of <u>Materials</u> hinges on magical creatures. The elephant-trunked, diamond-shaped Mulefa, which use seedpods as wheels, are connected to the mystery of the all-important Dust. The gallant Gallivespians are tiny spies who ride dragonflies and carry poison in their barbed heels. And don't forget the horrid harpies that feed on the spirits of the dead but ultimately lead an exodus from the underworld.

Reichert, Mickey Zucker
The Beasts of Barakhai. <u>Books of Barakhai</u>. 2001. DAW, ISBN: 0756400406, 352p.

Lost and hungry in an alternate world, grad student Benton Collins kills and eats a rabbit. This is a mistake, as in Barakhai everyone spends half of life in an animal body. Collins is sentenced to death for eating a sweet old woman. But all is not as it seems, and a last-minute rescue gives him the chance to fulfill his destined role in ending an old curse.

Rowling, J. K.
⇨ *Harry Potter and the Prisoner of Azkaban.* <u>Harry Potter series</u>. 1999. Scholastic, ISBN: 043965548X, 560p. `YA`, `AW`.

    Wonderful creatures are everywhere in Rowling's series, nowhere more so than in this third volume. You'll fear the horrid soul-sucking Dementors, ponder the natures of a frightening black dog and a suspicious sickly rat, and thrill to the fierce but noble hippogriff Buckbeak. Rowling makes you long to learn the care and feeding of magical creatures from the big-bodied, bigger-hearted Hagrid.

Smaug Gets in Your Eyes: Fantasy's Formidable Dragons

    Thick, scaly skin, flame-throwing breath, filling passersby with terror and awe . . . but enough about me in the morning. The subject is that ubiquitous fantasy creature, the dragon. If you have a fixed conception of the big flying lizards, open your mind—scores of authors portray them in myriad ways. Dragon lovers may be familiar with the creations of Tolkien, Le Guin, and the newly hyped Christopher Paolini, but here are some fine dragon novels that are less known.

Bertin, Joanne
The Last Dragonlord. 1998. Tor, ISBN: 0812545419, 512p.

    Linden's starting to believe he's the last weredragon. He has pined for a soultwin (mate) for six centuries, but none has come, and the evil Fellowship would destroy his kind once and for all. Hope comes from Maurynna, a feisty sea captain who Linden suspects may be hiding a dragon side of her own. If the idea of half dragons, half humans as romance icons intrigues you, find this book.

Hobb, Robin
Assassin's Quest. <u>The Farseer trilogy</u>. 1997. Bantam Spectra, ISBN: 0553565699, 757p.

    Hobb's first trilogy climaxes with discovery of huge stone dragons. But are these stony sentinels more than a sculpture garden? Fitz, Regal, and their allies must find the answer if they hope to save the realm. If you like this unusual depiction of dragons, continue to the <u>Tawny Man</u> trilogy.

Kerner, Elizabeth
Song in the Silence. <u>Lanen Kaelar series</u>. 1997. Tor, ISBN: 0812550447, 416p.

    Lanen dreams of dragons, so when a chance to travel in search of them arises, she takes it. On a far isle, she finds the dragons and an ability to speak with them telepathically. The dragon king falls for her in a big way, but that's trouble (and not just in the boudoir), as most of his kind don't like humans.

Kerner follows her solid debut with *The Lesser Kindred* and *Redeeming the Lost.*

Knight, E. E.
Dragon Champion. Age of Fire series. 2005. Roc, ISBN: 0451460472, 384p.

Knight's gray dragons are something of an enigma. Born without scales, flame, or wings, their beginnings are relatively defenseless. Young Auron, the sympathetic protagonist, must use wits and determination to survive past adolescence. *Dragon Avenger* follows.

McCaffrey, Anne
⇨ *The Dragonriders of Pern.* 1968–1978. Del Rey, ISBN: 0345340248, 832p.

McCaffrey's far-future science fiction has a fantasy air. The telepathic, empathic connection between dragons and riders works like magic, as does the teleportation of riding dragons "between." This classic trilogy (in omnibus) with strong-willed heroine and haughty dragons may seem familiar to genre readers who have read one of its many imitators, but it's still a great introduction to dragons for newcomers.

Vande Velde, Vivian
Dragon's Bait. 1992. Magic Carpet, ISBN: 0152166637, 208p. YA.

Accused of witchcraft, Alys is condemned to death by dragon. Luckily, the dragon to whom she is sacrificed (who also shifts to human form) offers to help her seek vengeance on her inquisitors instead. One question remains: Is Selendrile trustworthy, or is he using Alys for his own means?

Walton, Jo
Tooth and Claw. 2003. Tor, ISBN: 0765349094, 304p. AW.

When a father dies in a Jane Austen-like world, his children must divide the inheritance. Oh, by the way, this world is populated entirely by dragons, and their inheritance is the father's body, which his children will consume to gain strength. Quirky and stocked with wonderfully distinct Victorian dragon characters, this novel won the Campbell Award.

Watt-Evans, Lawrence
Dragon Venom. Obsidian Chronicles. 2003. Tor, ISBN: 0765341700, 480p.

Arlian wreaks vengeance against the dragons who enslaved him in youth, but he must decide if this makes his world a better place or results in unforeseen ills. If you prefer dragons as villains, try the Obsidian Chronicles, a satisfying selection of complex characters and puzzling ethical dilemmas that concludes with this third volume.

Just off the Turnip Cart: Country Folk Who Make Good

In *The Grapes of Wrath,* John Steinbeck wrote these lines for Ma Joad: "We keep a-comin'. We're the people that live. They can't wipe us out. They can't lick us. We'll go on forever." Many readers agree with her philosophy, enjoying books in which country folk persevere despite the machinations of evil city slickers. In the words of Jeff Foxworthy, "You know you're a redneck" if you relate to this strand of fantasy. I reckon y'all will feature these'ns.

Dickinson, Peter
The Ropemaker. 2001. Delacorte, ISBN: 0385730632, 384p. `YA`, `AW`.

For almost twenty generations, magic has hidden the Valley from its neighbors: a culture of raiders to the north and a monolithic empire to the south. But now the magic's breaking down, and two tired seniors and two green teens must sally forth in search of help. In a world of magic, their best hope lies in the absence of magic.

Drake, David, Flint, Eric, Kuttner, Henry, and Spoor, Ryk E.
Mountain Magic. 2004. Baen, ISBN: 0743488563, 480p.

Stories and novelettes in this collection are all set in strange worlds where hillbillies meet speculative fiction. In particular, look for Drake's stories about Old Nathan the Wizard, a hick with a bit of magic and a whole lot of woodlore who has to face the devil himself.

Eddings, David
Pawn of Prophecy. <u>The Belgariad</u>. 1982. Del Rey, ISBN: 0345335511, 272p.

Garion is a farm kid who lives simply with Aunt Pol and his roving grandfather. Well, except that Polgara is the world's most powerful sorceress, and grandfather is a wizard who likes to roam in the form of a wolf. Did I mention that Garion is heir apparent to their world? Fans of simple folk will especially like devoted Durnik, who leaves the smith he calls home to guard his beloved Polgara.

Feist, Raymond E.
Talon of the Silver Hawk. <u>Conclave of Shadows</u>. 2002. Eos, ISBN: 0380803240, 400p.

Lone survivor of his mountain tribe's massacre, gullible Kieli spends his youth avoiding the pitfalls of the more sophisticated society into which he falls. He reshapes himself as the educated, swashbuckling noble Talon, but can he play his new part well enough to exact revenge?

Jordan, Robert
The Eye of the World. <u>The Wheel of Time</u>. 1990. Tor, ISBN: 0812511816, 832p.

As <u>The Wheel of Time</u> turns, the country-boy-and-girl series leads long to see the world. They learn to be careful of what one wishes for, as the wish just may come true. As the series progresses, they yearn (sometimes repetitively) to return to the simple life. In this first book, however, viewing their amazing world through naive eyes is a joy.

Kay, Guy Gavriel
Lord of Emperors. 2000. Eos, ISBN: 0061020028, 576p.
    In this sequel to *Sailing to Sarantium,* a country doctor named Rustem joins Crispin, the mosaicist summoned to the capital in the first book. The two men must summon all their native wit to maneuver successfully in the truly Byzantine (after all, Sarantium is a stand-in for Byzantium) and perilous culture of the imperial household.

Moon, Elizabeth
The Deed of Paksenarrion. 1992. Baen, ISBN: 0671721046, 1040p.
    Did you hear the one about the sheep farmer's daughter? No, not that farmer's daughter: Young Paks longs for adventure—anything but farm life. Over the course of this trilogy (now in one book), she's transformed into a soldier, finding more adventure than she hoped for, in fact a good sight more than she wants.

Tolkien, J.R.R.
⇨ *The Hobbit.* 1937. HarperCollins, ISBN: 0618162216, 320p. `YA`.
    No country homeland is more beloved than The Shire and no lead less prepared for adventure than Bilbo Baggins. But a world full of dwarves, elves, trolls, goblins, and wizards will turn on the actions of a simple hobbit whose only expertise is at the dinner table. Bilbo's only competition for fantasy's bravest and most lovable bumpkin is another hobbit, Sam of *The Lord of the Rings*.

Bastards! And Other Returns of the King

For the by-blows of fantasy fiction, *bastard* isn't a pejorative but a clarion call to a future leadership role. An orphan wandering in the wilderness is almost always an Aragorn, biding time until someone needs a king. This fits the romantic fantasy tradition of the lowliest rising to greatness. If you feel a vicarious need to rise above your circumstances, try these.

Benjamin, Curt
⇨ *The Gates of Heaven.* Seven Brothers trilogy. 2003. DAW, ISBN: 0756401984, 528p.
    Barbarians conquer a nation, kill the king and queen, and sell their seven sons into slavery. It falls on the youngest, the likable Llesho, to find his brothers and retake their homeland. This book brings the saga, notable for its Asian flavor and superb protagonist, to a climax.

Brown, Simon
Inheritance. Keys of Power trilogy. 2000. DAW, ISBN: 0756401623, 432p.
    On the death of Queen Usharna, three of her children are unhappy that half brother Lynan receives an inheritance equal to theirs, including the Key of Union, crucial to their realm. When the heir, King Berayma, is killed, Lynan

is blamed and must go on the run. The aid of loyal friends is his only hope to survive the distrust of his siblings.

Lewis, C. S.
Prince Caspian. <u>Chronicles of Narnia</u>. 1951. HarperTrophy, ISBN: 0064471055, 256p. YA.

    In the fourth <u>Chronicle</u>, Peter, Susan, Edmund, and Lucy return to Narnia years after their glorious reign (that began at the end of *The Lion, the Witch, and the Wardrobe*). The siblings come to the aid of a new generation. This time, the rightful king has been murdered. Prince Caspian needs help to overcome the usurper, his evil uncle Miraz.

Martin, George R. R.
A Storm of Swords. <u>A Song of Ice and Fire</u>. 2000. Bantam Spectra, ISBN: 055357342X, 1216p. AW.

    If you've come this far (book three) in the epic, then you know Martin splits time between a large cast of characters. One highlight of this great book is the rise of Jon Snow, a natural leader who merits great success but is held back by self-doubts and his status as a bastard.

Tarr, Judith
Rite of Conquest. 2004. Roc, ISBN: 0451460022, 375p.

    Tarr writes historical novels, usually with a strong dose of fantasy and romance. Here she presents William the Conqueror as the bastard of a duke and a druid goddess, intent on crossing the Channel to reclaim England from the Saxons and reopen it to the Fey folk.

Tolkien, J.R.R.
The Return of the King. <u>The Lord of the Rings</u>. 1955. Houghton Mifflin, ISBN: 0618574972, 500p.

    He's no bastard, but Aragorn's return from exile to reclaim Gondor from Sauron's threat and Denethor's insanity will always be *the* return of the king for fantasy lovers.

Weis, Margaret
Dragon's Son. <u>Dragonvarld trilogy</u>. 2004. Tor, ISBN: 0765343916, 320p.

    Two half-dragon brothers grow up in different circumstances, one in privilege and one in poverty, but they must reunite to avenge their mother's death and restore her kingdom. Preceded by *Mistress of Dragons* and followed by *Master of Dragons,* this is the rare middle book in a series that doesn't lag at all.

The Ancient Races: The Best Fantasy Featuring Dwarves and Elves

When I think of dwarves and elves, I'm reminded of Yogi Berra's befuddled quote: "Nobody goes there anymore, it's too crowded." Bearded rock dwellers and graceful forest folk are considered such clichés that few fantasy authors write about them. For cynics who suspect every fantasy is the same, every dwarf might look like Tolkien's Gimli, and every elf like his Legolas, but fantasy lovers welcome these characters to their council of races. Here are books in which the ancient races play an important part.

Kerr, Katharine
A Time of Exile. **Deverry series**. 1991. Bantam Spectra, ISBN: 0553298135, 432p.

Lord Rhodry has a secret: He's half elf. As a result, he ages very slowly. His people are starting to talk, and his son is anxious for his turn to rule. Rhodry's old flame, Jill, a wizard, convinces him to fake death and return to his father's people in the elf lands of the west. In Kerr's Deverry, in which reincarnation is real and the present, past, and future are interwoven, a search for roots is certain to result in complexities.

Lackey, Mercedes, and Norton, Andre
Elvenborn. **Halfblood Chronicles**. 2002. Tor, ISBN: 0812571231, 480p.

The third book in a series by two all-time greats turns its focus to elves. Pressured by treacherous elf lords into leading a war against half-blood elves and dragons, strategic genius Kyrtian begins to suspect he allied himself to the wrong side. Both the cruel and noble sides of elves are examined here. One downside: Norton died in 2005, and series closer *Elvenbred* may not be forthcoming.

McKiernan, Dennis
⇨ **The Silver Call**. **Mithgar**. 2001. Roc, ISBN: 0451458613, 528p.

For those who dream of more Middle Earth, this book tells the story (with assumed names) of what would have happened if dwarves—with the help of hobbits (I mean warrows), humans, and an elf—had attempted to retake Moria. McKiernan's no Tolkien—but then nobody is—and this loving tribute is fun in its own right.

Pratchett, Terry
Lords and Ladies. **Discworld Witches**. 1992. HarperTorch, ISBN: 0061056928, 400p.

Pratchett's elves are beautiful in the way that suave serial killers are as they convince you to jump in the van. If there were such a van in Lancre, the folk of that kingdom would be piling in and fighting to ride shotgun. Luckily, Granny Weatherwax and the other witches recognize the danger behind the beauty and fight to save the Discworld. Also appearing is the dwarf Casanunda, the world's second greatest lover ("he tries harder").

Rhodes, Jenna
The Four Forges. **The Elven Ways**. 2006. DAW, ISBN: 0756402743, 368p.

A generation before the start of Rhodes's promising series opener, the Vaelinar, an elvish people, were transported by a magical disaster to a strange world devastated by war. They used magic to rule their new world, but now that control is breaking down. Rhodes draws her elves as fierce, martial people whose arrogance breeds both success and problems. The fate of a world may rest in the hands of Sevryn, a half-breed.

Salvatore, R. A.
The Dark Elf Trilogy. 1990–1991. Wizards of the Coast, ISBN: 0786915889, 816p.
    Let your inner fan boy or girl out of the cage to play in the dark elf drow culture of the action-and-emotion-packed, gore-soaked adventures of two-sword-wielding hero Drizzt Do'Urden. The Forgotten Realms line delivers elvish characters that many fantasy readers still crave, and this omnibus trilogy is one of the best.

Spencer, Wen
Tinker. 2003. Baen, ISBN: 0743498712, 448p.
    When young genius Tinker saves the elven governor, he turns her into an elf and makes her his consort. Set in an alternate universe in which the Chinese built a faulty hyperphase gate that transported Pittsburgh into the elf world, Spencer's creation features elves who are quirky and sexy in this pleasing concoction of fantasy, sci-fi, romance, and humor.

The Long and Short of It: Giants and Little Folk

It's not the size of the body, but the size of the heart that beats within it. In fantasy, folk at both ends of the size spectrum regularly prove this point. As they are usually portrayed, both little people and giants laugh easily, exhibit tremendous loyalty, and have big hearts beating in their chests. From little Merry, Sam, and Pippin to Harry Potter's big buddy Hagrid, these characters come in charming packages that are lovable at any size.

Donaldson, Stephen R.
The One Tree. **The Second Chronicles of Thomas Covenant.** 1982. Del Rey, ISBN: 0345348699, 496p.
    Donaldson's giants are hearty enough to charm the notorious antihero Thomas Covenant (and balance his bitterness for readers). Saltheart Foamfollower is the highlight of the first book, *Lord Foul's Bane,* and the fate of the giants is the emotional core of *The Illearth War.* In this second book of the second trilogy, Covenant and Linden Avery travel by giant ship in search of the One Tree.

Jarvis, Robin
Thorn Ogres of Hagwood. **Hagwood trilogy.** 1999. Magic Carpet, ISBN: 0152051228, 264p. YA.

In this trilogy opener, the Werlings—tiny shape-shifters who live in tree-tops—are drawn into a fight with the spidery Frighty Aggie, the evil Faerie queen Rhiannon, and her horrible thorn ogres. Jarvis has a way with the small, whether they are her Deptford Mice, the Werlings, or the young readers who enjoy her books. She makes adults feel small, too, but in the best way: young again.

Jones, Diana Wynne
Archer's Goon. 1984. HarperTrophy, ISBN: 0064473562, 336p. YA.

Howard's dad makes a pact with a devilish wizard named Archer, promising 2,000 words a month in exchange for freedom from writer's block. When the words don't arrive one month, Archer sends a Goon to collect. Howard discovers his father's words are used as tools in a seven-wizard war. With sister Awful and the dumb but bighearted Goon, Howard must decide which of the seven to support and which to stop.

Odom, Mel
The Rover. **Rover series.** 2001. Tor, ISBN: 0765341948, 512p.

Odom joins Terry Brooks and Dennis McKiernan in the vanguard of Tolkien imitators with this book about Wick, a hobbitlike dweller and librarian. He'd rather be home reading in bed, but his confidence grows as he encounters goblins, pirates, and dragons in a string of mostly merry adventures. Three sequels follow.

Pratchett, Terry
The Wee Free Men. **Discworld, Tiffany Aching.** 2003. HarperTempest, ISBN: 0060012382, 400p. YA.

Who are blue, tattooed, habitually drunk, six inches tall, and speak in an indecipherable brogue? It's not extras from *Braveheart* on a portable TV; it's the Nac Mac Feegle, fairy terrors who become the tiny army of Tiffany Aching, a nine-year-old witch in search of the Fairy Queen. Pratchett brings Discworld to young adults, if they can steal the book from their cackling parents.

Salvatore, R. A.
The Crimson Shadow. 1994–1996. Warner Aspect, ISBN: 0446698504, 784p.

It's not the rather bland prince hero, but Oliver DeBurrows, a halfling rogue who steals scenes and delivers all the best lines in this series in omnibus. Oliver comes across as the love child of Robin Hood and the Monty Python troupe.

. . . And Some Visits with Even Stranger Peoples and Races

Although some readers appreciate familiar character types, others come to fantasy for its creative potential. Such readers relish characters they have never considered before, characters that spark the imagination and suggest the possibility of new ways of being. Here are some books in which you'll find folks who are altogether different.

Abraham, Daniel
⇨ *A Shadow in Summer.* <u>Long Price Quartet</u>. 2006. Tor, ISBN: 0765313405, 336p. (hbk.)
> Abraham's first novel features poets who create and control shape-shifting creatures called andat (much as fantasy writers create characters). For instance, the andat Seedless can remove seeds from cotton (a djinn gin?) but also unborn children from wombs. He's trying to drive his creator mad and gain his freedom. That would be bad, because Seedless also keeps opposing armies at bay.

Atwater-Rhodes, Amelia
Hawksong. <u>Kiesha'ra series</u>. 2003. Laurel Leaf, ISBN: 044023803X, 256p. YA.
> Two shape-shifting cultures, one serpentine and the other avian, try to end a long war through an arranged marriage. Will the loathing bred into the prince and princess get the best of them, or can they rise above it?

Caine, Rachel
Heat Stroke. <u>Weather Warden series</u>. 2004. Roc, ISBN: 0451459849, 335p.
> In Caine's second book, weather warden Joanne returns from death as a Djinn. Brimming with power, but awkward in its use, Joanne struggles to master her new self while waging battle on human and ethereal planes. Caine takes familiar genres—contemporary romance and urban fantasy—and makes them new by blending them. Her pacing is brisk and her characters fresh and distinct.

Miéville, China
Perdido Street Station. <u>Bas-Lag</u>. 2003. Del Rey, ISBN: 0345459407, 640p.
> Original characters? How about an insectoid artist who vomits her paint, a desert nomad birdman who lost his wings, cactus people, armies of folk who are surgically augmented with contraptions, amphibious folk who shape water with magic, and monstrous slake-moths that feed on dreams and suck souls in the quest to reproduce. Dark, and sometimes difficult, this novel is so unique that you'll feel like you found a new genre.

Shinn, Sharon
Jovah's Angel. <u>Samaria series</u>. 1997. Ace, ISBN: 0441005195, 368p.
> Shinn's science-fantasy series may be the first populated by genetically engineered angels. Using technology and song, they try to keep a second apocalypse at bay. Who says religious philosophy and romance don't mix?

Stevenson, Jennifer
Trash Sex Magic. 2004. Small Beer, ISBN: 1931520127, 292p.
> Stevenson's characters are recognizable—tree and animal spirits, sirens, water witches—but she places them in the milieu of contemporary trailer

dwellers. With a love for alcohol and sex that fits surprisingly well with their magical identities, the whole group is unexpectedly likable.

Weber, David
Oath of Swords. <u>War God series</u>. 1994. Baen, ISBN: 1416520864, 400p.
　　　Hradani aren't completely unlike roguish humans in other fantasies, but they're huge, with foxlike ears, freakish endurance, and a tendency to berserk rages. Weber's other species don't like them, but you will, particularly series hero Bahzell Bahnakson. Did I mention they speak in thick Scottish brogues?

Ye Gods! Deities in Fantasy

　　　Where else but in fantasy novels do people frequently interact with gods? (Unless you can prove it, your local cult doesn't count.) As characters, powerful gods create new possibilities and challenges for writers. These novels can be controversial, as fantasy gods are often portrayed with everything but reverence. Readers open to examining human-god relations will find these books full of laughs, thrills, and intriguing ideas.

Cook, Glen
The Black Company. <u>Black Company series</u>. 1984. Tor, ISBN: 0812521390, 320p.
　　　In the first novel of a long-running series, the gods are like comic book superheroes and villains (it's often difficult to tell which side they are on). They are seen through the thoroughly jaded eyes of members of a mercenary company, trying to survive a war that they only partially comprehend. Gritty, violent, but very entertaining.

Fallon, Jennifer
Harshini. <u>Demon Child trilogy</u>. 2000. Tor, ISBN: 0765348683, 499p.
　　　Following *Medalon* and *Treason Keep,* Fallon caps the first of what will be two trilogies. Three countries face devastation unless half-breed demon child R'Shiell can successfully navigate an on-the-job training of capricious gods and political intrigues to defeat a nasty god named Xaphista and his zealot followers.

Gaiman, Neil
⇨ *Anansi Boys.* 2005. HarperTorch, ISBN: 0060515198, 416p. AW.
　　　Gaiman brings gods out of the heavens and into human lives in <u>Sandman</u> graphic novels, *Good Omens,* and *Neverwhere.* He's at it again in this distant cousin to the darker *American Gods.* Fat Charlie, an average guy, discovers at his father's funeral that dad was a god. Even worse, his long-lost trickster brother sends him stumbling through bizarre encounters with gods from many traditions.

Moore, Christopher
Coyote Blue. 1994. Harper, ISBN: 0060735430, 304p.
Sam Hunter, a Native American man, has made a "life" for himself as a successful but straight-arrow Santa Barbara insurance salesman until Coyote throws him a few curves. Moore's trickster humor is a fine match for the trickster god that enlivens this tale.

Patton, Fiona
The Silver Lake. Warriors of Estavia. 2005. DAW, ISBN: 0756403669, 496p.
Six gods protect a small land from barbarians and spirits that would otherwise overrun them. In the exciting first book of Estavia, two orphans seek their destiny in the service of these gods, facing opposition from a third boy claimed by the hungry spirits.

What, Leslie
Olympic Games. 2004. Tachyon, ISBN: 1892391104, 286p.
As they turn New York City into the playing field for their infighting, Zeus, Hera, and the other Greek gods are not very likable, but they are extremely funny in a charmingly cheeky little book.

Rainbow Warriors: Cultural Diversity in Fantasy

Fantasy fiction was vulnerable for most of its history to the accusation that the characters were almost universally white and that most heroes were male. To be fair, many fantasy writers are open to difference. They explore diversity through magical races and species instead of skin color or sexual preference. In contemporary fantasy, they have done better, with many books that feature people of color and nontraditional sex and gender roles.

De Lint, Charles
Forests of the Heart. Newford series. 2000. Tor, ISBN: 0312875681, 400p.
De Lint is known for mixing a mélange of cultures in urban fantasies. This book, for instance, features a Mexican-Indian faith healer leading a diverse group of art colony dwellers. They want to protect their native Canadian spirits from displaced Irish "Gentry " spirits who plan to raise a Green Man.

Hopkinson, Nalo, ed.
Mojo: Conjure Stories. 2003. Aspect, ISBN: 0446679291, 320p.
One serious inequity remains in fantasy: Few stories appeal to readers of African descent by using that continent's rich folklore. It's especially nice to see this anthology, which passes by overworked European myths for 19 colorful stories rooted in West African magic. Well-known writers like Barbara

Hambly, Tananarive Due, and Neil Gaiman mix with new talents to make an unusual, satisfying blend.

Kushner, Ellen
Swordspoint. 1987. Bantam Spectra, ISBN: 0553585495, 368p.

Mix mannered Regency melodrama with a classic swashbuckler, cast gay leads, and you get *Swordspoint.* Master swordsman Richard St. Vier is hired by nobles to fight their duels. His lover, Alec, is a death obsessed scholar full of wicked wit. Although this is political fantasy, the joy is subtle interaction between well-drawn characters. Almost twenty years later, Kushner published a welcome sequel, *The Privilege of the Sword.*

Lackey, Mercedes
Magic's Pawn. **The Last Herald Mage.** 1989. DAW, ISBN: 0886773520, 352p.

Unable to accept his son's homosexuality, Vanyel's father sends him to live with his aunt. Vanyel falls for his aunt's protégé and with Tylendel's help begins to come out of his shell. Lackey, a pioneer of portraying diversity and angsty teen emotion in fantasy, is in top form in this poignant tale of romance found and lost.

Marks, Laurie J.
Fire Logic. **Elemental Logic series.** 2002. Tor, ISBN: 081256653X, 384p.

Same-sex couples, gender role benders, and people of many colors are common in Marks's fantasy. She treats them as normal, not exceptional, writing a book in which bigotry isn't present but strong, believable emotion remains. Her unusual narrative style makes the reader work but rewards the effort with complex politics and gripping characters. Followed by *Earth Logic.*

Pinto, Ricardo
The Chosen. **Stone Dance of the Chameleon.** 1998. Tor, ISBN: 081258435X, 640p.

A Portuguese Scot writes about gay people of color in Asian-inspired societies. This series beginning novel pulses with ornate detail and dreamlike (often nightmarish) prose. An intricate book suggested for readers who value style as much as substance.

Pratchett, Terry
Night Watch. **Discworld, The Watch.** 2002. HarperTorch, ISBN: 0060013125, 432p.
Thud! **Discworld, The Watch.** 2005. HarperTorch, ISBN: 0060815310, 416p.

If you prefer to combat bigotry with satire, then read the books about Ankh-Morpork's finest, The Watch. Pratchett is not just a comedian, he's a marvelous social theorist. His pointed barbs about ethnic violence between trolls and dwarves, discrimination against werewolves and vampires, and social posturing by the rich and poor cut straight to the quick of narrow-mindedness.

Looking for Some Hardheaded Women: Fantastic Female Characters

In the pulp past, the most likely position for a woman in fantasy was thrown over Conan's bulky shoulder. That's changed: The days of female characters who are absent, perpetually prone, or present only as generic love interests are receding. Writers like Marion Zimmer Bradley, Katharine Kerr, and Katherine Kurtz blazed a trail that has grown to one busy side of the fantasy freeway. Contemporary fantasy characters test gender boundaries and put old roles to new uses. These books arc bursting with interesting women.

Alexander, Alma
The Secrets of Jin-shei. 2004. HarperSanFrancisco, ISBN: 0060750588, 512p.
> In an alternate China, eight women from disparate backgrounds accept the bond of jin-shei: special secret friendships that create benefits and impose obligation. Over time, the responsibility of their bond draws them into a dangerous world of magic and the search for immortality.

Forsyth, Kate
⇨ *The Pool of Two Moons.* <u>The Witches of Eileanan.</u> 1998. Roc, ISBN: 0451456904, 560p.
> The <u>Eileanan</u> series is loaded with great women, with the focus characters changing in each volume. In this second book, the solemn warrior maid Iseult and her mentor, the aged-but-active witch Meghan of the Beasts, develop a deep friendship while questing to find a magic scepter in a creepy forest. Forsyth's characters are plucky and easy to like.

Hambly, Barbara
Sisters of the Raven. 2002. Aspect, ISBN: 0446615366, 512p.
> The magic of men holds Yellow City together, but now it's failing. When women show magical gifts for the first time, some men blame the women for disrupting their spells. Even worse, someone is killing women magicians. Against this backdrop, Summer Concubine (the king's consort), Pomegranate Woman (an aging widow), and Raeshaldis (a student) must combine powers to save their society. Followed by *Circle of the Moon.*

Kelleher, Anne
Silver's Edge. <u>Shadowlands series.</u> 2004. Harlequin Luna, ISBN: 0373811144, 544p.
> When the Silver Caul that separates three worlds begins to break down, three young women from diverse backgrounds—a blacksmith's daughter, a faery lady-in-waiting, and a queen—must stop the goblin invasion that could destroy them all.

Lackey, Mercedes
Oathbreakers. Vows and Honor. 1989. DAW, ISBN: 0886774543, 320p.

Tarma, a swordswoman, and Kethry, a sorceress, are the sworn companions at the center of Lackey's Valdemar-set trilogy. In this middle book, the two search for Idra, the captain of their mercenary troop, who has disappeared. Male companions questing together are a dime a dozen, but to see two women interact like this is something special.

Locksley, Rebecca
The Three Sisters. 2004. Eos, ISBN: 0380814005, 512p.

Yani is a warrior bodyguard for the queen. Marigoth is a child sorceress who has chosen to stunt her own growth. Elena has legendary beauty said to spur men to mad behavior. The three sisters are of the Tari, a people who feel the death agonies of anyone whose life they take. When marauding Mirayans steal Elena away, her sisters come after her.

Pierce, Tamora
The Woman Who Rides Like a Man. Song of the Lioness quartet. 1986. Simon Pulse, ISBN: 0689878583, 304p. YA.

Alanna doesn't just ride like a man. She has a gruff way, prefers solitude, and is dangerous with a sword. In the third book of the quartet, Alanna is challenged to a duel to the death by a sexist desert tribesman. She wins and begins training three young women to take on the role of shaman, but her challenges have just begun.

West, Michelle
The Sun Sword. Sun Sword series. 2004. DAW, ISBN: 0756401704, 832p.

This book completes West's six-book series. Big and sprawling, it takes time to get moving, but if you like fantasy with dozens of well-defined characters, you'll enjoy this tale of evil patriarchal southern clans building toward war with a northern kingdom that needs to get its act together. Women in this series grow and develop impressively.

If They Hit You in the Head, Keep Your Wits Gathered about You: Resourceful Lead Characters

There's a downside to heroes with lightning-fast swords, muscles that twitch like giant anacondas, or spell-casting in high definition with Dolby surround sound: Their success is too easy, and they become predictable. After reading about so many chosen ones, you may yearn for a hero who succeeds not through predestination but by thinking quickly on his or her feet and finding believable solutions to tough problems. It's easier to relate to someone who muddles through, making the most of limited resources. These books feature inventive, capable leads.

Berg, Carol
Son of Avonar. **The Bridge of D'Arnath**. 2004. Roc, ISBN: 0451459628, 480p.

Refusing a king-to-be, Seri marries a forbidden magician. He's caught and killed, along with their son, and Seri is exiled. Ten years later, she discovers another young magician—mute, naked, unable to remember his past, and on the run. Because of her loss of station, to help him is punishable by death, but she does it anyway. Seri uses her wits to stay a step ahead of wizard hunters and dark wizards in this series beginning.

Foster, Alan Dean
A Triumph of Souls. **Journeys of the Catechist**. 2000. Aspect, ISBN: 044652218X, 406p. (hbk.)

This book concludes Foster's series about a humble herdsman who agrees to rescue a seer he doesn't know. To get through an endless series of dilemmas, Etjole has only curiosity and the wisdom of his people.

Kay, Guy Gavriel
⇨ *Sailing to Sarantium.* 1998. Eos, ISBN: 0061059900, 560p. (out of print).

With reluctance, hero Crispin travels to the capital to aid the emperor. A great warrior? A powerful magician? No, Crispin is a mosaicist, and making pictures won't help when you get caught up in intrigue, assassinations, and magic. With simple decency as his greatest weapon, Crispin must put all the political tiles in place. Followed by *Lord of Emperors.*

Lynch, Scott
The Lies of Locke Lamora. **The Gentlemen Bastards**. 2006. Bantam Spectra, ISBN: 055358894X, 832p.

Locke Lamora isn't the strongest or nimblest of the Gentlemen Bastards, but he's audacious and resilient. His improvisational gifts make him the obvious leader of his gang of scam artists. This witty caper was the most hyped debut of 2006, with film rights sold before the book arrived. If you don't mind rough language and action, you'll probably like this new series opener too.

McKenna, Juliet
Southern Fire. **Aldabreshin Compass**. 2003. Tor, ISBN: 0765352753, 512p.

Aldabreshin Archipelago is a simple barter-based society. When reports of magical invaders come from the south, warlord Kheda tries first to form alliances against the foe and then to confront them. Out of his depth, he solves problems creatively, although his answers don't bode well for his own future. McKenna's series will visit the four compass points.

Turner, Megan Whalen
The King of Attolia. **The Queen's Thief.** Greenwillow, 2006. ISBN: 006083577X, 400p. **YA**.

Let's give King Eugenides a hand. The queen he married cut off one of his in *The Thief.* As this trilogy finisher begins, the Attolians still can't believe Eugenides and Queen Irene love each other. They think he's using her for political gain. Two strong leads move adroitly behind the scenes to hold together their kingdom and relationship.

Watt-Evans, Lawrence
Ithnalin's Restoration. Ethshar. 2002. Tor, ISBN: 0765340550, 272p.

Like a riff on *The Sorcerer's Apprentice,* Watt-Evans writes about a wizard-in-training who's in trouble. Arriving home to find her master turned to a statue, with his soul split between household objects that are now animated and running around the city. With limited magical skill and less help, Kilisha labors to put her master back together.

Whiny, Self-Interested, and Undependable . . . I Can Relate to That: Fantasy's Antiheroes

Antiheroes are about self-acceptance. They screw up, usually cause most of their own problems, but readers stay with them because they hang in there and clean up after themselves—a trait most of us aim to replicate. These books generate deeply divided opinion. If you like heroes blemish free, read elsewhere, but if you find comfort in the idea that even the best make mistakes and have problems, then these books are for you.

Cook, Glen
Shadows Linger. **The Black Company.** 1984. Tor, ISBN: 0812508424, 320p.

Entering their second book, the members of The Black Company still aren't even sure they're fighting for the right side. The mercenary crew is full of character flaws and depravity. Individually, they are weaker than the beings they battle, but they are collectively strong (when they stop fighting each other), good at staying alive (usually), and committed to honoring their contract.

David, Peter
⇨ *Sir Apropos of Nothing.* **Apropos of Nothing series.** 2001. Pocket, ISBN: 0743412346, 672p.

Apropos is lame and duplicitous, the bastard son of a whore. And those are his good qualities. In the first few chapters, he betrays friends, becomes a drunk, sucker punches a hero, and runs from an attack on the princess he is to protect. But despite his best efforts to dodge it, Apropos's destiny stays with him as he cheats and grovels his way to success. This pun-filled, off-kilter series starter will please those who want a break from fantasy clichés.

Donaldson, Stephen R.
Lord Foul's Bane. **The First Chronicles of Thomas Covenant**. 1977. Del Rey, ISBN: 0345348656, 496p.

 If Thomas Covenant had gone to Oz, he would have lit the Scarecrow on fire, left the Tin Man to rust, bullied the Cowardly Lion, and then blamed the trio for his problems. A leper transported to a world in which he is a powerful hero, his only care is that he isn't deluded by his new health. Fantasy's ugliest antihero stars in a series starter that is fantastic but not for the faint of heart.

Douglass, Sara
The Nameless Day. **The Crucible**. 2000. Tor, ISBN: 0765342820, 576p.

 Thomas Neville's betrayal of a woman led to her death. To forget his past, he becomes a monk. He's still obnoxious, hypocritical, misogynistic—a real piece of work. But Archangel Michael calls on Thomas to protect the world from demons. This novel starts the series; you'll have to read on to find if Neville's trials forge him into better stuff.

Feist, Raymond
Exile's Return. **Conclave of Shadows**. 2004. HarperTorch, ISBN: 0380803275, 384p.

 Vanquished by Tal Hawkins earlier in the series, evil, once-powerful Kaspar is now exiled to the harshest part of Midkemia. He has nothing but dark wishes for retaliation left, but his vengeance quest turns into a journey of self-redemption.

Martin, George R. R.
A Clash of Kings. **A Song of Ice and Fire**. 1998. Bantam Spectra, ISBN: 0553579908, 1040p. `AW`.

 Don't get attached to hatred for Martin's so-called villains. As you read on, you may discover they have become your favorite characters. No author is better at showing why villains act as they do. In some cases, such as that of nasty Tyrion Lannister in this second series entry, you may discover that they are heroes (in their fashion).

Wolfe, Gene
Sword & Citadel. **The Book of the New Sun**. 1981. Orb, ISBN: 0312890184, 416p. `AW`.

 Severian is not a dependable narrator. He claims his memory is photographic but omits scenes that don't flatter him. He grows from a torturer into something better, but readers must keep a sharp eye on him, maybe even rereading books to understand this complex series, now in two omnibus editions, of which this is second.

Chapter Three

Setting

This chapter includes lists to help you find books with a variety of settings: worlds based on many different historical periods, countries, and geographic terrains. Twenty years ago, it would have been considerably shorter. Back then, the great majority of fantasy was set in vaguely British, vaguely rural, vaguely medieval worlds. There were always a few exceptions to the rule, but not enough. That was a shame, because fantasy readers tend to be fascinated by history and in love with the idea of roaming the world.

Fortunately, times (and places) have changed. In the last couple of decades, fantasy authors have found success in a variety of time periods, from ancient to modern. Urban fantasies, set in cities of many time periods, have become a hot commodity. There is a growing trend to create fantasy lands based on many world countries, not just Britain, Rome, and Greece.

Setting is a crucial appeal factor for many fantasy readers, but we call it *world building*. The term implies a godlike power for the author, a role that carries great responsibility. It's about more than time and place. It requires creation of believable political and social systems; development of peoples, creatures, and their interrelations; and definition of the world's magic. This may be fantasy, but readers demand that the author present a believable and detailed world.

What a Wonderful World: Fantasy Settings You'll Long to Visit

Some say fantasy fans want escape, but that's not strictly accurate. We are travelers, not escape artists. It's not that we want to run away so much as that we want to go places. Our authors oblige us by building irresistible new worlds. Sometimes these worlds are like no place on earth. Other times they are like places we have been, but more so: more vivid, colorful, alive with magic. If you are among fantasy's fellow travelers, book a trip to these destinations.

Abraham, Daniel
> *A Shadow in Summer.* **Long Price Quartet.** 2006. Tor, ISBN: 0765313405, 336p. (hbk.)
>> Our first stop is Saraykhet, a bustling seaport in the Summer Cities. Seedy docks (fantasy readers like seedy) press against the palaces of the noble quarter. In this city, the most powerful people are the Poets who create magical demi-gods that keep the economy humming. Abraham sets the stage masterfully for his forthcoming quartet.

De Lint, Charles
> *Someplace to Be Flying.* **Newford.** 1997. Orb, ISBN: 076530757X, 384p.
>> De Lint's turf is the bizarre fantasy land of . . . Canada! Not *just* Canada, but Newford, where hidden within the city is a melting pot of myth. Celtic creatures try to gain inroads on Native American spirits. This book shows the city through the eyes of a cabbie, whose attempt to save a woman opens his vision to the true nature of the streets he drives.

Donaldson, Stephen R.
> ⇨ *Lord Foul's Bane.* **The First Chronicles of Thomas Covenant.** 1977. Del Rey, ISBN: 0345348656, 496p.
>> In The Land, stonelore and woodlore nurture a place where you can frolic in your happiest dreams. The soil is healing, as are the ailantha berries that grow along traveler's ways. Wraiths dance under the moon to bring the spring, and the Ranyhyn gallop across the plains. I could go on, but Donaldson already did. All you have to do is read it.

Joyce, Graham
> *Requiem.* 1995. Tor, ISBN: 0312864523, 288p.
>> Contemporary Jerusalem is the most compelling character in Joyce's dark fantasy. Crumbling walls and shrines, bustling modern culture, and ancient religious strife all mix to make a horrific setting for this tale of a grieving

husband, on the run from his feelings, who stumbles across a fragment of the Dead Sea Scrolls.

Manguel, Alberto
The Dictionary of Imaginary Places. 2000. Harcourt, ISBN: 0156008726, 804p.
 If you love maps in fantasy books, if you want to preview new worlds or review past journeys, then get this nonfiction classic, now updated and expanded. From Homer's Greece to Harry's Hogwarts, they're all here. Each entry has a descriptive summary and copies of original maps.

May, Julian
Conqueror's Moon. <u>The Boreal Moon Tale</u>. 2003. Ace, ISBN: 0441012116, 464p.
 A volcano tips the balance of power between four warring kingdoms when fumes and ash destroy crops that made some of the island kingdoms wealthy. Complex political, social, and magical systems make High Blenholme vivid and believable, and absence of obvious heroes and villains creates sympathy for all sides in this series starter.

Rowling, J. K.
Harry Potter and the Chamber of Secrets. <u>Harry Potter series</u>. 1998. Scholastic, ISBN: 0439064872, 352p. YA.
 Take the Express from the secret platform for another year at Hogwarts. The second book provides an extended tour of the campus and its environs: the shops of Diagon Alley, the Whomping Willow, the spider-filled forests, the Quidditch fields, and the extensive secret tunnels beneath classrooms and dormitories. A girl's bathroom is the most important location of all in a novel full of distinctive places.

Stackpole, Michael
A Secret Atlas. <u>The Age of Discovery</u>. 2005. Bantam Spectra, ISBN: 0553382373, 480p.
 The Aturansi family's maps have made Nalenyr into an empire. The family has become rich by exploring the unknown, but new magic and old rivals endanger their status as this series opens in a tale that recalls the age of exploration but sets it in a vibrant new world.

Tolkien, J.R.R.
The Lord of the Rings. 1954–1956. Houghton Mifflin, ISBN: 0618517650, 1216p. (hbk.)
 One of the reasons this classic is evergreen is Tolkien's loving description of Middle Earth. From the depths of Moria to the heights of the Misty Mountains, from the green home places of The Shire and Rivendell, through the forests of Lothlorien or Fangorn, and across the blighted landscapes of Mordor: Every physical detail is memorable.

It Seems Like Old Times: The Best Fantasy of the Ancient World

Attention fantasy writers: When in doubt, set novels in the ancient world. We know the setting well enough that you won't strain yourself making it up, but time's passage has obscured the period, so you need not bother with pesky historical accuracy. Complete with recognizable cultures, the attractive settings are still draped in veils of mystery. Brushes with magic, legendary acts of heroism, and encounters with the gods all seem plausible when they are draped in the mist of ancient times.

Douglass, Sara
Hades' Daughter. <u>The Troy Game</u>. 2002. Tor, ISBN: 0765344424, 672p.
> When Theseus deserts Ariadne, she works a curse that destroys the magic labyrinths and cultures of Atlantis, Troy, and other Aegean civilizations. Thus begins <u>The Troy Game</u> of greed, cruelty, and revenge that spans the ancient world. Douglass plays loose with history and legend, creating an ancient world that is savage, complex, and very readable.

Threshold. 2000. Tor, ISBN: 0765342774, 464p.
> If an Egypt-like setting and pyramid magic intrigue you, try Douglass's stand-alone novel about a slave girl brought to work on a pyramid. She's confused by alternating cruel and kind treatment from the slave master but sure of one thing: her budding magical skills tell her to beware the pyramid as it nears completion.

Fisher, Catherine
The Oracle Betrayed. <u>Oracle Prophecies</u>. 2005. Eos, ISBN: 0060571594, 352p. **YA**.
> Fisher blends Egypt and Greece in The Two Lands, where the Speaker for the Oracle has become corrupted. She concocts a plot to kill the Archon. Only a young priestess, a scribe, and a musician can stop the plan and appease the offended Rain Goddess. Readers will feel the claustrophobia of the tombs and tunnels where the story climaxes.

Gemmell, David
⇨ *Lion of Macedon.* 1990. Del Rey, ISBN: 0345485351, 528p.
> A half-Macedonian, half-Spartan general becomes the right-hand man of Philip of Macedon, serving him in both worldly conquests and a voyage into Hades to retrieve the newborn Alexander the Great. If you like Gemmell's take on the ancient world, you also will enjoy his last series, a superb reimagining of the Trojan War.

Harlan, Thomas
The Shadow of Ararat. <u>Oath of Empire</u>. 1999. Tor, ISBN: 0812590090, 816p.
> In this alternate history, mages and legions keep the Roman Empire running into the seventh century, but a showdown between the Romans and the

Persians is brewing. Harlan's strength is his eye for detail. Descriptions of clothing, architecture, weapons, and warfare anchor a complex story involving many ancient lands. The first of a four-book series.

Holdstock, Robert
Celtika. <u>The Merlin Codex</u>. 2001. Tor, ISBN: 0765349043, 384p.
Holdstock mixes the legends of Merlin and Jason of the Argonauts. When Merlin brings the enchanted Argo out of limbo, he begins a quest that includes a search for Jason's lost sons and a Celtic invasion of Greece. Blending legends and dropping mythic references by the dozens, Holdstock is never an easy author, but he's worth the effort.

Watson, Jules
The White Mare. <u>The Dalraida Trilogy</u>. 2004. Overlook, ISBN: 1585677507, 480p.
In the first century, the Romans intend to conquer Alba (Scotland). Ragtag tribes are the only opposition. In this first book of a trilogy, a druid priestess and her new Irish husband attempt to rally the tribes while resolving the difficulties of a political marriage.

Eric the Well-Read: The Best of Viking Fantasy

Picture it: sacking and looting on a winter morning with Lucky Eddie by your side. After some wacky pillaging, take the longship home to Helga, Honi, Hamlet, your duck Kvack, and your dog Snert. On second thought, maybe Hagar cartoons aren't the best facsimile of Viking life. I can suggest better options in fantasy. But does anyone else miss Hagar the Horrible cola?

Anderson, Poul
Mother of Kings. 2001. Tor, ISBN: 0765345021, 544p.
Gunnhild marries Eirik Blood-Ax in the tenth century and then leads him to unite Norway under one throne. After his death, she uses magic and maneuvering to maintain rule for her nine sons. The book's epic style at times dwarfs the characters, but accurate history and culture will please Viking fans.

Farmer, Nancy
Sea of Trolls. 2004. Simon Pulse, ISBN: 0689867468, 480p. **YA**.
Apprentice bard Jack and sister Lucy are kidnapped by Viking berserkers. When his inept spell makes the half-troll Viking queen's hair fall out, Jack must quest northward across the Sea of Trolls to Mimir's Well or his sister's life will be forfeit. Hearty epic fun in which vivid Norse legends are interwoven with the realities of village life and culture.

Harrison, Harry
⇨ *The Hammer and the Cross.* <u>The Hammer and the Cross trilogy.</u> 1993. Tor, ISBN: 0812523482, 480p.

Harrison's historical fantasy sets up several conflicts: between Vikings and English kingdoms, within factions on each side, and between Christians and a new Viking sect called the Way. At the crossroads of the conflicts is Shef, a young smith despised by his own Northumbrians who proves himself a brilliant inventor and leader for the Vikings.

Kay, Guy Gavriel
The Last Light of the Sun. 1993. Roc, ISBN: 0451459857, 512p.

The Vikings, English, and Welsh get new names, but readers will recognize them. Set in an era of growing Anglo-Saxon power, the Viking lifestyle is threatened, and you know it won't end well for them. Kay's style here is bleak, less lush than in his other novels, but fit to the harsh, desolate climate.

Marillier, Juliet
Foxmask. <u>Children of the Light Isles.</u> 2004. Tor, ISBN: 0765345919, 576p.

Set in Scotland's northern isles, this follows the next generation from *Wolfskin.* When hotheaded Thorvald discovers that his real father is an exiled king-slayer, he decides to seek him. He finds Creidhe (who loves him) stowed away after he sets sail and it's too late to turn back. Their journey to the western isles traps them in a conflict between two tribes.

Saberhagen, Fred
Gods of Fire and Thunder. 2002. Tor, ISBN: 0765341514, 320p.

Haraldur and Baldur aren't dwarf brothers from *The Hobbit.* They're Norsemen after treasure and a Valkyrie. Their quests draw them to a Valhalla besieged by giants, with Wodan crazy and Thor and Loki missing. In a high-spirited tale of Norse gods and heroes, the Last Battle is brewing.

Wilkins, Kim
Giants of the Frost. 2005. Warner, ISBN: 0446617288, 544p.

After two failed engagements, Victoria wants a quiet place to finish her thesis. She retreats to an isle in the Sea of Norway but finds it to be a magic place of wights, hags, and supernatural weather: hard discoveries for a scientist to reconcile. As she encounters Norse gods, Victoria has a sense of déjà vu: In another life she loved Vidar, son of Odin, and he's not over her. One of the genre's new talents crafts an atmospheric romantic fantasy.

Cam-a-Lot: The Many Faces of Arthurian Fantasy

No tale is retold so many ways as that of Arthur, Merlin, Guinevere, Morgan le Fay, and the rest of the Round Table gang. It's dropped into dozens of historical settings. It's treated as coming-of-age tale, romance, war story, straight history, or magical myth. On film, it appears as cartoon, comedy, musical, action-adventure, or artsy, anthropological fable. I've heard people say they don't like Arthurian fiction, but given the number of variations, that isn't an easy statement to back up. There's a book in the Arthurian library for every borrower. Here are 10 good versions of the saga from which each reader can select his or her own Camelot.

Bradley, Marion Zimmer

⇨ *The Mists of Avalon*. <u>Avalon</u>. 1979. Del Rey, ISBN: 0345350499, 912p. AW.

It's goddess worship versus Christianity in Bradley's feminine take on the legend. On one side Viviane (the Lady of the Lake) and Morgaine try to maintain the ways of the druids. Opposing them is Gwenhwyfar, the Christian princess. Both compete for Arthur's favor, and his decision to back his wife begins the downfall of his reign.

Cornwell, Bernard

⇨ *The Winter King*. <u>Warlord Chronicles</u>. 1995. St. Martin's, ISBN: 0312156960, 433p.

Arthur is baby Mordred's regent, a warlord trying to unite Celtic tribes against Saxon invaders. Druid Merlin loves relic quests. Lancelot's a pretty-boy creep and Guinevere a schemer. Arthur's brave warriors are the heroes here, as they slog in the muck and battle against the political currents of the sixth century. Cornwell's known for Napoleonic adventures, so it's no surprise that his <u>Warlord Chronicles</u> stress military action.

David, Peter

Knight Life. <u>Modern-Day Arthur</u>. 1987. Ace, ISBN: 0441010776, 352p.

Arthur returns . . . as a mayoral candidate in New York City. Merlin, a 10-year-old genius (he ages backward) manages him. Troubled Gwen (reincarnated) lives with abusive Lance, a failed writer, but falls for Arthur. Morgan has become a TV junkie but her fighting spirit rekindles when she discovers Merlin is free. David gives the legend a satirical Manhattan-romantic-comedy treatment.

Lawhead, Stephen

Taliesin. <u>The Pendragon Cycle</u>. 1987. Eos, ISBN: 038070613X, 496p.

Reversing Bradley's framing of the legend, <u>The Pendragon Cycle</u> portrays Arthur and his cohorts as Christian warriors battling Morgian's pagan magic. The series starts here, a generation earlier. After her homeland sinks, Charis, princess of Atlantis, moves to Britain, marries the bard Taliesin, and has little Merlin. Lawhead's unusual portrayal of Arthur as a Christian divides fans of the legend.

Malory, Sir Thomas
Le Morte d'Arthur. Fifteenth century. Signet, ISBN: 0451528166, 512p.

  Written (from prison) in the fifteenth century, this isn't the first telling of the Arthur legend (Geoffrey of Monmouth's twelfth-century account is the most significant predecessor), but it is the most famous early effort. Keith Baines translated this edition from Middle English. Arthurians could do worse than starting their comparative journey by reading this classic.

Radford, Irene
Guardian of the Balance. <u>Merlin's Descendants</u>. 1999. DAW, ISBN: 0886778751, 608p.

  The first book in the <u>Descendants</u> series is told from the pagan point of view of Merlin's daughter Wren, who loves Arthur, mostly from afar. Subsequent books follow further descendants as they protect Arthur's ideals in later eras. The recent fifth book, *Guardian of the Freedom,* advances to the time of George III and the American Revolution.

Stewart, Mary
Mary Stewart's Merlin Trilogy. 1970–1979. Eos, ISBN: 0688003478, 928p. (hbk.)

  Stewart focuses on Merlin, who in her version is not a wily plotter nor tremendously powerful but an earthy man with a little psychic power and a lot of wisdom. In Stewart's descriptive series, Arthur's rise and fall corresponds with the wax and wane of Merlin's power.

Taylor, Holly
Night Bird's Reign. 2005. Medallion, ISBN: 1932815538, 506p.

  In *Reign,* Celtic names and myths are mixed so thoroughly that you may not realize you are reading Arthurian fiction. But at its core, this is the story of dreamer Gwydion (Merlin), whose prophetic dreams lead him to protect Arthur and search for a mythic sword.

White, T. H.
The Once and Future King. 1938–1958. Ace, ISBN: 0441003834, 688p.

  White tells the basic story well but sometimes distracts the reader with modern references or long digressions outside his main narrative. You may or may not like Merlin as comic relief. Still, this book brought Arthur to the attention of modern readers and into the ranks of popular fiction.

Whyte, Jack
The Skystone. <u>Camulod Chronicles</u>. 1992. Tor, ISBN: 0812551389, 512p.

  In Whyte's <u>Chronicles</u>, fantastic elements are all explained in realist terms as the imaginings of pagans. Merlyn (who arrives in the third book; the first two are about Romans and Excalibur) trains young cousin Arthur in the old

Roman values. This series is popular among readers who don't like magic but do like sex and historical detail.

Medieval-Doers: Fantasy's Favorite Setting

When I was young, medieval settings and fantasy were synonymous. Novels were almost always set in a loosely European world of castles, kings, queens, swords, and sorcery. Fantasy fans played Dungeons & Dragons, and campaigns set in the modern world, Victorian times, or (gasp!) America just weren't thinkable. Settings have become much more diverse in the last twenty years, and the genre is better for it. Still, I have a soft spot in my heart (or is it my head?) for medieval fantasy. These books succeed in making this old setting feel fresh.

Douglass, Sara
  The Wounded Hawk. **The Crucible.** 2001. Tor, ISBN: 0765342839, 624p.
    Trained as a lecturer in medieval history, Douglass always frames her stories with spot-on details that re-create the era. In this second book of a trilogy, a worldly monk tries to keep demons from destroying the earth. Conflict between Richard II and Prince Henry of Bolingbroke is at the center of the story.

Duncan, Dave
  Paragon Lost. **The King's Blades.** 2002. Eos, ISBN: 0380818353, 448p.
    A group of young knights adventures in a country modeled after medieval Russia, complete with a mad czar and the beginnings of secret police. A disgraced knight must stop Igor from gaining the service of his own Blade.

Elliott, Kate
  King's Dragon. **Crown of Stars.** 1997. DAW, ISBN: 0886777712, 640p.
    If you love medieval settings, Elliott's complex society will fascinate you. The story has class conflict, succession politics, mysticism, and clashes of religion and royalty. Elliott changes enough to make this world distinct from historical Europe, but it remains believable. An intricate plot involving a large cast of characters sets up her series nicely.

Jordan, Sherryl
  The Hunting of the Last Dragon. 2002. Eos, ISBN: 0064472310, 256p. **YA**.
    A peasant boy joins forces with a Chinese orphan after rescuing her from a traveling fair in an alternate fourteenth-century England. The pair enters a hunt for the last dragon against a background that includes monks, the Black Death, and early use of gunpowder.

Kay, Guy Gavriel
⇨ *The Lions of Al-Rassan.* 1995. Eos, ISBN: 0060733497, 528p.

Kay sticks to medieval settings, pulling new stories from its well-worked ground. His Al-Rassan is an analog of Moorish Spain—an empire crumbling into warring states. Kay doesn't rely on magic for pyrotechnics. He gives strong characters moral dilemmas and divided loyalties in a vivid world. The results are always dramatic, never boring.

Kurtz, Katherine
In the King's Service. **Deryni.** 2003. Ace, ISBN: 0441012094, 384p.

Religion, state, and magic clash in this latest return to *Deryni* court politics. As you read into Kurtz's series, you gain a sense of history for her fantasy world. It's not hard: The books are short. Although this return to the series was long awaited, you may want to start at the beginning with *Deryni Rising.* Fans of the medieval period also will enjoy Kurtz's *Knights Templar* series, written with Deborah Turner Harris.

Tarr, Judith
Kingdom of the Grail. 2000. Roc, ISBN: 0451460049, 512p.

Historical fantasist Tarr blends the Arthurian saga and the Song of Roland, two key medieval legends. Roland, a warrior and shape changer in the service of Charlemagne, must win the love of a beautiful Moor, combat the evil monk Ganelou, and find a way to free Merlin from captivity. The author puts her doctorate in medieval history to fine use.

Celtic-kle Your Fancy:
Fantasy in the Celtic Tradition

Far back in the mists of time, before the Anglo-Saxons, there were the Celts, a mysterious (cue fog machines and dancing druids) nature-and-goddess-worshipping culture with a folklore that has powerful pull for the fantasy community. By the fifth century, the Celts had been pushed into Ireland, Scotland, and Wales, where they integrated elements of Norse culture and Christianity into their potent mix. This is fertile ground for fantasy, with rich mythology, a fierce history of war against Romans and Saxons, herbal lore, and musical and artistic traditions. With many options to choose from, you can pick from many approaches to this material.

Chadbourn, Mark
World's End. **The Age of Misrule.** 1999. Gollancz, ISBN: 1857989805, 557p.

For a primer in ancient Celtic myths in a modern British setting, try this trilogy-opening thriller about reawakening Celtic gods and mythical beasts. The Tuatha De Danann and their modern charges, the Brothers and Sisters of the Dragon, must collect four objects of power from around Britain or humanity will be swept away by the evil Formorri.

Forsyth, Kate
  The Witches of Eileanan. Witches of Eileanan. 1998. Roc, ISBN: 0451456890, 416p.
    The world of Eileanan has a richly Celtic feel. In dialect Scottish brogue, several narrators tell this tale of redhead twins and their aging mentor. On the day Isabeau (a witch, her twin is a warrior maid) enters the coven, it's attacked, and she must go on the run from evil Queen Maya. Adventures come in a flurry in a creature-packed quest that starts a six-book series. (Published as *Dragonclaw* in Forsyth's native Australia.)

Guest, Lady Charlotte
  The Mabinogion. 1838–1845. Kessinger, ISBN: 1419171097, 232p.
    Before you launch into Celtic fantasy, familiarize yourself with the original lore and period detail in this translation of 11 Welsh myths. This edition has drawings by Tolkien illustrator Alan Lee and a charming (though censored) text adapted by a nineteenth-century lady. If you don't care about pictures, try the Jones and Jones translation.

Hetley, James A.
  The Summer Country. 2002. Ace, ISBN: 0441012205, 368p.
    A Maine convenience store clerk is nearly raped by a troll-like creature. Her rescuer, a knight, tells Maureen that she is an "Old One," wanted in the Summer Country. The world she finds there is beautiful, but the behavior of the residents is ugly. Maureen must find new strength to survive. If you like Celtic myth but not the gentle fashion in which it's usually told, try this raw, modern book. Followed by *The Winter Oak.*

Holdstock, Robert
  The Iron Grail. The Merlin Codex. 2002. Tor, ISBN: 0765349876, 336p.
    Holdstock blends myths in pursuit of archetypal truth (heavy, huh?). His results have a generally Celtic feel. In the Codex, he pairs Jason (of the Argonauts) with Merlin. After chasing the Golden Fleece in *Celtika,* Merlin returns to pre-Britain Alba to aid King Urtha (now who could that be?) by retrieving his stolen children from the Otherworld.

Kerr, Katharine
  ⇨ *Daggerspell.* Deverry. 1986. Bantam Spectra, ISBN: 0553565214, 480p.
    Following traditions of Celtic culture, in which certain souls are bound together across the realms of time, *Daggerspell* follows a core group of characters through multiple incarnations. With romance, magic, elves, intrigue, and adventure, there's a little bit for everyone here. The 13-book Deverry saga opened in grand style with this book.

Lawhead, Stephen
The Paradise War. <u>Song of Albion trilogy</u>. 1991. Lion, ISBN: 0745924662, 410p.

A graduate student follows his roommate into the Otherworld of Albion, where the two become active participants in Celtic myths. Unlike most writers of Celtic fantasy, who prefer the pagan path, Lawhead chooses a Christian interpretation.

Llywelyn, Morgan
Druids. 1991. Del Rey, ISBN: 0804108447, 416p.

The queen of Celtic historical fiction examines the culture's early defeat by Romans in ancient Gaul. Magic is only in the perception of practitioners, so this isn't purely fantasy, but it reads like it. The book lavishly portrays druidic ritual and Celtic daily life.

Melling, O. R.
The Hunter's Moon. <u>The Chronicles of Faerie</u>. 1992. Amulet, ISBN: 0810992140, 305p. YA.

Two 16-year-old cousins who love Celtic lore go backpacking in Ireland. When they decide to sleep on a faerie mound, you know things won't turn out well. Irish Findabhair is abducted by—who else?—the Faerie king, and timid American Gwen has to go after her. The plot moves briskly, and Melling, an Irish scholar, blends in myth effectively.

Tuttle, Lisa
The Mysteries. 2005. Bantam Spectra, ISBN: 055358734X, 384p.

Tuttle mixes Texas urban fantasy noir with Celtic fairylands. Detective Ian Kennedy, haunted by the disappearance of his love years ago, takes the case of another vanished woman. This isn't standard detective fiction: Ian specializes in cases of people who he believes have traveled to the world of the Sidhe—elves. Recommended to all readers except those who need strongly resolved endings.

London Calling: The Grand Tradition of Fantasy in an English Setting

When it comes to books, Brits dominate the cultural landscape, and not just (nose in the air) *literature,* but also genre writing. In mystery, Conan Doyle, Christie, and Sayers are major benchmarks, and contemporary police procedural writers push the tradition forward. Romance is still a world of Regency manners, country manors, and men in kilts. Fantasy is the most British of all genres. No one can overestimate the influence of Tolkien and Lewis. Sales of

Harry Potter show that interest in English fantasy is not flagging. Britain is not just home to fantasists; it's the setting for much of the action as well. Here's a small taste of great recent fantasy set in Britain.

Douglass, Sara
God's Concubine. The Troy Game. 2004. Tor, ISBN: 0765344432, 624p.
> In The Troy Game, mythic heroes reborn every few millennia continue an epic struggle. In this second book, the conflict resumes in eleventh-century England. William the Conqueror and Harold Godwineson are among the reincarnate combatants. Book three, *Darkwitch Rising,* moves to seventeenth-century England.

Gaiman, Neil
Neverwhere. 1996. Harper Perennial, ISBN: 0060557818, 400p.
> London Underworld takes on new meaning in Below, a bizarre alternate London that is frightening but fascinating. Protagonist Richard Mayhew is like those befuddled men who stumble into Monty Python skits or Terry Gilliam films. The mixture of his buttoned-down mind with the weirdness he encounters results in a very British conflict.

Hoyt, Sarah A.
Any Man So Daring. Shakespeare trilogy. 2003. Ace, ISBN: 0441012086, 336p.
> Hoyt concludes a trilogy about encounters of Shakespeare with the elf king Quicksilver. In this entry, Will is nagged by guilty suspicions that his success as a playwright is related to his experiences in the land of Faerie. He's forced to return when an evil usurper there kidnaps his son Hamnet. If you like the Elizabethan era, give this series a try.

MacLeod, Ian R.
House of Storms. 2005. Ace, ISBN: 0441013422, 464p.
> MacLeod continues to develop the alternate Victorian world of *The Light Ages.* It's a technology-enhanced Britain based on magical aether. Alice, a powerful guild mistress and overprotective mother, uses magic that leads to class conflict and a civil war.

Rowling, J. K.
Harry Potter and the Goblet of Fire. Harry Potter series. 2000. Scholastic, ISBN: 0439139600, 752p. YA, AW.
> From the tent village on the moors built by Quidditch fans to the invasive tabloid journalism of Rita Skeeter, this book is full of reminders that Harry Potter and friends are a very English lot indeed. The behavior of the Hogwarts students contrasts nicely with that of their French and eastern European counterparts in this fourth series entry.

Stroud, Jonathan
> ⇨ *The Golem's Eye.* **Bartimaeus trilogy.** 2004. Miramax, ISBN: 0786836547, 576p. YA, AW.
>
> Despite similarities, Stroud's series, about boy magician Nathaniel and the loquacious djinn Bartimaeus, does not steal from *Harry Potter*. In this middle book, Nathaniel works for Internal Affairs in an English government controlled by magicians. New lead Kitty is in the resistance that wants to end rule by magic. Famous English landmarks, such as Westminster Abbey and the British Museum, serve as backdrop for the action.

Wrede, Patricia C.
> *Mairelon the Magician.* **Mairelon.** 1991. Starscape, ISBN: 0765342324, 288p. YA.
>
> Regency romance meets fantasy in this novel. Plucky Kim's days posing as a boy street thief end when the dashing Mairelon catches her stealing. He takes her under his wing for a chase through the English countryside in search of magical silver. Followed by *Magician's Ward*.

Easterns: Fantasy with the Flavor of Asia

The folklore source material has always been there, but fantasy writers are only beginning to make use of Asian settings. Perhaps the success of films like *Crouching Tiger, Hidden Dragon, Hero,* and *The House of Flying Daggers* is stirring authorial imagination. Sales of manga and anime among younger generations also should impact fantasy novels. With the quality of books such as those that follow, Asian-themed fantasy will be a boom market in years to come.

Banker, Ashok
> *The Prince of Ayodhya.* **The Ramayana.** 2003. Aspect, ISBN: 0446611999, 592p.
>
> *The Ramayana* is a cultural touchstone for Indian Hindus, but Banker's update isn't dry, dusty folklore, an exotic, inaccessible delicacy, or a religious education. After a slightly slow start, this is, simply put, a fast-paced fantasy action epic set against the vivid backdrop of ancient India, particularly the magnificent city-state of Ayodhya. The five follow-up books, available only in English editions, are worth the hunt.

Benjamin, Curt
> *Lords of Grass and Thunder.* 2005. DAW, ISBN: 0756403421, 576p.
>
> Mongolian history inspires this follow-up to Benjamin's Seven Brothers trilogy. Prince Tayy returns home as hero and heir to the leadership of his people. His jealous cousin Qutula, corrupted by a snake demon, plans to

murder Tayy and his own father, the Khan. Eluneke, a shaman in training who loves Tayy, becomes his best hope for survival.

Feist, Raymond, and Wurts, Janny
Daughter of the Empire. **Riftwar: The Other Side.** 1987. Bantam Spectra, ISBN: 055327211X, 432p.

The Tsurani Empire is a viper's nest of spies and assassins. When Mara's father and brother die in battle, she's thrust to the head of house Acoma. Mara is determined to maintain her family name but hampered by inexperience and the rigid patriarchal culture of her world (think feudal Japan). Wurts and Feist each bring their own strengths as writers to this top-notch trilogy opener.

Hearn, Lian
Across the Nightingale Floor. **Tales of the Otori.** 2002. Riverhead, ISBN: 1573223328, 320p.

Takeo grows up in the village of a secret religious clan, but when it is burned, he becomes ward to Lord Otori Shigeru. Takeo enters a larger world in which feuding warlords clash and the Tribe, a ninjalike group of supernatural assassins, claims his loyalty. Spare, fluid language makes it easy to become immersed in the romance and intrigue.

Hughart, Barry
The Bridge of Birds. **Master Li series.** 1984. Del Rey, ISBN: 0345321383, 288p. AW.

Silly and bawdy, this funny mystery is set in magical ancient China. Number Ten Ox—a brave, strong, gullible young man—is sent after relief for the children of his village, who have fallen into deep sleep. He gets aid from Master Li, a wise sage, who is also drunken and devious. Rambling around China on the trail of magical ginger, the two have picaresque adventures while trying to get to the root of the problem.

Johnson, Kij
Fudoki. 2003. Tor, ISBN: 0765303914, 320p.

Princess Harume, dying after a long life circumscribed by the customs of the imperial court, tells the story of Kagaya-hime, a twelfth-century warrior woman who began life as a cat. The sole survivor of an estate fire, the cat takes to the road for adventures around Japan. This story within a story captures many aspects of Japanese culture.

Novik, Naomi
Throne of Jade. **Temeraire.** 2006. Del Rey, ISBN: 0345481291, 432p.

The second entry in the Temeraire series finds Captain Laurence taking the dragon to China. The duo sail around the world to find intrigue in the Imperial Court. Novik's novel is successful as a Napoleonic-era naval thriller, as an odd-couple buddy story, or as a tale of fish-out-of-water Westerners experiencing a new civilization.

Pratchett, Terry
Interesting Times. **Discworld, Rincewind series**. 1994. HarperTorch, ISBN: 0061056901, 400p.

The full curse is "May you live in interesting times," and that's what the Empire gets when they request a "Great Wizzard" to save them. Ankh-Morpork can spare only inept Rincewind, who falls in with a goofy Red Army. Meanwhile, aging Cohen the Barbarian arrives with his wheelchair-bound Silver Horde and decides to become Ghengiz Cohen.

Russell, Sean
The Initiate Brother. 1991. DAW, ISBN: 0886774667, 480p.

Canadian fantasist Russell creates a new world by blending medieval China, Japan, and imagination. Brother Shuyun becomes spiritual advisor to the family of a warlord. The fate of ancient Wa will depend on his success. This is elegant, well-characterized fantasy set against a fully realized background. Followed by *Gatherer of Clouds.*

Wells, Martha
The Wheel of the Infinite. 2000. Eos, ISBN: 0380788152, 400p.

Vivid settings are part of Wells's success. For *Wheel,* she turns from her usual European settings to the Celestial Empire, a creation based on Southeast Asia, particularly Angkor Wat. The interesting magical system, tropical climate, sand painting rituals, and descriptions of architecture jump off the page, bringing an unfamiliar world to life.

Steampunk: Forward-Looking Fantasy in Victorian Settings

The cyberpunk movement of 1980s science fiction spawned a spin-off. Set in the Victorian era in early industrial times, steampunk places magic alongside the dawn of technology. Antiauthority, anti-class-structure punk attitude is also on display. The mixture of science and fantasy excites some readers while turning off others. If you think that public transportations suffers from lack of dirigibles or suspect that Victoria might have been the faerie queen as well as that of England, you might be in the target audience for these books.

Dahlquist, Gordon
The Glass Books of the Dream Eaters. 2006. Bantam, ISBN: 0385340354, 768p. (hbk.)

A prim plantation owner's daughter, a street-toughened thief, and a military surgeon are the protagonists in this tale set in a quasi-London. Set against backdrops like creepy operating theaters and rambling country manors and full of cliffhangers, the Victorian tone of this literary dark fantasy will remind readers of classic serialized novels.

Frost, Mark
The List of Seven. 1993. Avon, ISBN: 0380720191, 416p.

Young Arthur Conan Doyle becomes allied with Jack Sparks, one of Queen Victoria's secret agents. Frost, creator of TV's *Twin Peaks,* cooks up a story of séances, occult plots, monsters, and a mix of historical and fictional characters, positing Sparks as Doyle's model for Sherlock Holmes. Followed by *The 6 Messiahs.*

MacLeod, Ian R.
The Light Ages. 2003. Ace, ISBN: 0441011497, 464p.

In a style akin to Dickens's darker works, MacLeod builds alternate history from aether. The magical substance, source of technology and industry, is monopolized by great guilds. Commoners process the stuff, which turns some into changelings. Robert Borrow, son of one such victim, tries to make his way in a cruel world on the verge of revolution.

Moore, Alan, and O'Neill, Kevin
The League of Extraordinary Gentlemen, Vol. 1. 2002. Wildstorm, ISBN: 1563898586, 192p.
The League of Extraordinary Gentlemen, Vol. 2. 2004. Wildstorm, ISBN: 1401201180, 228p.

Victorian adventure fiction meets superhero team comics as heroes Alan Quartermain, Captain Nemo, Dr. Jekyll and Mr. Hyde, Mina Murray (née Harker), and the Invisible Man fight "M" (whose identity I can't reveal). Moore writes with dry English humor, and O'Neill's graphics mix Victorian futurism and vivid gore.

Powers, Tim
⇨ *The Anubis Gates.* 1983. Ace, ISBN: 0441004016, 400p.

Time travel, romantic Victorian poets, the Egyptian underworld, London sewers, an evil (there are no other kind) clown, body swapping, Knights Templar, tiny killers on an eggshell fleet, and a werewolf: Mystical and groovy, only Tim Powers could render such an odd combination this believably.

Priest, Christopher
The Prestige. 1995. Tor, ISBN: 0312858868, 416p. AW.

At the turn of the twentieth century, the bitter rivalry of two magicians consumes them. They push each other to new heights, perhaps too far. Meeting almost a hundred years later, their descendants feel a mysterious connection, which leads them to compare their ancestors' journals and uncover what happened long ago.

Stoddard, James
 The High House. 1998. Aspect, ISBN: 0446606790, 336p.
> Chaos clashes with stiff-upper-lip Victorian religion in a manor house called Evenmere. Young Carter Anderson has grown up there, but when he unknowingly gives the keys to an evil society, he starts a chain of events that seals his fate as master of the High House. Don't be surprised by anything you find when doors to these rooms are opened.

Wells, Martha
 The Death of the Necromancer. 1998. Eos, ISBN: 0380788144, 544p. (out of print).
> Nicholas Valiarde leads a band of thieves in Ile-Rien (which has the feel of Vienna or Paris). Thieving covers their preparations for revenge on Count Montesq, who framed Valiarde's mentor, but encounters with horrible creatures, vivisected corpses, and magical devices in the city cellars and sewers interrupt their plans. The Fall of Ile-Rien, a follow-up series in the same setting, is still in print.

Alternate America: Finding Fantasy in a New World

Ask the average American about fantasy, and they'll tell you it's that land straight down Main Street on the far side of the castle. The United States is fantasy challenged. We think of ourselves as pragmatic and serious. When we do indulge in fantasy, it's generally borrowed. In a country where history hasn't yet receded into the mists and indigenous cultures have been marginalized, myth and folklore are a patchwork stolen from other nations. But a few brave fantasists are successfully setting fantasy in the New World. This list is dedicated to them.

Card, Orson Scott
 Seventh Son. The Tales of Alvin Maker. 1987. Tor, ISBN: 0812533054, 256p. AW.
> Card's imagined frontier America intrigues even when the plot stutters. He starts with folksy vernacular language and an American magic of hexes, healings, and heartfires. Historical figures of the early 1800s appear, and side plots concern Native Americans and slaves. This fantastic reimagining of early Mormonism is worth a look.

De Lint, Charles
 ⇨ *Dreams Underfoot.* Newford. 1993. Orb, ISBN: 0765306794, 416p.
> Committed to creating fantasy from the melting-pot cultures of Canada and the United States, de Lint blends indigenous cultural myths with immigrant myths and then sets them against urban landscapes. *Dreams* makes a fine entry to Newford, but de Lint's achievement is collective: Jump into any book and read in any order.

Gaiman, Neil
American Gods. 2000. HarperTorch, ISBN: 0380789035, 624p. AW.
 Just released from prison, Shadow Moon finds that his new job involves traveling the United States to recruit Old World gods (who came over with immigrants but are now shambling remnants of their former selves) for a showdown with new gods of U.S. technology. The whole novel is a metaphor for—and sometimes a satire of—the self-contradictory core of U.S. culture.

Irvine, Alexander C.
The Narrows. 2005. Del Rey, ISBN: 0345466985, 352p.
 In Irvine's reimagining of World War II–era Detroit, Henry Ford's plants also build golems to fight the Germans. Caught in a game of spies, counterspies, and sabotaging imps, one worker tries too hard to contribute more to the war effort, unleashing a dangerous dwarf from the depths.

Keyes, J. Gregory
Empire of Unreason. **The Age of Unreason.** 2000. Del Rey, ISBN: 0345406109, 416p.
 In an alternate eighteenth century, a comet brought to earth by malevolent demons has created a new ice age. From Charleston, Ben Franklin leads Native Americans, liberated slaves, and European refugees in defense of the continent. A slew of historical characters grace the pages of this intriguing science fantasy, the third in Keyes's series.

King, Stephen
The Drawing of Three. **The Dark Tower.** 1985. Signet, ISBN: 0451210859, 480p.
 Wounded hero Roland enters a violent, alternate New York City, where he tries to recruit help from three different decades. A wheelchair-bound, schizophrenic civil rights activist, a junkie, and a murderer all play crucial roles in his quest. King's series hits its stride with this second book, surpassing the intriguing but often vague opener, *The Gunslinger.*

Palwick, Susan
The Necessary Beggar. 2005. Tor, ISBN: 0765349515, 320p.
 An extended family is forced to immigrate to Reno, Nevada (a near-future Reno that is uglier than the real one). Some members adjust, but others can't take the culture shock. The twist is that this family hails from the abundant magical world Gandiffri. Mystery, romance, coming-of-age, and fantasy adventure combine for a potent mix.

Powers, Tim
Earthquake Weather. 1997. Tor, ISBN: 0812555198, 640p. AW.
 In a loose sequel to *Last Call* and *Expiration Date,* Powers returns to his fantastic urban United States and his tale of an American Fisher King. His ghostly Las Vegas, California vineyards, and earthquake-prone Los Angeles are vivid and satisfying, even in sections in which the plot becomes confusing.

Resnick, Mike
  Dragon America. **Dragon America.** 2005. Phobos, ISBN: 0972002693, 259p.
    Forget dragoons, Resnick's American Revolution has *dragons.* Washington sends Daniel Boone to recruit Shawnee warriors to fight the British. Unable to raise troops, Boone heads west in pursuit of the fire-breathers. Later books will set dragons in other American eras.

Windling, Terri
  The Wood Wife. 1996. Orb, ISBN: 0765302934, 320p. `AW`.
    When her mentor dies, Maggie Black travels to the poet's estate in the desert hills outside Tucson, Arizona. She intends to write his biography while nursing some of her own hurts. As she begins to explore the mystery of his death, Maggie enters a fantastic world. Lushly romantic, this original work is as beautiful and frightening as its Sonoran Desert setting.

Zicree, Marc Scott, and Wilson, Robert Charles
  Magic Time: Ghostlands. Magic Time. 2004. Eos, ISBN: 0061059609, 496p.
    The last volume of the Magic Time trilogy takes questers to postapocalyptic Manhattan, Chicago, and the Old West, where a lawyer, a woman warrior, a Russian doctor, and a bipolar wizard are among those looking for the source of the Change, which shoved the United States into a magical dimension.

Contemporary Style Is Not Just for Furniture: Modern Worlds with Fantastic Spins

A few fantasies have always featured factories instead of forests, but when writers like Charles de Lint hit big with books that make modern magic, contemporary fantasy became one of the genre's hottest fields. For many, contemporary fantasy is more accessible than mythic pasts. (Although for others, modernity destroys the magic.) If you eschew fantasy for more up-to-date, edgy fair, your excuse no longer applies. Get current with these novels.

Brooks, Terry
  Running with the Demon. **The Word and the Void.** 1997. Del Rey, ISBN: 0345422589, 448p.
    An all-out battle of good and evil brews in small-town Illinois (where Brooks grew up, as the level of detail in this novel shows). Young Nest tries to protect a park with magic, but instead she becomes a target of demons. Events will come to fruition at the Fourth of July picnic, and the fireworks might be more than anyone expected.

Caine, Rachel
Ill Wind. <u>Weather Warden series</u>. 2003. Roc, ISBN: 0451459520, 352p.

With a sarcastic demeanor and a taste for fast cars and faster men, Joanne Baldwin is a modern woman. Her job is to moderate weather with magic, but false accusations leave her facing death or deactivation. Fast-moving fun ensues as Joanne races across the modern United States. Caine crosses contemporary romance, thriller, mystery, and fantasy.

Card, Orson Scott
Magic Street. 2006. Del Rey, ISBN: 0345416902, 416p.

A classic story of mischief at the borders of the fairy world and the human is placed in an African American Los Angeles neighborhood instead of the English countryside. Card mixes suspenseful writing with ethical questions.

De Lint, Charles
⇨ *Spirits in the Wires.* <u>Newford</u>. 2003. Tor, ISBN: 0312869711, 448p.

Fairy world meets cyberspace in this entry in de Lint's loose series set in a Canadian city. Newford residents who may share origins on the Internet are pulled into Wordwood, a Web site with a physical reality infected with mischievous spirits. De Lint deserves credit for popularizing urban fantasy. He has a gift for making the shaggiest stories believable.

Lackey, Mercedes, and Guon, Ellen
Bedlam's Bard. <u>Bedlam's Bard series</u>. 1990–1992. Baen, ISBN: 0671878638, 624p.

A Southern California street musician accidentally wakes an elf lord while playing at the local Renaissance fair. Veteran Lackey tried contemporary fantasy with this work and must have liked it. She's returned to both this series and *Bardic Voices* many times since.

Powers, Tim
Strange Itineraries. 2004. Tachyon, ISBN: 1892391236, 224p.

Ghosts, quirky characters, and California settings collide in a book of short stories with a more serious tone than is typical for Powers, considered by many the king of contemporary fantasy. Think of him as the fantasy alternative to Philip K. Dick.

Shetterly, Will
Nevernever. <u>Bordertown</u>. 1993. Magic Carpet, ISBN: 0152052100, 240p. **YA**.

With wife Emma Bull *(War for the Oaks),* Shetterly built the shared world *Bordertown,* an urban landscape full of runaways, motorcycle gangs, and other street people on the border of the human and faerie worlds. In <u>Bordertown</u>, many of the locals are elves, and neither magic nor technology is predictable. This is a sequel to *Elsewhere.*

Battle-Tested: Fantasy That Puts You in the Middle of the War

Some people find war stories exciting and prefer an older style of battle in which skill makes more of an impact than it does with modern weapons. This preference is more easily satisfied by fantasy than any other genre. Some readers like tactics, thrilling to the well-executed plan or battlefield surprise. Others want the vicarious experience of what it is like to be a soldier in the midst of the fray. If you're among the legions of fans for such martial material, here are the books for you.

Bunch, Chris
 Dragonmaster. <u>Storm of Wings trilogy</u>. 2002. Roc, ISBN: 0451460308, 416p.
   Dragonmaster starts a trilogy of adventures featuring Hal Kailas. Beginning his career as a cavalry soldier, Hal finds his place as a dragon rider. Bunch draws strong parallels between the use of dragons for war and the development of combat aviation in World War I.

Cook, Glen
 The Black Company. <u>Black Company series</u>. 1984. Tor, ISBN: 0812521390, 320p.
   Told by a company surgeon and historian, this tale recreates the mercenary life. Using choppy and sometimes disorienting storytelling, Cook re-creates the feeling of life in wartime. There's no glorification: The Black Company isn't even sure what it's fighting for. They just move from skirmish to skirmish, trying to stay alive. A battle to defend the Stair of Tears is the best sequence in this throwback to an earlier, pulpy style.

Erikson, Steven
 ⇨ *Memories of Ice.* <u>Malazan Book of the Fallen</u>. 2001. Tor, ISBN: 0765310031, 784p.
   Dark military fantasy taken to the nth degree; you'll love this or hate it. It's gruesome and cryptic. Read this third book right after the opener, *Gardens of the Moon,* as it picks up directly on its events. There are too many characters, battles, and shifting alliances for a tidy plot summary, but Erikson pulls off not one but two military climaxes with aplomb.

Gemmell, David
 Troy: Lord of the Silver Bow. <u>Troy series</u>. 2005. Del Rey, ISBN: 0345494571, 496p.
   Gemmell has a gift for battle scenes, so it's exciting when he turns to a subject like the Trojan War. Although he uses the same characters, it's immediately clear that this tale will take different turns than *The Iliad.* For one thing, Aeneas is Gemmell's protagonist.

Moon, Elizabeth
The Deed of Paksenarrion. 1988. Baen, ISBN: 0671721046, 1040p.
    War is seen from a very personal level in this excellent trilogy that started Moon's career. The reader experiences every step of Paks's development, first as a simple fighter, then as someone who can battle with magic, and finally, after surviving true adversity, to the exalted rank of paladin.

Pratchett, Terry
Jingo. **Discworld, The Watch.** 1997. HarperTorch, ISBN: 0061059064, 448p.
    For a break from fighting, try the "war" in Discworld's 20th novel. Both Ankh-Morpork and Klatch claim a new island that rises between their two lands. Ankh-Morpork has no army to back its claim, but it does have a bewildering array of hilarious propaganda and diplomacy and intelligence operations. As usual, it falls on Sam Vimes and his Watch to find the solution.

Turtledove, Harry
An Emperor for the Legion. **Videssos Cycle.** 1987. Del Rey, ISBN: 0345330684, 336p.
    In the series, a Roman legion is transported magically to Videssos (a world much like Byzantium). In this second book, the Romans retreat across a gauntlet of hostile territory. The stretches of boredom and political maneuvering an army can experience between its actual battles are rendered especially well.

Borderline: The Weirdest, Most Whimsical Trips into Fantasy Realms

    This book is dedicated to identifying patterns in the fantasy genre. There's irony, however, in focusing on common themes in a genre that breaks rules. What category is proper for books that are just plain bizarre? How can one group books set in worlds that aren't like anywhere else? This list collects journeys to places stranger than third-tier tourist attractions, odder than your in-laws' Christmas party, more surreal than cable television at 3:00 A.M. This is your ticket to Weirdsville: Settings so fantastic that only fantasy can imagine them.

Carroll, Jonathan
Glass Soup. 2005. Tor, ISBN: 0765311801, 320p.
    Isabelle, who brought her husband back from death in *White Apples,* is now pregnant, and little Anjo's origins draw the interest of Chaos (who takes several forms) and God (most often appearing as a polar bear named Bob). Carroll's story of everyday Americans in Vienna focuses on themes of love,

friendship, and responsibility. But that's like saying that Salvador Dali painted everyday objects. Carroll's world is truly surreal.

Carroll, Lewis
⇨ *Alice's Adventure in Wonderland and Through the Looking Glass.* 1865–1871. Signet Classics, ISBN: 0451527747, 240p. `YA`.

This is what happens when math professors write fiction. One hundred forty years later, Wonderland is still as weird as ever. You don't need to sit on a mushroom and smoke a hookah to feel a little trippy as you travel with Alice, chase the White Rabbit, take tea with the Mad Hatter, or play croquet with the terrifying Queen of Hearts and her pig baby. Take *Alice* away from your children and read it again yourself.

Holt, Tom
The Portable Door. 2003. Orbit, ISBN: 1841492086, 416p.

With plenty of Pratchett and Douglas Adams novels to read, few Americans have discovered Holt, whose style is even more distinctly British. His bumbling English everymen have funny run-ins with magical worlds, as in this tale of a dim clerk who does his best to ignore mysterious goings-on at the strange, whimsical, yet very bureaucratic firm of H. W. Wells until the woman he loves is stolen by goblins.

Pratchett, Terry
Carpe Jugulum. **Discworld, Witches.** 1998. HarperTorch, ISBN: 0061020397, 378p.

Selecting the weirdest Pratchett is like picking which of Michael Jackson's surgeries changed his looks. King Verence invites everyone to his daughter's christening in Lancre, a kingdom with more local color than the *Wizard of Oz* set. Unfortunately, some debonair vampires make Verence's guest list, and the witches must employ headology to send them packing. Igor makes hith firtht funny appearanth here too.

Spencer, Wen
Tinker. 2003. Baen, ISBN: 0743498712, 448p.

Wealthy teenage inventor Tinker runs a junkyard in Pittsburgh, but due to malfunctioning world gates, the city resides in the world of Elfhome most of the time. An elvish lord whose life Tinker saved is courting her (rather vigorously), and Japanese demons are after Tinker's ability to build another world gate. Followed by *Wolf Who Rules.*

Wolfe, Gene
The Knight. **The Wizard Knight.** 2004. Tor, ISBN: 0765313480, 432p.
The Wizard. **The Wizard Knight.** 2004. Tor, ISBN: 0765314703, 480p.

Wolfe has made a career of writing mystical stories with undependable narrators who travel hallucinatory worlds. This two-book series set in a world of knights and quests is no standard fantasy. A boy enters a fantasy world and the body of Sir Able, whose strapping physique makes a strange container for a preteen mind. If you like straightforward narrative, this may not be for you, but if you want original reading, you'll enjoy puzzling out the meaning and purpose of the protagonist's strange transformation.

Fan-to-Sea: The Best of Nautical Fantasy

The pitch of the deck, the wind in your face, a hammock to sleep in, and galley food . . . no doubt about it, sea travel is miserable. But the romance of the briny deep is grand. You can experience it in historical series with endless binnacles, spinnakers, and mizzenmasts, but if you don't know your scuttlebutt from your poop deck, then shipboard fantasy might be for you. Sea monsters, underwater kingdoms, and wizard pirates are more exciting than another mannered account of the Napoleonic Wars any day! Cross the gangplank and set sail on these adventures.

Hobb, Robin
Ship of Magic. **Liveship Traders**. 1998. Bantam Spectra, ISBN: 0553575635, 832p.

Hobb has all the elements for hearty nautical adventure: sentient ships with distinct personalities, sea serpents, a family of merchant traders, a ruthless would-be pirate king, a port settled by convicts, and evil barbarian slavers. This trilogy starter emphasizes careful development of great characters in a vivid, complex world.

Kearney, Paul
The Mark of Ran. **The Sea Beggars**. 2003. Bantam Spectra, ISBN: 0553383612, 320p.

Rol Cortishane grows up in a fishing village, but a mob comes after his grandfather, forcing him to sea and a literal voyage of self-discovery. Rol is Weren, a race powerful in the days before the world of Umer went into decay. In this series starter, Rol falls in with questionable companions and begins training in dark skills.

McKiernan, Dennis
Voyage of the Fox Rider. **Mithgar**. 1993. Roc, ISBN: 0451454111, 592p.

Lady Jinnarin, of the foot-tall Pysk race, reveals the existence of her long-hidden people in a desperate attempt to find help in tracking her missing mate. She enlists mage Alamar and elfin sea captain Aravan in a search for the green sea and black ship that haunt her dreams. The leisurely pace of McKiernan's writing is well suited to this shipboard milieu.

McKillip, Patricia A.
The Changeling Sea. 1988. Puffin, ISBN: 0141312629, 144p.

A foggy sea village is the perfect setting for McKillip's dreamy, hazy narrative. Because her father's life and mother's sanity were lost to the sea, Peri places curses on it. When a strange prince asks her to deliver a message to the sea along with her hexes, strange things emerge from the depths that will change Peri and her village forever.

Miéville, China
The Scar. **Bas-Lag.** 2001. Del Rey, ISBN: 0345460014, 608p. AW.

Bellis, a linguist on the run, is shanghaied and brought to Armada, an enormous flotilla of stolen ships. She and the other strange folk press-ganged aboard Armada are at the mercy of the Lovers, leaders who hope to harness a gargantuan sea monster and use its power to take them to the Scar. Miéville's groundbreaking settings are fantasy's most original.

Nix, Garth
Drowned Wednesday. **Keys to the Kingdom.** 2005. Scholastic, ISBN: 0439436567, 400p. YA.

Neurotic, asthmatic Arthur Penhaligon returns in his third adventure. The hospital in which he's recovering floods, sending his bed adrift on the Border Sea. There he meets Lady Wednesday, who has been turned into a whale. She'll give young Arthur the third key he needs if he defeats the pirate Feverfew. The best entry yet in a whimsical series.

Novik, Naomi
⇨ *His Majesty's Dragon.* **Temeraire series.** 2006. Del Rey, ISBN: 0345481283, 384p.

Patrick O'Brian meets Anne McCaffrey in tales of the Napoleonic Wars at sea with one addition: dragons used to provide air support during battle. Our story is told from the British view, as young Captain Laurence bonds with a jet-black dragon. Two more well-received books have followed in a series that could become a fantasy mainstay.

In Forest Deep: Fantasy Journeys into the Woods

The trouble with fantasy set in forests is that the characters are wooden. (Sorry.) Endlessly branching plots can leave readers out on a limb. (Forgive me.) Some say their bark is worse than their bite, but deep inside these books ring true. (Really, I am sorry.) Seriously, even those who can't tell an oak from a pine realize that the forest is the home of fantasy. When you wander in the woods, anything can happen. Forests can serve as everything from a shelter for outcasts to lairs of terrible evil. Get ready for a quick trip into the fantasy woods.

Holdstock, Robert
Mythago Wood. **Mythago Wood series.** 1984. Orb, ISBN: 0765307294, 336p.
AW.
    Britain's last primeval forest is home to every myth ever believed. A solder returning from World War II finds his brother obsessed with the woods. Soon, he, too, fights to win the love of a woodland princess and locate the Umscrumug, the myth before all others. Layers of symbol and archetype accumulate as you read deeper into a haunting book. Several loose sequels, beginning with *Lavondyss,* follow.

Keyes, Greg
The Briar King. **Kingdoms of Thorn and Bone.** 2002. Del Rey, ISBN: 0345440706, 608p.
    Aspar White is a holter: protector of the King's Wood. He's gruff, ornery, and hard to frighten with tales, but even he can't deny that something is wrong in the woods. An encounter with a greffyn, a creature with killing touch and breath, confirms his fears. The trouble, however, is even more grave: Someone's awakening the Briar King (a kind of Green Man), whose return will doom them all.

McKillip, Patricia A.
Solstice Wood. 2006. Ace, ISBN: 0441014658, 288p.
    Fantasy forests are often the home for the Faery folk, as in McKillip's latest. Sylvia returns home for her grandmother's funeral and discovers that grandma's sewing circle is actually a coven of witches who keep the fay at bay in the nearby woods. When Sylvia's family begins to fall apart, along with the barrier dividing the two worlds, she goes into the woods in search of her origins.

Pyle, Howard
The Merry Adventures of Robin Hood. 1883. Signet Classics, ISBN: 0451530268, 416p. YA.
    As easily as Errol Flynn bests Kevin Costner on film, this classic beats the recent novels. Robin, Little John, and Friar Tuck sound merriest in rousing, poetic medieval English. Sherwood is evergreen, sheltering, and never bleak. Pyle's woodcut illustrations are great, too. Robin McKinley and Jennifer Roberson have contemporary takes on this story, but start here.

Roberson, Jennifer
Karavans. 2006. DAW, ISBN: 0756404096, 448p.
    In Roberson's new series, a family travels among many refugees on the run from foreign invaders. They journey in a karavan (remarkably like a caravan) toward a new home but soon find themselves blocked by the Alisanos, a sinister woodland with the nasty habit of shifting its position. How's that for a moving (ha!) forest tale.

Tolkien. J.R.R.
⇨ *The Two Towers*. **The Lord of the Rings**. 1954. Houghton Mifflin, ISBN: 0618002235, 352p.

  Tolkien had a gift for forests. *The Hobbit*'s Mirkwood has ethereal wood-elves and dwarf-wrapping spiders. In *The Fellowship of the Ring*'s Lothlorien, Galadriel rules. In the end, the best Tolkien forest of all is Fangorn, where Ents herd unruly trees and deliberate slowly at the entmoot. You'll never see forests in the same way again.

Urban Developments: Big-City Fantasy

  Have you seen more telephone poles than trees in your lifetime? Prefer bustling streets to mountaintops and forests? Would you rather take a subway than sit in a saddle? Fantasy once avoided metropolitan settings, but now there's a growing body of fantasy literature set in big cities. Readers even can choose between past, present, and future time frames for their urban fantasy fix. Go to town on this reading.

Abbey, Lynn, ed.
Thieves' World: Turning Points. 2002. Tor, ISBN: 076534517X, 368p.
Thieves' World: First Blood. 2003. Tor, ISBN: 031287488X, 464p.
Thieves' World: Enemies of Fortune. 2004. Tor, ISBN: 0312874901, 352p.

  Many writers have contributed inhabitants to *Thieves' World* and its bustling city Sanctuary. The series began as an anthology of stories edited by Robert Asprin. It continued in that mode for 10 years but also spawned hit-and-miss novels in the 1980s. Current editor Abbey restarted the enterprise, first with her novel *Sanctuary* and then a return to the series' roots with these three anthologies.

Bishop, K. J.
The Etched City. 2004. Bantam Spectra, ISBN: 0553382918, 400p.

  A mercenary gunslinger and a battlefield doctor are on the run from the Army of Heroes, a group created to eradicate revolutionaries. They try to lose themselves in the crowds of Ashamoil, a violent melting pot of a city where cultures clash and the citizens are torn between the decadent pursuit of beauty and the struggle to stay alive.

Klasky, Mindy
The Glasswrights' Apprentice. **The Glasswrights' Guild**. 2000. Roc, ISBN: 0451457897, 336p.

  In a caste-conscious society, a middle-class family invests everything to buy their daughter an apprenticeship in the powerful glasswrights' guild. One day she sneaks away from work to see the new prince but ends up implicated in his assassination. Rani must go into hiding among the lowest of the low, the street-dwelling Touched. Klasky opens a consistent five-book series.

Lee, Tanith
A Bed of Earth. **Secret Books of Venus.** 2002. Overlook, ISBN: 1585674559, 345p.

In Venus (an alternate Venice), two powerful families have feuded over the title burial ground for centuries. A grave maker unearths evidence of the horrible events that underlie the dispute. The shadowy but feverishly romantic city is the unifying element of the Secret Books of Venus, dark fantasies that can be read in any order.

Miéville, China
Perdido Street Station. **Bas-Lag.** 2000. Del Rey, ISBN: 0345459407, 640p.

Look at the map and read the descriptions in the first few chapters of this book. If you appreciate cities, you'll be hooked. Miéville provokes your senses as he details New Crobuzon's smells, tastes, sounds, and visions. A fascinating mix of technology, Victorian squalor, and corrupt magic, this city is ugly, but you won't want to turn away.

Pratchett, Terry
Feet of Clay. **Discworld, The Watch.** 1996. HarperTorch, ISBN: 0061057649, 368p.

Ankh-Morpork! Where the Watch keeps a fragile peace between dwarves and trolls (but fight among themselves); where Cut-Me-Own-Throat Dibbler sells sausages made of gods-know-what; where the wizards of Unseen University regularly endanger the populace. The city's in almost every *Discworld* entry, but for a taste of its pleasures (swallow quickly), try this entry about an investigation of golem suicides.

Shetterly, Will
Elsewhere. **Bordertown.** 1991. Magic Carpet, ISBN: 0152052097, 264p. **YA**.

For fantasy street life, look *Elsewhere*. Runaway Ron finds himself on the mean streets of Bordertown, where elf gangs stalk, drugs and violence coexist with magic, and technology is undependable. If you like this world, you'll find it's the shared territory of many writers, particularly Shetterly's wife, Emma Bull, and anthologist Terri Windling.

Thurman, Rob
Nightlife. 2006. Roc, ISBN: 0451460758, 352p.

Thurman's alternate New York City is even stranger than the real place. With a used-car salesman faun and a beautiful vampire, young Cal searches the city's underbelly for his half-demon roots. Along the way, he finds psychotic elves, a troll under the Brooklyn Bridge, and muggers that just don't stand a chance. A dark fantasy series is forthcoming.

Fantasy Underground: Dark Trips into Dungeons and Deep Places

You can drive paved roads to most places on earth without even dropping a cell phone call. So what's an author to do? There are few mysterious places left on which to model fantasy environments. Well, one such realm is right under our feet. It's perfect for fantasy: dark, spooky, and labyrinthine, and things SNEAK UP BEHIND YOU THERE! (That works better with a campfire.) Ever since Dante envisaged hell, writers have imagined and reimagined the world below. Start shoveling if you want, but an easier way underground is to pick up these books.

Browne, N. M.
  Basilisk. 2004. Bloomsbury, ISBN: 158234910X, 320p. **YA**.
     Authoritarian rule forced Lunnzians who wouldn't comply into underground catacombs. Rej is one of these "combers." He's never been Above, but when he begins to dream of a dragon in the sky, he's compelled to see if his dream is true. There he discovers a young woman who shares his dreams and a plot to destroy the world below.

Eddings, David
  Magician's Gambit. <u>The Belgariad</u>. 1981. Del Rey, ISBN: 0345335457, 320p.
     Garion, Ce'Nedra, Polgara, and company continue country-by-country adventures in this middle book of five. The best bits are in two underground sections: first, when they visit Ulgoland, home to devout, obsessive tunneling folk who can travel through rock walls, and later when they invade the lair of evil Ctuchik to capture the Orb of Aldur.

Gaiman, Neil
  ⇨ *Neverwhere.* 1996. Avon, ISBN: 0380789019, 400p.
     When a drudge aids a woman in distress, he's conveyed from London Above to London Below, a shadow city populated by sinister inhabitants. Richard's only hope to regain his life above is to follow the woman, Door, in a search for her family's killers. It's a quest across a surreal, treacherous landscape, a Hieronymus Bosch painting brought to life.

Goldstein, Lisa
  Dark Cities Underground. 1999. Tor, ISBN: 0312868278, 256p.
     As a child, Jerry's stories inspired his mother's books about the world of Neverwas. Years later, a biographer writing about Jerry's estranged mother asks to interview him. As he responds to the questions, strange memories emerge. So does a man who believes Neverwas is real and wants Jerry to show him the way in. Subways, Egyptian myth, and the archetypes of childhood mix in this intriguing tale.

Le Guin, Ursula K.
The Tombs of Atuan. <u>Earthsea Cycle</u>. 1971. Simon Pulse, ISBN: 0689845367, 192p. YA.

A highlight of the spare, beautiful <u>Earthsea Cycle</u>, this second entry is set in fantasy's best labyrinth. Wizard Ged, in search of the second half of an amulet, becomes trapped in the maze below the Temple of Atuan. Only Tenar, priestess and guardian of the tombs, can save him, but to do so, she must admit that everything she has been taught is a lie.

Norton, Andre
Three Hands for Scorpio. 2005. Tor, ISBN: 0765304643, 304p. (hbk.)

Telepathic triplet princesses are kidnapped and left to die in the underground Dismals in the late, great Norton's last solo credit. She still had the gift at 93 (!) years of age. The triplets battle across the underground landscape, fighting a variety of mammoth insectoid creatures, but will they find their way back home?

Russell, Sean
Beneath the Vaulted Hills. <u>Rivers into Darkness</u>. 1997. DAW, ISBN: 0886777941, 480p.

In an alternate nineteenth century, the last mage, Eldrich, tries to stamp out magic. Almost successful, he hears of one last trove of magical lore hidden in a labyrinth. Battling the church and the promagic Tellerites, Eldrich leads an expedition underground. Scenes beneath the earth are especially effective, capturing the claustrophobia of spelunking.

Running Hot and Cold: Fantasy Thrills on the Thermometer

In the library where I work, we stagger through mind-numbing heat, fighting hallucination as library pages fan us with reference manuals. Our tongues swollen, we stumble to the fountain, but inevitably find *no* water pressure. Downstairs in our cinderblock lunchroom, we brave the other extreme, shivering in icy cold, burning books to keep from freezing. When someone stays down too long, we have to chop off their frostbitten toes. If you want to know how simple tasks of obtaining food, water, and shelter become nearly impossible in cold and heat, then I suggest fantasy novels. In their pages, you can caravan through blistering deserts or snowshoe over jagged ice floes, all without leaving the climatized comfort of your favorite chair.

Jones, J. V.
A Cavern of Black Ice. <u>Sword of Shadows</u>. 1999. Tor, ISBN: 076534551X, 792p.

Ash, a girl troubled by bad dreams and a menacing foster father, joins Raif, a hunter whose clan has been destroyed. The pair quest across frozen wastes to reach the title cavern, the only place Ash can release the magic energy that threatens to annihilate her. More than a backdrop, cold is a constant danger that impacts every scene of this series opener.

Martin, George R. R.
⇨ *A Storm of Swords*. **A Song of Ice and Fire**. 1998. Bantam Spectra, ISBN: 0553579908, 1040p. **AW**.

The series isn't called *Ice and Fire* for nothing. In the third book, Jon Snow and the Night Watch fight undead Others and desperate wildling invaders in the frozen north, while in the south, Dany quests with dragons through sun-baked lands. In Martin's vivid settings, harsh climate has clear effects on both culture and individual behavior.

McKiernan. Dennis
The Eye of the Hunter. **Mithgar**. 1992. Roc, ISBN: 0451452682, 592p.

Warrows (small folk like hobbits), elves, and a shape-shifting bear-man chase the evil Baron Stoke across extreme climates in Mithgar, from a frozen glacier to a broiling desert. This environmentally concerned novel is derivative, a bit preachy . . . and page-turning fun.

Pattou, Edith
East. 2003. Magic Carpet, ISBN: 0152052216, 516p. **YA**.

In rural Norway, Rose is North-born: She's destined to the unpredictable life of a traveler. Her fate is fulfilled when she allows a great white bear to take her away from her family. The bear is more than he seems, but after making a mistake that forfeits his life to the Troll Queen, Rose must travel across arctic lands to save him.

Sachar, Louis
Holes. 1998. Laurel Leaf, ISBN: 044022859X, 288p. **YA**.

Stanley Yelnats is off to Green Lake for the summer. The catch is that there is no longer a lake, just a juvenile detention camp where boys dig holes in the withering sun and then fill them again. Stanley escapes into the Texas wastelands, where he finds the mythic past of Green Lake and his own heritage. This absurdist tall tale disguised as a young-adult novel will appeal to adults, too.

Strauss, Victoria
The Burning Land. 2004. Eos, ISBN: 0380817721, 560p.

Suffering many depredations, Gyalo crosses the desert on a rescue mission. He's been sent by the Brethren of Arata to save (he believes) a community of refugees. In the oasis where he finds them, some believe him a prophet and others think him a demon. The fervor of Strauss's theocratic cultures fits well in her book's climate of shimmering heat.

It's All Academic: Fantasy Books for School Are Fun to Read

I attended a magical school, full of spell casting, adventure, and mythic creatures. Unfortunately, magical school was held in my head, concurrent with real-world classes. Most of my teachers (particularly Mrs. Miller, who made algebra seem like alchemy) did not appreciate the time I spent attending my alternate courses. I'd rather have been reading novels like these, which will appeal to students and anyone interested in revisiting the fantastic classrooms of their daydreams. These are good follow-up suggestions for the legions of <u>Harry Potter</u> readers.

Bray, Libba
A Great and Terrible Beauty. 2003. Delacorte, ISBN: 0385732317, 432p. ▰YA▰.
   Mix equal parts Victorian gothic thriller, comedy of manners, young-adult angst, and colorful fantasy and you get *Terrible Beauty.* When friends at an English boarding school follow Gemma into the realms of her visions, they find an exotic escape but unleash trouble. Bray nails the details of behavior in a girls' school. Followed by *Rebel Angels.*

Dean, Pamela
⇨ *Tam Lin.* 1991. Puffin, ISBN: 014240652X, 480p.
   There are many versions of the ballad Tam Lin, but none like this (and perhaps none so good). Dean moves the tale from Scotland to the classics department of a Minnesota college in the 1970s. The fantasy hides below the surface of campus events until late in the book, when it rises surprisingly to the surface. If you relate to the excited bookishness of liberal arts students, this may become a favorite.

De Lint, Charles
Blue Girl. 2004. Puffin, ISBN: 0142405450, 384p. ▰YA▰.
   When she intervenes with bullies, brash new girl Imogene becomes a friend of mousy, studious Maxine. The girls moderate each other's extremes and are doing well until they meet the ghost of Adrian, a boy killed in the school parking lot. These days he hangs out with prankish fairies, and his attention to Imogene leads her into real danger.

Jones, Diana Wynne
The Year of the Griffin. <u>Derkholm</u>. 2000. HarperTrophy, ISBN: 006447335X, 400p. ▰YA▰.
   Under Professor Corkoran, Wizards' University has degenerated into little more than an extended scheme to extort student money, but led by griffin Elda, this year's freshmen aren't falling for his tricks. They are, however, having

magical misadventures. This sequel to *Dark Lord of Derkholm* can be read as a goofy YA adventure or a spoof of academia.

Lackey, Mercedes
 A Wizard of London. Elemental Masters. 2004. DAW, ISBN: 0756403634, 384p.
 Harton School teaches only lower magic: clairvoyance, telepathy, and communication with the dead. It's a surprise when two girl students become the targets of a formidable wizard. The school's mistress calls in favors from a powerful former lover to protect them. This loose adaptation of *The Snow Queen* is part of a loosely connected series.

Rowling, J. K.
 Harry Potter and the Order of the Phoenix. Harry Potter series. 2003. Scholastic, ISBN: 0439358078, 870p. `YA`.
 It's quite a feat that Rowling's descriptions of Hogwarts make every reader wish they could attend boarding school. In the fifth entry, officious, cruel Dolores Umbridge turns the school into a bureaucratic shambles. Banned from Quidditch, with girl trouble and multiplying classwork, Harry takes on the burden of leading a student rebellion.

Stevermer, Caroline
 A Scholar of Magics. 2004. Starscape, ISBN: 0765353466, 432p.
 Edwardian light adventure awaits in this witty magical romance, sequel to *A College of Magics*. A visiting Wild West show sharpshooter and a fashionable young math instructor become involved in very British derring-do. Stevermer's Glasscastle University gently parodies hidebound English academia.

Wright, John C.
 Orphans of Chaos. Chaos series. 2005. Tor, ISBN: 07565349957, 336p.
 If V. C. Andrews and Edith Hamilton wrote Harry Potter, it would be something like this. Five orphans (who are *very* curious about sexuality) are kept in a school run by Greek gods. Like students everywhere, they go through strange, magical changes and suspect they are being held hostage, but these are not typical teens. A highly atmospheric book sets the scene for a forthcoming series.

Rated RPG: The Best Fantasy for Gamers

Role-playing games (RPGs) are an alternate media dimension. Gamers have their own lines of books connected to their favorite game settings. They like novels that read like their games play, with many character races, magical implements, beasts, and enough action to keep their minds spinning like a 20-sided die. Although they can be gateways to other fantasy reading, these books appear so rapidly that their (often young) readers may never depart from RPG land. A quick production schedule can hinder the quality of these books, but strong titles can be found. This list also includes novels that depict the RPG lifestyle.

Baker, Keith
> *The City of Towers.* <u>**Eberron: The Dreaming Dark**</u>. 2005. Wizards of the Coast, ISBN: 0786935847, 384p.
>
> Eberron is the new campaign setting for Dungeons & Dragons. Its designer also published this novel of Tolkienesque characters (elves, dwarves, and the like) placed in a world where magic and technology intermingle.

Faust, Minister
> *Coyote Kings of the Space-Age Bachelor Pad.* 2004. Del Rey, ISBN: 0345466357, 544p.
>
> Faust's first novel brims with references to gaming, comics, and fandom. Hamza and Yehat, two roommates in multicultural Edmonton, find themselves caught between drug dealers peddling "Crème" and a woman with connections to ancient Egypt. In a clever touch, RPG character sheets are used to introduce the characters.

King, J. Robert
> *The Thran.* <u>**Magic: The Gathering**</u>. 1999. Wizards of the Coast, ISBN: 0786916001, 311p.
>
> Fans of Magic: The Gathering will enjoy this book, the first and best of the novelizations published in connection with the card game. King provides the background of characters like the demon Yawgmoth and his disciple Gix.

Knaak, Richard A.
> *The Legend of Huma.* <u>**Dragonlance: Heroes**</u>. 1988. Wizards of the Coast, ISBN: 078693137X, 384p.
>
> Another common Dungeons & Dragons campaign setting is <u>Dragonlance</u>. Nearly two hundred books have been placed in this world. Most are dreck, but a few authors have turned in fine efforts. Weis and Hickman are probably the best known, but Knaak's books are also good. This one, about Huma, a dragon-riding knight, is a worthwhile example.

Niles, Douglas
> *Darkwalker on Moonshae.* <u>**Forgotten Realms: Moonshae**</u>. 1987. Wizards of the Coast, ISBN: 078693560X, 384p.
>
> The best-known Dungeons & Dragons setting is <u>Forgotten Realms</u>, and this was the very first novel set there. Back in print after many years out of print, it's still worth reading, especially for those with nostalgia for gaming days of the past.

Norton, Andre, and Rabe, Jean
 Return to Quag Keep. 2006. Tor, ISBN: 0765312980, 304p. (hbk.)
    Published in 1978, Norton's original *Quag Keep* was the first novel to
incorporate references to RPGs. Although that book is in print, its gaming references are dated. This sequel, published after Norton's death, updates the tale
of seven gamers thrust into a magical world. You can tell the authors know and
enjoy gaming.

Salvatore, R. A.
 ⇨ *The Icewind Dale Trilogy.* 1988. Wizards of the Coast, ISBN: 078691811X,
    1056p.
    Salvatore's name is practically synonymous with Forgotten Realms. This
omnibus contains the three Drizzt Do'Urden tales—*The Crystal Shard, Streams
of Silver,* and *The Halfling's Gem*—that began that association (although his
Dark Elf Trilogy is a prequel).

Vande Velde, Vivian
 Heir Apparent. 2002. Magic Carpet, ISBN: 0152051252, 336p. YA.
    Giannine is playing a virtual reality game at the arcade when the owner
gives her bad news. Parents protesting fantasy gaming have sabotaged the machine. Giannine can escape only by beating the game quickly, otherwise her
brain will be damaged. Young adults and other virtual gamers will enjoy this
novel and its multiple restarts.

Weis, Margaret, and Hickman, Tracy
 ⇨ *The Annotated Chronicles.* 1984. Wizards of the Coast, ISBN: 0786918705,
    1312p.
    You can read the Dragonlance Chronicles as separate books or in this big
three-in-one omnibus, complete with annotations. This is the core story for
the series and Dungeons & Dragons campaign setting. Even at this length, it's
action-packed, quick-reading fantasy.

Chapter Four

Mood

The appeal factor of mood or tone is a slippery concept because it arises through collaboration between the writer and the reader. The writer creates his or her part through a mixture of language, pacing, and subject matter, and the reader contributes his or her own attitudes, preferences, and whims to the mix. Lists in this chapter identify some of these moods and provide books that may satisfy them.

Many of these lists bridge genres. If you normally read mysteries, horror, historical fiction, literary fiction, science fiction, or romance and would like to ease into fantasy, this chapter is for you. Genre blending is one of the hottest trends in contemporary fiction, and these lists point the way to books that combine fantasy and other genres.

Some of these lists are entry points into the genre for people who don't usually read novels. There are lists in this section for those who prefer movies and comic books, as well as lists that should appeal to young or less-experienced readers.

Finally, fantasy veterans will find lists here to facilitate a return to the genre's roots or, conversely, to explore its newest currents. Fantasy fans also can use these lists to investigate other genres without ever leaving the familiar comforts of fantasy fiction.

Fantasy for Fantasy Lovers: Right down the Middle of Genre Conventions

This is fantasy's mac and cheese: The taste isn't subtle, but it's hearty. Books in this list don't attempt to stretch boundaries. They revel in the genre's best traditions. These books go down nicely until you have them once too often, at which point they may start to taste like rancid cheese. I recommend these books to young readers, those who have not read much fantasy, or those who take comfort in familiar styles and concepts. If you are sensitive to clichés or looking for something different, these may not be for you. Give these authors credit: Anyone can heat up a box of Kraft, but making a fresh dish from familiar ingredients is harder than you'd think.

Brooks, Terry
   The Sword of Shannara Trilogy. 1977–1985. Del Rey, ISBN: 0345453751, 1200p. (hbk.)
       In the early 1980s, it seemed like every kid in the world was reading this series about the humble Ohmsford family, whose members are called (in several generations) to save Shannara. It borrows much from Lord of the Rings, but Brooks has a faster pace, a plus for those with short attention spans. As the series advances, Brooks, whose strength is storytelling, finds a more original voice.

Eddings, David
   The Malloreon, Vol. 1. 1985–1988. Del Rey, ISBN: 0345483863, 816p.
   The Malloreon, Vol. 2. 1989–1991. Del Rey, ISBN: 0345483871, 528p.
       This second series of five books follows The Belgariad. This quest rehashes the first, which wasn't original itself: An assemblage of stock characters must interpret a prophecy to defeat ultimate evil, and so on. But Eddings is such a good-natured writer that you'll be charmed by his characters and their exciting adventures, even if you've seen it before.

Feist, Raymond E.
   ⇨ *Magician: Apprentice*. **The Riftwar Saga.** 1982. Bantam Spectra, ISBN: 0553564943, 528p.
       Boyhood friends Pug and Thomas come from low beginnings but dream of becoming a magician and a warrior (respectively). They pursue these goals through troll encounters, battles, and alien capture. Feist ends with a cliffhanger: You'll be ready to continue the saga. His strengths are characterization, quick pace, and compelling depiction of cultures.

Goodkind, Terry
Wizard's First Rule. **The Sword of Truth**. 1994. Tor, ISBN: 0765300273, 576p.
 The first rule is that people will believe anything. A cynic might say this is especially true of Goodkind fans. This tale of a chosen one, a mysterious woman, and a hermit wizard battling a nasty villain is sometimes sadistic, but Goodkind has an eye for action. Many readers object to his formulaic, preachy style, but others respond avidly to his philosophy.

Jones, J. V.
The Baker's Boy. **The Book of Words**. 1995. Aspect, ISBN: 0446670979, 528p.
 When the paths of a noble girl and a common boy with magical powers collide, they join forces to fulfill a prophecy and stop the advance of absolute evil. Jones started her career with this solid effort (and keep reading, because she gets even better).

Norton, Andre, and Lackey, Mercedes
The Elvenbane. **Halfblood Chronicles**. 1991. Tor, ISBN: 0812511751, 576p.
 Elves tyrannize humans but fear a prophecy that a halfblood wizard will end their reign. Enter Shana, a halfblood raised by a shape-shifting dragon. Vigorous pacing makes this swift reading. Experienced readers will recognize which of the authors wrote each section. A caveat: With Norton's death, the final book of this series may never be written.

Thompson, Eldon
The Crimson Sword. **The Legend of Asahiel**. 2005. Eos, ISBN: 0060741511, 720p.
 Eldest son Soric becomes an evil wizard and arranges to assassinate his father after King Sorl disinherits him. He claims the kingdom of Alson, but widowed Queen Ellebe has a surprise: a younger son who was secreted away at birth. Young Torin has been raised as a mushroom farmer, but now he must go on a quest to find the title sword and defeat Soric.

Weis, Margaret, and Hickman, Tracy
Dragon Wing. **Death Gate Cycle**. 1990. Bantam Spectra, ISBN: 0553286390, 480p.
 The representative of a race of powerful sorcerers meets with a dwarf who is plotting a revolution and an assassin who has formed an alliance with his intended victim. Brand-name fantasy can be clichéd, with characterization sacrificed for action. Rapid deadlines make creativity difficult. A few writers, like Weis and Hickman, somehow thrive in this environment. If you get hooked, a seven-book series (and many other books) follow.

Reinventing the Genre:
The New Weird

There's a paradox in classifying the fantasy genre: As soon as it's defined, it becomes more familiar than fantastic. That's where the very loose confederation of writers called the New Weird comes in. As far as I know, they don't have secret meetings or handshakes, but they share a goal of stretching boundaries and shattering conventions. These kids color on the lines instead of inside them, intentionally blurring and blending genres. If you're in the mood for a challenge, for a book that will take you beyond traditional "rules" of fantasy, try the New Weird.

Blaylock, James P.
The Digging Leviathan. 1984. Babbage, ISBN: 193023516X, 292p.
    A California boy with webbed fingers and gills invents a digging machine. With his friend Jim and Jim's loopy father, Giles begins to burrow. Their efforts attract the attention of evil Dr. Frosticos. As these characters pursue various goals—the earth's center, immortality, and, most unusually, mermen—an eccentric mix of fun, fear, and fantasy results.

Carroll, Jonathan
The Wooden Sea. 2001. Tor, ISBN: 0765300133, 304p.
    McCabe is police chief in a small town that is turning ever stranger. Haunted by a dead dog that won't stay buried, his teenage hoodlum self, and images of a strange feather, he is drawn into a mind- and time-bending mystery. Carroll's refusal to accept conventions keeps him on the fringe. It's worth your trip to join him there occasionally.

Ford, Jeffrey
The Fantasy Writer's Assistant and Other Stories. 2002. Golden Gryphon, ISBN: 193084610X, 280p. (hbk.)
    In the title story, the fantasy writer's assistant discovers that his employer has been exploiting characters in the world he has created. Ford mixes bizarre premises, philosophical inquiry, and subtle humor in genre-defying stories. If you like this, try his other collection, *The Emperor of Ice Cream*, or his first novel, *The Physiognomy*.

Harrison, M. John
Viriconium. 1971–1984. Bantam Spectra, ISBN: 0553383159, 480p.
    Collecting three novellas and seven stories from previous works, Harrison depicts a civilization in its long twilight period and descent into evening. The reader must piece together these snapshot views, working like an archaeologist to reveal the history of Viriconium. Harrison's style is descriptive and cryptic at the same time.

Link, Kelly
Stranger Things Happen. 2001. Small Beer, ISBN: 1931520003, 266p.
In Link's stories, fantasy illuminates contemporary life. She combines horror with humor and a smattering of cultural references. Unlike much of the fiction in this list, her work is quite accessible. Her second collection, *Magic for Beginners,* is also superb.

Miéville, China
Iron Council. Bas-Lag. 2004. Del Rey, ISBN: 0345458427, 576p. AW.
The crumbling decadence of New Crobuzon and Bas-Lag is again the setting for Miéville's third novel in the loosely related series. This entry is about anarchists on a train. More than any other writer, Miéville is associated consistently with the New Weird. Strong imagery, superb world building, and socialist politics are his trademarks.

Powers, Tim
Strange Itineraries. 2004. Tachyon, ISBN: 1892391236, 224p.
Powers was new and weird long before any movement was named. Written over twenty years, these nine stories reveal fantastic events that are still personal—part of quiet, everyday life, not the epic or earth-shattering. My favorite is the disturbing "Pat Moore," about the collision of several characters, alive and dead, who share the same name.

Sarrontonio, Al, ed.
Flights: Extreme Visions of Fantasy. 2005. Roc, ISBN: 0451460367, 592p.
Neil Gaiman, Orson Scott Card, Patricia McKillip, Gene Wolfe, Tim Powers, Charles de Lint, Harry Turtledove, and other luminaries contributed to an anthology that asked writers for the fantasy equivalent of stories in Harlan Ellison's legendary science fiction collection *Dangerous Visions.* Everything and anything but typical fantasy can be found here.

VanderMeer, Jeff
City of Saints and Madmen. 2006. Bantam Spectra, ISBN: 0553383574, 704p.
Ambergris is a city of horror tempered with unexpected humor. Adding new material to an earlier collection of the same name, VanderMeer creates a self-referential world with imagined bibliographies, glossaries, city records, and scientific documents.

Smashing of Bone, Spurting of Blood: High-Violence Fantasy

For some fantasy readers, slashing swords, hacking axes, and arrows falling thick as raindrops are what the genre is about. Executioner's axe dull? Swell!

Intestines on swords like spaghetti on forks? Nifty! Such readers want to wade into every melee, the bloodier the better. These stories obviously aren't for children, but fans of grotesque and gory will enjoy taking a stab.

Bakker, R. Scott
The Warrior-Prophet. **Prince of Nothing**. 2004. Overlook, ISBN: 1585677280, 624p.

Gruesome for graduates, Bakker's trilogy combines history, religion, and philosophy with warfare, plague, and torture. In this second book, the action really moves, with Holy War crusaders on the march. If you want thought with your atrocities, this is for you.

Erikson, Steven
Memories of Ice. **Malazan Book of the Fallen**. 2001. Tor, ISBN: 0765310031, 784p.

If the devastation of *Gardens of the Moon* wasn't enough, this volume adds an undead army that eats those it conquers. Erikson's abstract style makes readers work, but fans say this is his best yet, adding more emotion to the brutal, visceral impact of the first book. Read this third in the series second, as it picks up right after the events of *Gardens*.

Goodkind, Terry
Stone of Tears. **The Sword of Truth**. 1995. Tor, ISBN: 0812548094, 992p.

Richard Cypher and his love Kahlan defeated Darken Rahl in the first book of this epic, but their solution opened the door to the Keeper of the Underworld. Events in this book drive the lovers apart, leaving each to fight separate battles. With human sacrifice, torturous sex, and people skinned alive, this should satiate even the most bloodthirsty.

Keyes, Greg
The Charnel Prince. **Kingdoms of Thorn and Bone**. 2004. Del Rey, ISBN: 0345440714, 512p.

Ancient evil is awake and spreading as this second book in the series starts. Villagers are turned into flesh-eating fiends. Rogue monks leave piles of human sacrifices. A coven and girls school is razed. Monsters walk the land. And that's just the first few chapters! Even better, Keyes manages great characters and an exciting plot to go with the action.

Salvatore, R. A.
⇨ *The Thousand Orcs*. **Hunter's Blades**. 2002. Wizards of the Coast, ISBN: 0786929804, 384p.

The Lone Drow. **Hunter's Blades**. 2003. Wizards of the Coast, ISBN: 0786932287, 384p.

Salvatore's books are the equivalent of Hollywood action films: stoic leads, secondary characters used for comic relief, he-man sentimentality and philosophizing, and endless streams of bloody violence. These two books open the latest trilogy involving dark elf Drizzt Do'Urden. A hunt for a few pesky orcs turns into a battle against thousands. Characters name their weapons, which is good, because they appear in every scene.

Stover, Matthew Woodring
   Blade of Tyshalle. <u>Overworld</u>. 2001. Del Rey, ISBN: 0345421434, 800p.
       Future Earth is an overcrowded mess that uses the beautiful but deadly parallel fantasy Overworld as a violent, virtual entertainment playground. When Earth's oligarchy plans a nasty virus that will clear Overworld for wealthy earthlings, Hari Michaelson and his Overworld alter ego must stop them. Combat descriptions here are definitely X-rated.

Washing of Face, Breaking of Nail: Low-Violence Fantasy

Are you unable to stomach growing violence in fantasy? Even Tolkien, you may lament, with his genteel poetry and battles described in stirring-but-vague, after-the-fact speeches, has been translated into violent films. It's not necessarily a world without difficulty that you're after. You just don't want tragic events to spurt, ooze, or scream in pain. As a librarian, I have many tricks in my bag for those who dislike violence. In young-adult books, violence is usually less vivid. High-fantasy classics or folklore rarely include gory details. "But no," you say, "I want something new." Here's one more resource, a list of great reads without the icky mess.

Clarke, Susanna
   Jonathan Strange & Mr. Norrell. 2004. Bloomsbury, ISBN: 1582346038, 800p. AW.
       A reclusive scholar and his showy pupil struggle to rebuild English magic to oppose Napoleon. Their magic involves menacing bargains with the faerie world, but direct violence is not a factor. Clarke's language is droll and mannered Victorian English: all footnotes and fussy propriety.

Le Guin, Ursula K.
   Tales from Earthsea. <u>Earthsea Chronicles</u>. 2001. Ace, ISBN: 0441011241, 304p.
       Le Guin's understated style feels both ancient and ageless. She is a still water that runs deep and would never sink to the crassness of surface violence. Why not revisit Earthsea for this book of stories that add flesh to the lean frames of the original novels? If you are new to the series, start with *A Wizard of Earthsea.*

Russell, Sean
   The One Kingdom. <u>The Swans' War</u>. 2001. HarperTorch, ISBN: 0380792273, 544p.
       Opening a series, Russell gracefully weaves two plot lines. In the first, two noble houses engage in a lingering political feud. In the second, three young

friends meander down a strange river on a mystical trip into the past. Leisurely storytelling and intriguing characters are the draw here, not cheap thrills.

Shinn, Sharon

⇨*Mystic and Rider.* Twelve Houses series. 2005. Ace, ISBN: 0441013031, 432p.

Shinn doesn't send her heroes off to kill a villain or steal a treasure: They're on a fact-finding trip to investigate rumors of revolt. The focus is on group dynamics, romance, and intrigue as they visit the noble houses of Gillengaria. You'll feel like a comfortable member of the company in this easygoing opener to the series.

Tuttle, Lisa

The Silver Bough. 2006. Bantam Spectra, ISBN: 0553587358, 352p.

Appleton is a place of the past; even its namesake orchards are gone. But when an earthquake cuts it off from the rest of Scotland, a tree bears fruit and a renaissance may have begun. Three American women—a librarian, a widow, and an orphaned genealogist—witness the magic. With its gentle Celtic lore, this resembles *Brigadoon.*

Zettel, Sarah

A Sorcerer's Treason. Isavalta. 2002. Tor, ISBN: 0765343746, 512p.

When an orphaned Wisconsin lighthouse keeper is the heroine, you can expect gentility. In 1899, after saving a stranger from Lake Superior, Bridget travels with him to magical Isavalta, home of her birth father. She lands in the midst of shadowy political intrigues in the imperial court. This is the second book of the series, but read it first: It's a prequel.

Passing Fancies: The Best Fantasy to Pass around to the Whole Family

No genre is as likely to please an entire family of readers as fantasy. While Mom and Dad respond to history, complex political intrigue, and layered characters, the kids soak up magic and thrill to action and heroism. Young readers seem willing to try long page counts and complicated plots when they read fantasy, so adults can share these books without reading below their level. Most fantasy books also appeal to both sexes. Pick up these crowd-pleasers and start passing.

Alexander, Lloyd

The Book of Three. The Prydain Chronicles. 1964. Henry Holt, ISBN: 0805080481, 224p. YA.

Bringing Welsh myth to life, Alexander's Chronicles follow Taran the assistant pig keeper on his hero's journey. Young readers identify with the awkward boy's rise, and adults enjoy the humor. This book has provided a gateway to fantasy for more than forty years.

Cooper, Susan
The Dark Is Rising. **The Dark Is Rising series.** 1973. Aladdin, ISBN: 1416905286, 232p. YA.

Cooper uses British folklore to great result. Children can start the series with *Over Sea, Under Stone,* which has a simpler style than later volumes. Adults should head straight into *The Dark:* Its brooding, mythic tone makes this highly suspenseful children's writing. Young Will is drawn into conflict between the Old Ones and the Dark during an icy British winter.

Dean, Pamela
The Secret Country. **The Secret Country trilogy.** 1985. Puffin, ISBN: 0142501530, 384p. YA.

Like the Chronicles of Narnia, this book follows children who cross into a fantasy world. And like C. S. Lewis, Dean writes without the pandering or preciousness that makes some books for young readers unpalatable for adults. Her characters, however, find more challenge than Lewis's in rising to their roles in the fantasy world. First of a trilogy.

Jacques, Brian
Mossflower. **Redwall series.** 1988. Ace, ISBN: 0441005764, 384p. YA.

You might assume that Disney-like talking animals and upbeat heroics have little to offer adults. But with sometimes-wicked humor, a talent for describing landscape, varied characters, and a naturalistic worldview, Jacques charms grown-ups, too. The second Redwall book is first chronologically and is cited by many series readers as their favorite.

Pullman, Philip
The Golden Compass. **His Dark Materials.** 1995. Laurel Leaf, ISBN: 0440238145, 304p. YA.

Pullman's series has met controversy because some interpret it as antireligion. Although His Dark Materials certainly poses theological arguments, it's simplistic to say Pullman is against religion in general. It's precisely this complexity that makes the books delicious for adults (although many enjoy the fantasy without thinking much about the religious content). Kids will love the feisty heroine.

Rowling, J. K.
Harry Potter and the Sorcerer's Stone. **Harry Potter series.** 1997. Arthur A. Levine, ISBN: 043936213X, 400p. YA.

This series cannot be praised enough for how it brings together families of readers. Kids love the series from the first book, and adults are drawn in deeper as Harry, Hermione, and Ron begin to grow up. It all begins here, as the three friends have their first encounter with Hogwarts School.

Snicket, Lemony
The Bad Beginning. <u>A Series of Unfortunate Events</u>. 1999. HarperCollins, ISBN: 0064407667, 162p. (hbk.) `YA`.
    Children relate to the way that Klaus, Violet, and Sunny Baudelaire are consistently underestimated. Adults secretly smile as the children are subjected to mock-gothic dangers. Everyone enjoys the hammy villain Count Olaf. The first of 13 quick-reading books.

Tickle Your Fancy: Fantasy to Make You Giggle, Smirk, and Guffaw

Listing fantasy's funniest books is a gamble. As with beauty, humor is in the eye of the beholder. Well, perhaps it's not in the eye (although the Three Stooges tried to prove otherwise). Perhaps it is in the spleen or pancreas of the beholder (ranking internal organs for funniness is a challenge): some deep, internal place that brews up a different sense of humor for each of us. Or perhaps humor is in the bladder. I've known people who had a hard time keeping it there. If you aren't sure where you keep your sense of humor, these books may aid the diagnosis.

Flint, Eric
The Philosophical Strangler. <u>Joe's World</u>. 2001. Baen, ISBN: 0743435419, 448p.
    In the city of New Sfinctre, at a pub called the Sign of the Trough, readers find Greyboar, a strangler and philosopher; his diminutive agent, Ignace; and nearsighted swordswoman, Cat. The humor is bizarre and more than a little random: satirical barbs and bawdy humor tossed about like monkeys flinging excrement at the zoo. A big, delightful shambles.

Gaiman, Neil, and Pratchett, Terry
Good Omens. 1990. William Morrow, ISBN: 0060853964, 400p. (hbk.)
    I dread this book. Somebody in my book group always brings it up, and by the time we finish quoting the best bits, the evening's done. In this goofy Armageddon, the Antichrist is a boy named Adam; the Horsemen of the Apocalypse inspire biker wannabes; and Aziraphale and Crowley, Heaven and Hell's representatives, want to keep earth going because they like living there (they especially like Queen albums).

Holt, Tom
Tom Holt Tall Stories. 1987–1992. Orbit, ISBN: 1841493457, 568p.

    Expecting Someone Taller, one of two novels collected here, spoofs the Ring of the Nibelung. Malcolm Fisher runs over a badger who turns out to be Ingolf, last of the Giants. Ingolf charges his hapless killer with the protection of two magical Gifts of Power. Unless Terry Pratchett implodes, Holt is doomed to compete with Robert Rankin for the title of "that other British fantasy humorist," but those who love English humor will gladly welcome them to our shelves.

Jones, Diana Wynne
The Tough Guide to Fantasyland. 2006. Puffin, ISBN: 0142407224, 256p.

    Not a novel but a satirical catalog of fantasy clichés, this book ought to be mandatory reading for anyone who thinks that they, too, can write a trilogy. This is where you can turn for laughs and sanity after reading bad fantasy. *The Tough Guide* was out of print, but it's back, snarkier than ever, in this newly updated version.

Kotzwinkle, William
The Bear Went over the Mountain. 1996. Owl, ISBN: 0805054383, 320p.

    Now he's gone on to the sublime heights of *Walter, the Farting Dog,* but Kotzwinkle's best adult book is this charmer about Hal Jam, a bear who finds a manuscript under a tree and gets it published. Agents, publishers, other writers, and televangelists line up to curry his favor, seeing Hal not as a bear but as a gruff, he-man, Hemingway type. This is the perfect antidote if you've read one too many talking animal fantasies.

Moore, Christopher
A Dirty Job. 2006. William Morrow, ISBN: 0060590289, 416p.

    Poor Charlie Asher. His wife dies in childbirth, and others start dropping dead around him, too. Minty Fresh explains that they are Death Merchants, whose job is to gather souls before the Forces of Darkness get them. Moore has long teetered on the brink of fame. Start reading his weird backlog now, before it's so big that you'll never catch up.

Pratchett, Terry
The Truth. Discworld. 2000. HarperTorch, ISBN: 0380818191, 368p.

    Young noble William de Worde finds direction when he joins forces with dwarf printers, a vampire photographer who turns to dust when he uses his flash, and the perfect source of information, Gaspode the talking dog. Pratchett's worst book has dozens of funny bits in it, and he doesn't show any sign of slowing. Pterry (as he's sometimes known) isn't just a funny fantasy writer, he's the best satirist writing today, period. (Exclamation point, exclamation point.)

Rankin, Robert
The Hollow Chocolate Bunnies of the Apocalypse. 2002. Gollancz, ISBN: 0575074019, 352p.

    Rankin definitely prefers dark *Chocolate.* His mystery is set in a world populated by toys and nursery rhyme characters (who often take a raunchy twist, such as Madame Goose, who runs a brothel). Eddie the teddy bear (former sidekick to detective Bill Winkie) helps Jack, a 13-year-old seeking his fortune in the big city, track down a serial killer.

So Bad They're Good: Villains for Days When You'd Rather Join in the Evil Laughter

    The lowest form of fantasy life is the Mary Sue, a perky, relentlessly upbeat heroine. She bats her eyelashes or twirls a little knife like a baton and enemies fall down dead or fall over themselves to help her. Although you're supposed to love her, you wish she would *suffer.* There are male Mary Sues, too: bland, perfect heroes for whom everything comes easy. That's where the villain comes in: A first-rate scoundrel can wipe that ultrawhite smile off Prince Laughing Boy's face. If you're having a bad day, don't turn to evil. Satiate your vengeful mood with these books.

Carey, Jacqueline
Banewreaker. The Sundering. 2004. Tor, ISBN: 0765344297, 512p.
Godslayer. The Sundering. 2005. Tor, ISBN: 076535098X, 416p.

    Carey mirrors many aspects of The Lord of the Rings but tells the story from the point of view of Satoris (her Sauron). In this version, good and evil are replaced with shades of gray. One understands the motivations of the "dark lord" and his underlings. Moral ambiguity doesn't make light reading, but it will definitely leave you thinking.

Gentle, Mary
Grunts! 1992. Roc, ISBN: 0451454537, 464p.

    For maximum effect, read this after you finish a big bland fantasy epic. Gentle (an author whose surname seems a kind of sarcastic joke) takes the much-maligned orc, outfits him with futuristic weaponry, and sets him loose on the good guys. This is a spray of battery acid out of a fire hose—only for those with pitch-dark senses of humor.

Maguire, Gregory
Wicked. 1995. Regan, ISBN: 0060987103, 406p.

    Maguire takes on the ultimate rehabilitation, casting Elphaba, the Wicked Witch of the West, as a green-skinned girl victimized by bigotry and the Wizard of Oz's political manipulations. With its literary underpinnings, this is darker and more complex than either *The Wizard of Oz* or the hit musical that was derived from it. Wicked, indeed.

Marco, John
The Jackal of Nar. <u>Tyrants and Kings</u>. 1999. Bantam Spectra, ISBN: 0553578871, 768p.

    Marco's hero, Richius, is bland and makes bad decisions. It's hard to get excited about him. But hang on, his villain, Count Biagio, is a real fire-eater! He knows what feeds his appetites and goes after it. His henchman, Tharn, is no slouch either. As the series progresses, Biagio becomes even more of a focal point.

Martin, George R. R.
A Clash of Kings. <u>A Song of Ice and Fire</u>. 1998. Bantam Spectra, ISBN: 0553579908, 1040p. AW.

    Despite the huge cast of well-drawn characters in <u>A Song of Ice and Fire</u>, I have yet to meet a reader who doesn't like Tyrion Lannister best. A misshapen dwarf, he serves as a foil for his golden-haired siblings and nephews. But Tyrion has smarts and character to offset his deficiencies. It's a joy to watch him operate in the second book of the series.

Modesitt, L. E.
The White Order. <u>Recluce series</u>. 1998. Tor, ISBN: 0812541715, 480p.

    Cerryl, a chaos magician (who isn't really a villain, just treated as one), shows how chaos can be used for good. The surprising result is a twist on the familiar patterns of <u>Recluce</u> (this is the eighth book), producing what is easily one of the best books in a long series.

Salvatore, R. A.
The Servant of the Shard. <u>Sellswords</u>. 2000. Wizards of the Coast, ISBN: 0786939508, 384p.

    Up to this point in the Forgotten Realms, Jarlaxle and Artemis Entreri have been archvillains of the best leering, snarling sort, the clever enemies of Drizzt Do'Urden. But in the series that this book begins, the two begin an interesting rehabilitation.

Badass Fantasy: Heroes Who Don't Take Anything from Anyone

Go along to get along. Turn the other cheek. But if you've been bullied or belittled, if you serve customers who are always right (yet so wrong), your patience may be stretched as thin as that strained smile on your face. That's where knuckle-dragging, badass heroes come in handy. They aren't tolerant. They kill first and let the gods sort 'em out. They make great alter egos for people who are tired of being meek and want to inherit the earth *now*. If you've put up with too much, instead of getting proactive with sharp weapons, let off steam with these books.

Erikson, Steven
Gardens of the Moon. <u>The Malazan Book of the Fallen</u>. 1999. Tor, ISBN: 0765348780, 688p.
    Gardens is a convoluted view of war in a miserable world where alliances constantly shift. Only survivors remain, and they know how to look out for themselves. In a big cast, everyone is battle-hardened. You'll feel tough as nails, too, as you finish this challenging opener. Later books in the love-it-or-hate-it series get even better.

Gemmell, David
⇨ *The Sword in the Storm*. <u>Rigante</u>. 1998. Del Rey, ISBN: 0345432347, 439p.
    Englishman Gemmell is the best contemporary writer for fans of flawed but noble warrior heroes. *Sword in the Storm* starts his <u>Rigante</u> series. When his people are threatened by foreign invasion, young Connovar travels across the sea into the heart of enemy territory to find out what kind of foes he is up against.
Wolf in Shadow. <u>The Jerusalem Man</u>. 1987. Del Rey, ISBN: 0345379039, 336p.
    Any of Gemmell's books would fit this list, but try *Wolf in Shadow,* opener to a trilogy. In its postapocalyptic future, magic again rules. Hero Jon Shannow literally fights the forces of Hell. Like many of Gemmell's heroes, he tries to maintain his own humanity in the midst of all the violence.

Haydon, Elizabeth
Rhapsody. <u>Symphony of Ages</u>. 1999. Tor, ISBN: 0812570812, 672p.
    The title heroine, formerly trapped in child prostitution, is a bit too perfect, a Mary Sue. Read this book for her two sidekicks, Achmed the Snake, a witty assassin who can sense the heartbeats of every person in the world, and Grunthor, a gigantic, jolly fighting machine. Approach this as epic he-man romance, and you'll be likely to enjoy it.

Howard, Robert E.
The Bloody Crown of Conan. <u>Conan series</u>. 1934. Del Rey, ISBN: 0345461525, 384p.
    No hero is more full of himself or more able to back it up than Conan, and nobody writes him better than his creator, Robert Howard. This collection of two stories is the second compilation of unedited reissues of Howard's original writing, complete with illustrations. This muscular fantasy, from the heyday of the pulps, is still a joy to read.

Salvatore, R. A.
 The Dark Elf Trilogy. 1990–1991. Wizards of the Coast, ISBN: 0786915889, 816p.

   Drizzt Do'Urden is a drow (dark elf) made tough by years of shabby racist treatment. In response, he makes himself into a two-sword-wielding whirlwind of death. This omnibus covers his origins.

Wexler, Django
 Memories of Empire. 2005. Medallion, ISBN: 1932815147, 561p.

   Corvus, a mercenary in search of his roots, unintentionally rescues young Veil on her way into slavery. His memory isn't working, but as Corvus pursues his search, it becomes clear that he's been carving his bloody swath through the world for a long time. This first novel has rough patches, but the characters and setting make it very readable.

Flights of Fantasy: High-Flying Fantasy to Read on an Airplane

Readers know that getting high doesn't require illicit substances. You can go soaring anytime you want in the pages of fantasy novels. You can even choose your mode of flight: airship, magic carpet, djinn, or broomstick to name just a few. The next time you're in the claustrophobic middle seat of an airliner, stuck between the armrest hog and the woman who needs to use the bathroom again, rediscover freedom of flight by sampling these highfliers.

Brooks, Terry
 Ilse Witch. **Voyage of the Jerle Shannara.** 2000. Del Rey, ISBN: 0345396553, 480p.

   It's *Dirty Dozen* for the fantasy set: Walker Boh, last of the druids, assembles a crackerjack company of individuals with different skills. Their task is to take an airship into unknown territory in search of ancient magic. Vicarious fliers will enjoy descriptions of the ship and the acrobatics of wing (roc) riders in this start to another Shannara trilogy.

Forsyth, Kate
 The Tower of Ravens. **Rhiannon's Ride.** 2005. Roc, ISBN: 0451460324, 448p.

   Set in the same world as the Witches of Eilcanan, this series opener will give you a jolt of wild-girl power. Rhiannon is half satyricorn (unicorn crossed with satyr), half human. She's savage, ignorant, and yet likable. With no horn, she'll be killed by her herd when she hits adulthood, so she captures a winged horse and escapes, beginning a long flight.

Oppel, Kenneth
  Airborn. <u>Matt Cruse series</u>. 2004. Eos, ISBN: 0060531827, 544p. `YA`.
      Oppel is obsessed with flying things. His <u>Silverwing</u> trilogy flew fans into the world of bats. Here, he begins a new series (for slightly older readers) about Matt, a cabin boy on the airship *Aurora,* and Kate, a young heiress in search of cloud cats. Storms, pirates, and narrow escapes send this steampunk adventure soaring. *Skybreaker* follows.

Ruby, Laura
  The Wall and the Wing. 2006. Eos, ISBN: 0060752572, 336p. `YA`.
      The Wall is Gurl, an orphan who can make herself invisible. The wannabe Wing is Bug, a boy who wants to fly (as some others can in this alternate world). As residents of the Hope House for the Homeless and Hopeless, their adventures turn New York City inside out. Dark humor and eccentric characters make this book enjoyable for all ages.

Stroud, Jonathan
  The Amulet of Samarkand. <u>The Bartimaeus trilogy</u>. 2003. Miramax, ISBN: 0786852550, 480p. `YA`, `AW`.
      Forget Disneyworld's Peter Pan ride, the best way to soar over the rooftops of London is with the arrogantly hilarious 5,000-year-old djinn Bartimaeus. The <u>Bartimaeus trilogy</u> stands out from the piles of young-adult fantasy that followed the success of <u>Harry Potter</u>.

Volsky, Paula
  The Grand Ellipse. 2000. Bantam Spectra, ISBN: 0553580124, 672p.
      Volsky sets fantasy spying and intrigue against the background of an around-the-world race. Along the way, you'll experience almost every means of transportation available in a world where steam engines are the latest technology. My favorite bits are in the hot-air balloons. Here's a great update for those who love Jules Verne's romantic adventures.

Wells, Martha
  The Ships of Air. <u>The Fall of Ile-Rien</u>. 2004. Eos, ISBN: 0380807998, 496p.
      Impulsive, witty Tremaine Valiarde leads a squabbling group of refugees on a fast-paced journey in this middle book of three. The mysterious Gardier overrun Ile-Rien. Tremaine and company flee before them, searching for allies, solutions, and survival. Their travels take them on a spooky luxury liner and then to an encounter with enemy airships.

Magic between Two People: Fantasy for Romance Readers

With fiery, impetuous heroines and strong heroes who need someone to unlock their tortured inner worlds, fantasy is a kissing cousin of romance. The genres even share overripe covers with buxom women and long-haired men that make some books embarrassing to read in public. In the last few years, cross-pollination has increased, with fantasy published directly for the romance market and romances written by credible fantasy writers. These books await anyone in the mood for love, even men who would be mortified to be caught reading a romance.

Briggs, Patricia
Moon Called. <u>Mercedes Thompson series</u>. 2006. Ace, ISBN: 0441013813, 304p.
Dark fantasy romance is red hot, with writers like Laurell K. Hamilton, Kim Harrison, and Mary Janice Davidson. Briggs seems likely to join them as a top seller. This series starter introduces Mercy, a mechanic who can turn into a coyote. Mercy finds herself in the middle of a werewolf war, with a choice between vampire and werewolf lovers.

Cast, P. C.
Goddess of Spring. <u>Goddess Summoning</u>. 2004. Berkley, ISBN: 0425197492, 384p.
A romance hero is dark and brooding with a godlike body, so who better for the part than Hades? The Underworld needs a feminine touch, but Persephone isn't ready for the job. When a baker prays to her for help, Demeter sends daughter Persephone to Tulsa for experience, and local bakery owner Carolina goes to Hades. The god of the Underworld is tough to crack, but deep down, he's just misunderstood.

De Lint, Charles
Widdershins. <u>Newford</u>. 2006. Tor, ISBN: 0765312867, 560p.
Jilly, an artist, and Geordie, a fiddler, have walked widdershins (counterclockwise, a way into the fairy realm) around romance since the first <u>Newford</u> story. Now the two take the plunge, but all is not well. Jilly's trapped in a fay world of her dark memories. Geordie's attempt to save her lands him in a dark place of his own. You'll have to read this vintage de Lint gem to find out if love survives.

Gabaldon, Diana
Outlander. <u>Outlander series</u>. 1991. Dell, ISBN: 0440242940, 896p.
Gabaldon writes romance with a strong element of Scottish historical fiction. And also magical time travel. And a lot of adventure. And a dose of tragedy. And it's 896 pages long. OK, this isn't a typical romance, but it satisfies the same urges. The first of six books to date.

Marillier, Juliet
⇨ *Daughter of the Forest.* <u>Sevenwaters trilogy</u>. 2000. Tor, ISBN: 0765343436, 560p.
When her stepmother turns her brothers into swans, only Sorcha can rescue them: by weaving shirts from sharp plants while maintaining silence. Through

many tragic years, Sorcha keeps quiet and weaves. Saved from drowning by a Briton from her past, Sorcha finds love but faces one more terrible decision in Marillier's impressive first novel.

Rawn, Melanie
Dragon Prince. **Dragon Prince trilogy.** 1988. DAW, ISBN: 0756403014, 576p.
A shimmering desert landscape, an interesting magical system called sun-running, engaging, long-suffering leads, political twists and turns, and plenty of romance are the ingredients of Rawn's trilogy opener. Young readers seem especially pleased by this book. The dragons promised in the title make only a brief appearance.

Shinn, Sharon
Archangel. **Samaria series.** 1996. Ace, ISBN: 0441004326, 400p.
To get a gig leading a choir of praise for Jovah, angel-on-the-rise Gabriel must find a wife. An oracle sends him to the slave Rachel, whom he marries, but Rachel had other plans. She's angry, not grateful. Only the trials the two pass through together lead them to true love. An intriguing hybrid of fantasy, science fiction, and romance.

Wrede, Patricia, and Stevermer, Caroline
The Grand Tour. 2004. Magic Carpet, ISBN: 0152055568, 480p. **YA**.
The Regency period manners of Jane Austen meet fantasy in this novel about two newlywed couples taking the grand tour of Europe. Entry into adult society is interrupted by their encounter with the theft of magical objects. Soon they become embroiled in a plot to take over Europe.

Steaming Up the Looking Glass: When Romance Is Nice, but Sex Is Better

Pull down the shades and lock up the children! It's time to whisper in your ear about erotic fantasy. Not that kind of erotic fantasy. I'm talking about fantasy novels that edge into erotica. I'm talking about riding the dragon. I'm talking about letting the troll out from under the bridge. Romance novels are about building relationships, with the possibility of sexuality. Although not always explicit, erotica is about exploring sensuality and sexuality. When you're ready to tuck yourself away for a little private reading, you might find this list useful.

Boyd, Donna
The Passion. 1998. HarperTorch, ISBN: 0380790947, 416p.
Forbidden love, jealousy, and animal instincts are the subjects of Boyd's books about werewolves. In *The Passion,* werewolf Alexander warns his son

and heir about the dangers of loving humans. His tale flashes back to his own steamy past with human Tessa in atmospheric 1890s Paris. Followed by *The Promise*.

⇨ **Carey, Jacqueline**
  Kushiel's Dart. <u>Kushiel series</u>. 2001. Tor, ISBN: 0765342987, 816p.
  Phèdre trains in the Night Court in an alternate Europe where courtesans have a high place in society. She's devoted to demigod Kushiel—in short, she's a masochist. This may disturb some, but Carey handles the material gracefully. Protégé and heir to an influential nobleman, Phèdre finds herself at the center of a whirlwind of power and intrigue.

Hamilton, Laurell K.
  A Kiss of Shadows. <u>Meredith Gentry</u>. 2000. Ballantine, ISBN: 0345423402, 480p.
  Sensual undercurrents running beneath the Unseelie Court come gushing to the surface in this story of a half-faerie detective drawn into the sexually adventurous sidhe world. Hamilton made her reputation on <u>Anita Blake</u> paranormal romances, but the <u>Meredith Gentry</u> series exhibits a new degree of frank sexuality.

Haydon, Elizabeth
  Prophecy. <u>Symphony of Ages</u>. 2000. Tor, ISBN: 0812570820, 736p.
  The second book in the <u>Symphony</u> turns up the heat. In her quest to visit a dragon, Rhapsody needs a guide. The mysterious Ashe fits the bill, and the two of them . . . get to know each other very well. This is more romantic epic than pure erotica, but the sex is frequent and passionate. The saga that surrounds erotic scenes is worth reading as well.

McReynolds, Glenna
  The Chalice and the Blade. <u>Celtic saga</u>. 1997. Bantam, ISBN: 0553574302, 512p.
  Twelfth-century Wales is the setting for this tale of Ceridwen, a young woman who survives the marauding of her ancestral home, and Dain, the disillusioned, broken man who saves her. The protagonists bring out passion in each other, but the brutal Caradoc won't give up his relentless pursuit. Sexual tension is palpable in this series opener.

Rice, Anne
  The Witching Hour. <u>Mayfair Witches</u>. 1990. Ballantine, ISBN: 0345384466, 1056p.
  Rice builds sensuality out of physical detail and exotic situations. This story focuses on Rowan, who doesn't know her witch lineage, and Michael, the man she saves from the sea, but they're only part of the century-spanning saga of a witch family. (If you like domination themes, try the <u>Sleeping Beauty</u> series that Rice wrote as A. N. Roquelaure.)

Warren, Christine
Fantasy Fix. 2003. Ellora's Cave, ISBN: 1843605627, 248p.
>Vampires are a potent metaphor for obsession and dark longings, so it's no surprise that they are such a staple of erotic fiction. Ellora's Cave specializes in paranormal erotica. Warren's book is one of this publisher's better entries.

It Was the Dark Lord in the Conservatory with the Candlestick: Fantasy for Mystery Readers

As Sherlock Holmes and Hercule Poirot note, sleuthing is based on applying logic to physical evidence. Add magic—which breaks the rules of reality—and rational detection goes out the window. But with well-defined magical systems, emphasis on suspense and action, and a playful take on mystery conventions, skilled writers successfully blend the genres. Viewing clues through the magnifying glass *and* the looking glass, mystery and fantasy fans should find common ground in these novels.

Bull, Emma
Finder. **Bordertown**. 1994. Tor, ISBN: 0765347776, 320p.
>People will do anything to enter Nevernever. So when a drug claimed to change body chemistry appears, allowing users into the elf world, desperate Bordertown street people are quick to try it. The drug has a nasty side effect: death. To find the drug's creator, policewoman Sunny Rico recruits Orient, a young man pulled toward any object he's asked to find.

Butcher, Jim
⇨ *Summer Knight.* **Dresden Files**. 2002. Roc, ISBN: 0451458923, 371p.
>Harry Dresden is a down-on-his-luck gumshoe in the classic hard-boiled mode. He solves crimes, makes wisecracks, but can't get his personal act together. The difference is that Harry is a wizard. His fourth adventure brings him a true femme fatale: Mab, the Winter Queen. She wants to find out who killed her sidhe counterpart, the Summer Knight.

Cook, Glen
Whispering Nickel Idols. **Garrett, P.I. series**. 2005. Roc, ISBN: 0451459741, 368p.
>Rex Stout's mysteries inspired this long-running series. Cook's version of everyman Archie Goodwin is Garrett. He does legwork for his own immobile Nero Wolfe: the Dead Man. By this 11th entry, the enchanted yet gritty streets of their stomping grounds, TunFaire, are populated by a slew of quirky fantasy characters. Early books in the series are out of print but worth finding: You'll have to go sleuthing to find used copies.

Cunningham, Elaine
Shadows in the Darkness. <u>Changeling</u>. 2004. Tor, ISBN: 0765348519, 304p.

Fans of female detective writers like Paretsky and Evanovich have found dark fantasy analogs like Laurell K. Hamilton, but Cunningham awaits wide-scale discovery. Her heroine, GiGi Gelman, a vice cop turned private investigator in Providence, specializes in missing persons. This case turns up her own fantastic history. Followed by *Shadows in the Starlight.*

Garrett, Randall
<u>*Lord Darcy.*</u> 1964–1979. Baen, ISBN: 0743435486, 688p.

Here's the first of the great fantasy detectives. Lord Darcy uses rule-governed magic to solve murders in an alternate world where the Plantagenet line survived into the twentieth century. Garrett's writing is chock-full of puns and allusions to classic mysteries. This omnibus collects all of the Darcy stories and the novel, *Too Many Magicians.*

Hughart, Barry
Eight Skilled Gentlemen. <u>Master Li series</u>. 1990. Doubleday, ISBN: 0385417101, 268p.

Comedy, adventure, and vivid Chinese mythology are the hallmarks of this third and final adventure of Master Li and Number Ten Ox. This time around, the sleuths must clear the Celestial Master, the realm's top Taoist priest, from a murder charge. A sublimely silly execution, magical cages, smugglers, and a thrilling dragonboat race figure into the mix.

Jones, Tamara Siler
Ghosts in the Snow. <u>Dubric Byerly</u>. 2004. Bantam Spectra, ISBN: 0553587099, 496p.

Dubric Byerly sees dead people. As head of security at Faldorrah Castle Keep, that means work for him: He can see the ghosts until he solves their murders. Since a mutilating cannibal went to work, Dubric has too much company. He must use medieval forensics to catch the killer before another young woman dies. Two sequels follow to date.

Pratchett, Terry
Men at Arms. <u>Discworld, The Watch</u>. 1993. HarperTorch, ISBN: 0061092193, 400p.

The <u>Watch</u> novels spoof police procedurals (and anything else that wanders onto the page). Their second adventure puts Captain Vimes, the naive man-dwarf Carrot, Angua the werewolf, and the rest of the Watch in the middle of clowns, assassins, a wise-talking dog, exploding dragons, and Leonard de Quirm's dangerous invention, the gonne.

The Dark Fantasy Tradition: Spine-Chilling Fantasy for Horror Readers

Drawing bright line distinctions between fantasy and horror is difficult. The genres differ in how much focus is placed on the evildoer and how frightening results are intended to be, but such measures are highly subjective. If you don't know which genre a book is, call it *dark fantasy* and you'll be safe from the literary police, but you'll still have to cope with terror caused by the books. Then again, if you picked this list, terror may be exactly what you crave.

Barker, Clive
The Great and Secret Show. **The Art**. 1989. Harper, ISBN: 006093316X, 672p.
Talk about going postal: Jaffe finds the keys to the "Art" in Omaha's dead-letter office. Jaffe's convert, the scientist Fletcher, creates a drug that enhances the Art, but this drives Jaffe to evil madness. Realizing his error, Fletcher becomes Jaffe's archrival in an eternal battle for control of a sea of dreams called the Quiddity.

Bishop, Anne
The Black Jewels Trilogy. 1998–1999. Roc, ISBN: 0451529014, 1216p.
Two corrupt priestesses battle for control of the Realms, using sexual violence and other terrors. Young witch Jaenelle follows a torturous path to her own throne with the help of an undead prince named Saetan and his sons Daemon and Luciver, preparing the final battle between good and evil. This omnibus contains three disturbing but powerful books.

Feist, Raymond E.
Faerie Tale. 1988. Bantam Spectra, ISBN: 0553277839, 448p.
The Hastings family moves to a house on the edge of California woods for peace and quiet, but the cruel and mischievous faerie spirits that inhabit the woods have other ideas. Feist tries out a different, scarier style in his only stand-alone novel, and it works.

Flewelling, Lynn
The Bone Doll's Twin. **Tamir triad**. 2001. Bantam Spectra, ISBN: 0553577239, 544p.
King Elrius usurped a throne destined to fall to a warrior queen. To escape the prophecy, he has highborn girl children killed. A gender-disguising spell cast at her birth saves Tobin, but her twin brother is also changed and thus killed. Growing up as a boy, Tobin must survive Elrius and the demon spirit of his/her brother. First of a trilogy.

Hendee, Barb, and Hendee, J. C.
Dhampir. <u>The Noble Dead</u>. 2003. Roc, ISBN: 0451459067, 384p.
>   Magiere and her half-elf friend run a scam, pretending to rid villages of vampires. When she kills a real vampire, Magiere decides to settle down, but she unknowingly picks a village that is a nest of vampires. They recognize Magiere as a half-vampire *dhampir:* a hunter of their kind. Fast reading, mixing fun and frights, this book begins a series.

Klause, Annette Curtis
Blood and Chocolate. 1997. Laurel Leaf, ISBN: 0440226686, 288p. `YA`.
>   Vivian falls for a boy named Aiden and always thinks of sex, but this isn't typical teen angst: Vivian is a werewolf. Her father's death puts her in a struggle for control of the pack, and love for a human is forbidden. Worst of all, Vivian fears that she might be killing people.

Lovecraft, H. P.
⇨ *H. P. Lovecraft: Tales.* 1919–1935. Library of America, ISBN: 1931082723, 850p. (hbk.)
>   Seventy years after his death, Lovecraft is still the master of dark fantasy. His work remains very readable (although some find his prose rather baroque), as this anthology of 22 tales written between 1919 and his death proves. Peter Straub edited this excellent collection.

Yarbro, Chelsea Quinn
Better in the Dark. <u>Saint-Germain series</u>. 1993. Orb, ISBN: 0312859783, 416p.
Blood Roses. <u>Saint-Germain series</u>. 1998. Tor, ISBN: 0312872488, 384p.
>   History meets dark fantasy in 19 books. Saint-Germain is an elegant vampire who fights evil across the span of history. Series starter *Hotel Transylvania* and other early books are out of print, but these entries, set in a creepy tenth-century German keep and Plague-ridden fourteenth-century France, are good examples of why readers enjoy this vampire series.

The Mythic Past: Great Fantasy for Historical Fiction Lovers

Enjoy historical fantasy's evocation of the past without getting hung up on absolute accuracy. It is *fantasy* after all. (My historian friends just melted.) Fans *do,* however, demand that writers don't violate the spirit of the historical times they chronicle. Polite, mannered fantasy set in the last days of ancient Rome wouldn't fly, nor would a sex-crazed romp in alternative Victorian Britain. If you're in the mood to mix historic figures with fantasy fun, try these books.

Card, Orson Scott
Red Prophet. <u>The Tales of Alvin Maker.</u> 1988. Tor, ISBN: 0812524268, 320p. AW.
In alternate America, the "Reds" of Ta-Kumsaw and his brother the Prophet are trapped by the murderous schemes of William Henry Harrison, Andrew Jackson, and Napoleon (who's exiled in Detroit!). Meanwhile, protagonist Alvin Maker finds his power through Taleswapper William Blake's mentorship and contact with the Reds. Second in the series.

Irvine, Alexander C.
A Scattering of Jades. 2002. Tor, ISBN: 0765340984, 416p.
To reawaken an Aztec god, Riley Steen needs to sacrifice a virgin, so he steals typesetter Archie Prescott's daughter. A chase across nineteenth-century America to Mammoth Cave results, where slave Steven Bishop must choose between freedom and helping Prescott. Aaron Burr, Tammany Hall, P. T. Barnum, and Edgar Allan Poe all appear.

Keyes, J. Gregory
A Calculus of Angels. <u>The Age of Unreason.</u> 1999. Del Rey, ISBN: 0345406087, 448p.
In *Newton's Cannon,* possessed by evil angels, Louis XVI destroys London with a comet. As this follow-up opens, Ben Franklin and Isaac Newton try to stop Peter the Great from annihilating Prague. Meanwhile, Cotton Mather, Blackbeard, and a Choctaw shaman join a New World delegation seeking news from the suddenly silent Europe.

Lackey, Mercedes, Flint, Eric, and Freer, Dave
This Rough Magic. <u>Heirs of Alexandria.</u> 2003. Baen, ISBN: 0743499093, 944p.
Beginning in the colorful sixteenth-century Venice of its predecessor, *The Shadow of the Lion,* this sprawling romantic adventure moves to the island of Corfu, lynchpin for the defense of Venice and source land of Goddess magic. Benito Valdosta and his love, Maria, lead its defense against the demon-possessed Duke of Lithuania and the Hungarian Witch-King.

Lindskold, Jane
The Buried Pyramid. 2004. Tor, ISBN: 076534159X, 512p.
Victorian fascination with Egyptology comes to life in this tale of an obsessive English millionaire, his able American niece, and the search for the tomb of Neferankhotep (who may be Moses). They skirmish with a religious cult and solve puzzles on their way to a climactic encounter with Egyptian deities.

Powers, Tim
The Drawing of the Dark. 1979. Del Rey, ISBN: 0345430816, 336p.
Powers brews a heady mix of fantasy, myth, and history in this tale of an Irish mercenary who in 1529 hires on as the bouncer at Herzewsten, a mystical

Vienna brewery. When Suleiman attacks with a host of Ottoman Turks, Duffy defends the property with the help of the Fisher King and a collection of Arthurian and Norse legends. Cheers!

Radford, Irene
   Guardian of the Vision. **Merlin's Descendants.** 2001. DAW, ISBN: 0756400716, 560p.
      Descendants of Merlin guard England's shores in Radford's series. This third book takes place during the rivalry between Mary Queen of Scots and Elizabeth I. Telepathic twins Griffin and Donovan Kirkwood are next in line to take up the responsibilities of the Pendragon, but one is a pacifist and the other isn't sure he is up to the task.

Turtledove, Harry
   Into the Darkness. **Darkness series.** 1998. Tor, ISBN: 0812574729, 704p.
      In an alternate world, if Harry Turtledove didn't write alternate history, would the genre cease to exist? *Into the Darkness* starts six books about an alternate World War II fought with magic. Turtledove returns to alternate history based on fantasy instead of science fiction. For more such works, look for Videssos and Gerin the Fox novels from his early career.

Rocket Ship or Dragon Sticker?
Fantasy for Science Fiction Fans

In the ocean of literature, fantasy fiction is cast away in a lifeboat with science fiction, but it's a raft of confusion. Both groups have survival skills, but fantasy lovers find Atlantis, summon mermaids, or raid other boats, while science fiction fans make a positioning system from driftwood and seaweed or terraform ocean into land. Though they share interest in alternate worlds and love of adventure, the genres otherwise differ. One group yearns for the past, the other the future. Magic and technology compete as ideas: Abundance of one makes the other unnecessary, and faith in one often precludes faith in the other. Still, fans of the two genres agree on these books.

Cherryh, C. J.
   The Morgaine Saga. 1976–1979. DAW, ISBN: 0886778778, 720p.
      The science fiction practicality of heroine Morgaine and the fantasy idealism of vassal Vanye meet in this omnibus of *Gate of Ivrel, Well of Shiuan,* and *Fires of Azeroth.* The duo quest across space and time, camping on the hard ground and destroying gates that threaten to unravel time's continuum with Morgaine's mighty technological sword.

Friedman, C. S.
⇨*Black Sun Rising*. The Coldfire Trilogy. 1991. DAW, ISBN: 0756403146, 496p.
Descendants of Earth colonists struggle on volcanic planet Erna. Advanced technology fails, but some people can tap into and use the "Fae," a magiclike force that turns fears into reality. As this first book of The Coldfire Trilogy develops, it becomes clear that long-term use of the Fae increases the dark side of its power.

Garrett, Randall
Lord Darcy. 1964–1979. Baen, ISBN: 0743435486, 688p.
When science fiction fans read fantasy, they often complain of *deus ex machinas*: gods in the machine. They don't like it when arbitrary magical forces bail the characters out of problems for no apparent reason. Fantasy detective Lord Darcy appeals to them. Magic in his alternate history is governed by logical rules that are spelled out for the reader.

Keyes, J. Gregory
Newton's Cannon. The Age of Unreason. 1998. Del Rey, ISBN: 0345433785, 384p.
What science enthusiast can resist a fantasy that casts Ben Franklin and Isaac Newton as heroes? Newton's discovery of "Philosopher's Mercury" drives rapid advancement of technology in this series opener. When characters talk about science in a way that is rhapsodic, yet still methodical, even scientists won't mind that it's all make-believe.

Kirstein, Rosemary
The Lost Steersman. Steerswoman Saga. 2003. Del Rey, ISBN: 0345462297, 432p.
Clarke's Third Law—that sufficiently advanced technology is indistinguishable from magic—is apropos to this medieval world where wizards wield technology. In this third book, a resigned steersman knows more than he'll tell about the evil wizard heroine Rowan seeks. Is this series science fiction or fantasy? You won't know until you finish.

Silverberg, Robert
Lord Valentine's Castle. Majipoor. 1980. Eos, ISBN: 0061054879, 528p. AW.
An amnesiac joins a juggling troupe, performing around enormous Majipoor in a quest to discover his past. Valentine's travels show something isn't right in the world, and his dreams tell him *he* must put things right on Castle Mount. This series seems like fantasy in this opener, but Silverberg has surprises in store that will appeal to science fiction fans.

Stover, Matthew Woodring
Heroes Die. Overworld. 1998. Del Rey, ISBN: 0345421450, 560p.
Media companies dominate future Earth, pacifying the people with Overworld, a violent alternate existence in which heroes and villains battle

with magic. Tired of killing to entertain, Hari Michaelson wants to quit his Overworld role of Caine the Assassin, but moguls force him to confront evil Ma'Elkoth by trapping his wife in the fantasy realm.

Wells, Martha
The Wizard Hunters. <u>The Fall of Ile-Rien</u>. 2003. Eos, ISBN: 038080798X, 464p.
  Turn-of-the-twentieth-century technology mixes with magic in a world invaded by time-traveling aliens in impervious airships. So begins <u>The Fall of Ile-Rien</u>. Heroine Tremaine holds a magical device—her beleaguered world's only hope—but she doesn't know how it works. Nodding to Jules Verne, this fun fantasy blends past, future, and imagination.

Seriously Fantastic: Fantasy for Literary Fiction Readers

A strange race only enjoys reading when they are bettering themselves. These odd folk sojourn through the country of Literaria drawing strength from the magic of symbol and metaphor. Under illusion of allusion, they quest for deep meaning. The irony (they quiver with joy at irony) is that lost in the fantastic world of Literaria, these folk believe that reading about other fantasy worlds is not serious enough. If you or someone you love wanders in Literaria, these fantasy novels will aid the quest. Perhaps they will serve as a trail of bread crumbs you can follow home to fantasy.

Carter, Angela
The Bloody Chamber and Other Stories. 1979. Penguin, ISBN: 014017821X, 128p.
  Carter adapts folktales, but instead of scrubbing out dark content as others do, she ramps up horror and sexuality, bringing out feminist undercurrents running beneath stories like "Little Red Riding Hood," "Bluebeard," "Puss in Boots," and "Beauty and the Beast."

Clarke, Susanna
Jonathan Strange & Mr. Norrell. 2004. Bloomsbury, ISBN: 1582346038, 800p. `AW`.
  Bibliophiles love this book, perhaps even more than fantasy fans. Sure, the story of magic revived to aid England's fight against Napoleon is fantasy, but style is the point, not plot. Clarke revives the eighteenth- or nineteenth-century British novel of fussy manners, sly wit, and footnotes full of arcane fascinations. This is fantasy for fans of Dickens and Thackeray.

Crowley, John
  ⇨ *Little, Big.* 1981. Harper Perennial, ISBN: 0060937939, 560p. `AW`.
  After Smokey Barnable marries into the Drinkwater family, he discovers their deep connection to the world of fairy. That's the plot summary, but if

you're looking for action, try another book. Read this book for the author's elegant language. Crowley's prose is profound, romantic, luminous; any of his fantasy books could grace this list.

Donohue, Keith
The Stolen Child. 2006. Anchor, ISBN: 1400096537, 336p.

There are two Henrys, the human boy stolen into the world of hobgoblins at age seven and his changeling replacement. Donohue isn't after fantasy adventure. His thought-provoking fable will leave you thinking about what it means to be different from others and about the child that you once were. A subtle, mesmerizing first novel.

Goldstein, Lisa
The Red Magician. 1981. Orb, ISBN: 0312890079, 192p.

A Jewish girl named Kisci becomes friends with the title magician, who tries to warn the people of his Hungarian village about the coming horror of World War II. This holocaust story mixed with Jewish mysticism won the American Book Award for its first-time author.

Maguire, Gregory
Wicked. 1995. Regan, ISBN: 0060987103, 406p.

It's not easy being green. This story of the Wicked Witch of the West is told from her perspective. If you suspect that Dorothy was the ultimate Mary Sue or that the Wizard was a con man to the core, you'll enjoy this complex political take on the less-than-merry-old Land of Oz. If you like this, Maguire has reimagined other fantasy stories.

Miéville, China
Looking for Jake. 2005. Del Rey, ISBN: 0345476077, 320p.

Literary readers will love the rotting splendor of the Bas-Lag novels but might prefer to wade into Miéville's depths with this story collection, which mixes politics and terror in equal doses. Miéville's brooding style always leaves the reader with the feeling that something is lurking just beneath the surface.

Myers, John Myers
Silverlock. 1949. Ace, ISBN: 0441012477, 384p.

Myers's classic explores transformation through books. Shipwrecked, self-centered Clarence Shandon meets Golias, a bard and "maker," who guides him through a world populated by literary characters. As Silverlock, Shandon becomes a better person through contact with these heroes. How many of Myers's literary allusions can you identify?

Tiptoeing Hesitantly into the Real World: Literary Fiction for Fantasy Readers

I can't believe you're moving on from fantasy. You say people make fun of the princess on the cover. You want to be taken seriously. Before you take the train to Mundania, take a dose of realism: *magic realism*. Don't give up fantasy for an uptight teacher, your all-business boss, or the spouse who wants you to be more practical. Read right under their noses! Get praise for your highbrow taste! Just pick fantasies that pose as literary fiction. And remember: *Frodo lives!*

García Márquez, Gabriel
One Hundred Years of Solitude. 1967. Harper Perennial, ISBN: 0060883286, 448p.

Spend the best century of your life in Macondo, a town where layers of fantasy and reality blend until you cannot separate them. The story of the Buendía family is the story of everything: love, war, death, obsession, tragedy, and beauty. No other work is more associated with magic realism. Read García Márquez's *Love in the Time of Cholera,* too.

Greer, Andrew Sean
The Confessions of Max Tivoli. 2004. Picador, ISBN: 0312423810, 288p.

Escaping age is a common fantasy theme, but Greer explores the cost of growing young. Max is born in 1871 with a 70-year-old body. He grows physically younger as he ages, although his mind develops normally. Max is mistaken for a dirty old man as a boy, pines for Alice Levy through his middle years, and spends his "old age" as an unnaturally wise schoolboy father.

Harris, Joanne
Chocolat. 1999. Black Swan, ISBN: 0552998486, 319p.

A wind blows Vianne Rocher into a French village where she opens a *chocolaterie* during Lent, angering the local priest. Aided by a river gypsy, the town's oldest resident, and her daughter, Vianne battles Reynaud for support of the people: chocolate versus church. Charming characters, a vivid setting, and mystic undertones make this bittersweet fable delicious.

Helprin, Mark
⇨ *A Winter's Tale.* 1983. Harvest, ISBN: 0156031191, 768p.

Helprin's evocative, romantic life of Peter Lake is the most beautiful of urban fantasies. It's full of shimmering images that stay with you: milk horses that fly, the fever glow of Beverly Penn, sleep among the stars of Grand Central Station's ceiling, and flights from the villain Pearly Soames. Fantasy lovers wish for eternal winter after reading this book.

Martel, Yann
The Life of Pi. 2001. Harvest, ISBN: 0156027321, 336p.
> After a shipwreck, Christian, Muslim, *and* Hindu Pi Patel finds himself on a lifeboat with a zebra, a hyena, an orangutan, and a tiger named Richard Parker. Infighting reduces their numbers, but Pi and Richard Parker will spend 227 days lost at sea. In the end, the reader must decide what is real and what is hallucination.

Niffenegger, Audrey
The Time Traveler's Wife. 2003. Harvest, ISBN: 015602943X, 560p.
> Dashing librarian Henry (we're all dashing) has a problem. He's unstuck in time, randomly jumping forward and backward. He falls in love with young Clare, who ages normally. The book tells the story of their tender, poignant, but out-of-sync romance.

Saramago, Jose
Blindness. 1995. Harvest, ISBN: 0156007754, 352p.
> The Portuguese Nobel Prize winner uses imaginative premises as a starting point for insights on human nature. Here, an epidemic of blindness spreads rapidly, setting off societal disintegration. Saramago vividly describes the resulting savagery. This literary fable shares much with fantasy tales of societies teetering on the edge of obliteration.

Süskind, Patrick
Perfume: The Story of a Murderer. 1985. Vintage, ISBN: 0375725849, 272p. `AW`.
> Born in eighteenth-century Paris, Grenouille is full of contradictions. He has a perfect sense of smell but no personal odor. His perfumes are the most beautiful ever, but he's atrocious, a sociopath who kills people to add their scents to his creations. If you like dark fantasy, don't hold your nose at this thrilling study of obsession from a gifted German writer.

Picture This: Graphic Novels of Fantasy for the Visually Inclined

Whether you think of them as comic compilations or an important new media, the popularity of graphic novels is skyrocketing. Appealing to the new reader, the visually inclined, and the nostalgia seeker, these fast-reading, eye-popping novels have many fans. Readers try to picture their fantasy favorites, so it's no surprise that many have received graphic treatment.

Barker, Clive
Abarat. **Abarat series.** 2002. HarperTrophy, ISBN: 0064407330, 432p. `YA`.
> Barker evolves: He started with gory horror, shifted to dark fantasy, and after sojourning in film turned to young-adult novels. Candy, a midwestern

girl, plunges into a surreal quest across the islands of Abarat. This is not a true graphic novel, but Van Gogh-like illustrations raise the storytelling to a higher level. First of a foursome.

Busiek, Kurt, et al.
Conan Vol. 1: The Frost Giant's Daughter and Other Stories. 2005. Dark Horse, ISBN: 1593073011, 192p.

    Busiek adapts Robert E. Howard's original pulp tales, and the illustrators capture the savage beauty of Conan's world in a style reminiscent of fantasy art master Frank Frazetta. Volumes 2 and 3, *The God in the Bowl and Other Stories* and *The Tower of the Elephant and Other Stories,* follow.

Gaiman, Neil, et al.
The Sandman: Preludes and Nocturnes. The Sandman. 1991. Vertigo, ISBN: 1563890119, 240p.

    This series jump-started a surge in popularity of graphic novels for "serious" readers. In the first of 10 collections, Sandman (or Morpheus or Dream if you prefer) comes out of long captivity to reclaim his throne. Gaiman weaves a new mythology from many sources, backed up perfectly by vivid, often surreal artwork from many artists.

Martin, George R. R., et al.
The Hedge Knight. 2004. Dabel Brothers, ISBN: 097640110X, 164p.

    Here's something I hope we'll see more of: a graphic novel used to draw readers into established series. Through this prequel, fans can visualize the world of A Song of Ice and Fire, and the uninitiated may become interested enough to try some very big books.

Medley, Linda
Castle Waiting. 2002. Fantagraphics, ISBN: 1560977477, 448p. (hbk.)

    Medley is writer and artist for this lighthearted feminist fairy tale. The story begins by retelling Sleeping Beauty but continues after the prince and princess travel off into the "ever after." This funny collection appeals to readers (especially women) of all ages.

Pini, Wendy, and Pini, Richard
Elfquest Book #01: Fire and Flight. Elfquest. 1978. Warp Graphics, ISBN: 0936861169, 192p.

    Elfquest has been in production in one form or another for almost thirty years. DC Comics recently bought the rights and is due to begin reproducing some of the comics soon. *Fire and Flight* is the original beginning, about an Elf chief named Cutter trying to lead his Wolfrider people through a treacherous world.

Pratchett, Terry, and Kidby, Paul
The Last Hero: A Discworld Fable. <u>Discworld</u>. 2001. Eos, ISBN: 0060507772, 176p.

> One of Pratchett's best creations is his geriatric hero, Cohen the Barbarian. This graphic novel tells the story of Cohen's attempt to go out with a bang, blowing up himself, his wheelchair-bound Silver Horde, and the gods themselves. Many of <u>Discworld</u>'s standbys make an appearance, and it's great fun to see them in illustration.

Fantasy behind the Films: For Those Who Like to Compare Books with Movies

The biggest difference between books and movies is that in books, the hero or heroine bears an uncanny resemblance to the reader. (In my mind, my Legolas hair is stunning. Galadriel will dump Celeborn and be all over me.) Seriously, with computer-generated images, movies are being made from fantasies that once were not filmable. Happily, many have been terrific, and their popularity has led to sale of rights for more fantasy franchises. This list is limited to films that are made or in production, but if you enjoy comparing book and adaptation, cross your fingers for more.

Baum, L. Frank
The Wonderful Wizard of Oz. 1900. HarperTrophy, ISBN: 0688166776, 320p. `YA`.

> Baum's book, though more detailed and darker in tone, is not changed substantially for the 1939 film (though "Over the Rainbow" and the singing Munchkins are a wonderful bonus). The backstory of farmhands, Miss Gulch, and Professor Marvel is an addition; the book never implies that Oz is a fever dream. If you enjoy the movie, you'll enjoy the extra character detail of the book and its many fine sequels.

Jones, Diana Wynne
Howl's Moving Castle. 1986. Eos, ISBN: 006441034X, 336p. `YA`.

> This anime film about a castle that exists in four places and the girl turned crone who moves in comes from a British YA novel. But Jones's novel is something quite different, a playful tweaking of fairy tale conventions. The Miyazaki film inserts a background war. Although the animation is eye-popping, character development is stronger in the book.

Lewis, C. S.
The Lion, the Witch, and the Wardrobe. <u>The Chronicles of Narnia</u>. 1950. HarperTrophy, ISBN: 0064409422, 208p. `YA`.

Unlike many fantasies, <u>Narnia</u> novels are short. Instead of trimming, film-makers can fit every detail. Even so, the 2005 film is remarkably loyal. Many feared a Disney film would be too cute, but visuals of war with the White Witch and her minions make the film darker. More <u>Narnia</u> films are on the way, beginning with *Prince Caspian.*

Paolini, Christopher
Eragon. <u>The Inheritance trilogy</u>. 2002. Knopf, ISBN: 0375826696, 528p.

Plucky young Eragon discovers that his dragon Saphira is the last of her kind and that he is the last dragon rider. Together they must combat evil King Galbatorix. Teen Paolini became a media darling after his book appeared. For youngsters who haven't read the fantasies it mimics, this is a passable introduction to the genre.

Priest, Christopher
The Prestige. 1995. Tor, ISBN: 0312858868, 416p. `AW`

Priest won the 1996 World Fantasy Award for this story of two Victorian-age magicians whose obsessive rivalry leads to trouble. Cleverly told in diary entries, it captures the style of period literature. The 2006 film makes significant changes, particularly in dropping a modern subplot, but it also provides a dose of twisty fun.

Pullman, Philip
The Golden Compass. <u>His Dark Materials</u>. 1995. Yearling, ISBN: 0440418321, 399p. `YA`.

This vividly visual trilogy, in which young Lyra literally battles the forces of heaven and hell, begs to be made into films. I can't wait for Iorek Byrnison to outshine Coke's hucksters as the best polar bear on film. The first film is due in late 2007. The big question is how the film will handle the controversial religious content of the novels.

Rowling, J. K.
Harry Potter and the Prisoner of Azkaban. <u>Harry Potter series</u>. 1999. Scholastic, ISBN: 0439136369, 448p. `YA`, `AW`.

With child actors aging more quickly than their characters and a gaggle of directors, this franchise could easily have laid eggs, but so far, the films are good. The film of this third installment, in which Harry meets Sirius Black and battles Dementors, is this author's favorite, but all of the movies have fans. Make sure you still read the books, which include a level of detail that films cannot possibly contain.

Tolkien, J.R.R.
⇨ *The Lord of the Rings.* 1954–1955. Houghton Mifflin, ISBN: 0618640150, 1216p.

The films feature violent, harrowing battles that Tolkien describes only vaguely. The books have a lovely, leisurely pace that even four-hour films can't capture. Tom Bombadil gets the axe (you probably won't miss him), and Arwen grows from a note in the appendix to a featured role. In the end, the verdict isn't difficult: True fantasy fans should experience the masterworks of both J.R.R. Tolkien and Peter Jackson.

Chapter Five

Language

The appeal factor of language is easily overlooked, but those who advise readers *ignore it at their peril*. (Flick the lights on and off and laugh evilly as you read that last sentence again.) Language preferences create great divergence. Handing pulp fantasy to readers who want a literary approach will not win fans for the advisor or the genre. A gentle soul who stumbles into violent horror fantasy may be frightened away from the genre forever. And lengthy, descriptive novels are anathema to fans of fast-moving action, producing an effect similar to that of holy water on vampires, with lots of steam and hissing.

Unfortunately, language is not an easy appeal factor to research. Reviews often fail to describe the way in which the author weaves words. There aren't handy-dandy lists on the Internet or sections in the local bookstore that separate authors by linguistic style. The lists that follow should do the trick, identifying different ways that fantasy writers approach language.

Magic Words: Fantasy Writers with a Gift for Language

This list is for readers who enjoy a spiffy sentence. The writers herein may or may not have a strong sense of character, plot, or pacing, but they have a flair for knitting words together in elegant, often surprising ways. They have robust vocabularies but rarely leave you wondering what in the Valhalla they mean. If you're the sort who quotes favorite passages like lines of poetry, then these writers are required reading.

Beagle, Peter S.
⇨ *The Last Unicorn.* 1968. Roc, ISBN: 0451450523, 224p.

A sweet, brave little unicorn leaves home, joining forces with a wacky magician named Schmendrick to battle an evil king and the Red Bull. Such a recap may leave an adult reader feeling like a sixth-grade boy caught playing with Barbie dolls, but this book is recommended wholeheartedly to adults because the prose sparkles with clever metaphors, wry humor, and poetic passages that illuminate the page.

Bujold, Lois McMaster
The Hallowed Hunt. <u>Chalion series</u>. 2005. Eos, ISBN: 0060574747, 448p.

Bujold has the full package: vivid characters, involving plots, and page-turning pacing. In this darker, slower-moving book, with characters less deep than usual, one can really see her gift for language. Bujold never writes a jarring sentence. Every word matters. Even a less obviously lovable work from the owner of four Hugos and two Nebulas is a keeper.

Carroll, Jonathan
The Marriage of Sticks. 1998. Tor, ISBN: 0312872437, 272p.

Carroll is a writer's writer: a free-flowing faucet of deft little insights, read-it-again passages, and dead-on details. In the first half of this book, Carroll builds a sympathetic but normal life for his lead Miranda. In the second half, he pulls the ground out from underneath her and reveals all the strangeness that lurked beneath.

Kay, Guy Gavriel
The Lions of Al-Rassan. 1995. Eos, ISBN: 0060733497, 528p.

Two great men alternate between friendship and enmity in the shifting alliances of medieval Spain. Jehane, a female physician, is drawn to both. Descriptive, involving, and historically meticulous, Kay covers more in one book than most writers manage in three. In a genre that suffers from bloat, his ability to build full-bodied stories in compact packages is a treasure. With *Tigana* and *Song for Arbonne,* this ranks among his best.

Lindskold, Jane
Child of a Rainless Year. 2005. Tor, ISBN: 0765315130, 400p.

The prose is like the ancestral house to which Mira returns in this novel: colorful, sentient, and haunting. Quieter than most fantasy, this book has as much reality as magic, but the language pulls you into a fluid mystery that leaves you with plenty to think about.

Link, Kelly
Magic for Beginners. 2005. Harvest, ISBN: 0156031876, 320p.

When other writers attempt postmodern literary fantasy, it's often intriguing but obscure. Link obtains the same depth without the blurriness: Her stories are bright little snapshots that are somehow both whimsical and disturbing. My favorites here are "The Faery Handbag," the title story, "Some Zombie Contingency Plans," and "Stone Animals."

Miller, Keith
The Book of Flying. 2004. Riverhead, ISBN: 1594480664, 288p.
    A book about a poet working as a librarian in a city where people don't read was likely to press all the buttons in my elevator. Still, I don't think I'm the only one who will enjoy the poetry of this poignant little fable by a debut author. Perhaps it's a bit ripe in spots, but more often you'll be caught up in this tale of a gentle hero's attempt to fly.

Mirrlees, Hope
Lud-in-the-Mist. 1926. Cold Spring, ISBN: 1593600410, 288p.
    In this classic, the stodgy men of Lud taste forbidden fruit and rediscover the Fairyland next door. In the same way, every ten years or so, this classic is rediscovered (Neil Gaiman wrote the foreword for this edition). Read it for its poetry, its humorous oaths ("by my Great-Aunt's rump!"), and its understated symbolism.

Worth an Epic Effort: Complex Fantasy to Challenge the Reader

Some readers want fantasy to transport them away from ponderous questions. This list isn't for them. This list is for readers who like heavy books and heavier thoughts, for readers who gravitate to fresh literary challenges. Selecting these books is like choosing a spouse: There are issues to work through, but ideally it's worth the effort in the end. Take care: It may take longer to read these books than some relationships last. These books are worth that extra effort.

Bakker, R. Scott
The Darkness that Comes Before. <u>The Prince of Nothing</u>. 2003. Overlook, ISBN: 1585676772, 608p.
    When most writers engage in world-building, they really just sketch a country or two. Not Bakker. He stuffs a brutal world on the verge of war with a full complement of countries, religions, languages, history, and philosophy. It's hard to take in, but the effort is justified. <u>The Prince of Nothing</u> is brainy but raw, a big, bustling trilogy for adults.

Borges, Jorge Luis
Ficciones. 1956. Everyman's Library, ISBN: 0679422994, 192p. (hbk.)
    "Wait," you say, "how can 192 pages of short stories make a list of epic challenges?" Because the Argentinean gets inside your head if you let him and

will keep stretching your brain for the rest of your life. Borges had a major influence on postmodernism, magic realism, and metafiction. In his hands, fantasy is not an escape but the lifeblood of philosophy.

Coe, David B.
Seeds of Betrayal. <u>**The Winds of the Forelands**</u>. 2003. Tor, ISBN: 081258998X, 608p.

If you prefer intricate politics, this may be your series. In this follow-up to *Rules of Ascension,* a series of assassinations complicates matters for those trying to prevent civil war. Coe keeps many plots and characters moving without the loss of momentum that sinks many multistrand fantasies. To date, two more books in the series have followed.

Martin, George R. R.
A Feast for Crows. <u>**A Song of Ice and Fire**</u>. 2005. Bantam Spectra, ISBN: 055358202X, 1104p.

Feast takes 70 pages (!) to list the characters. Martin admits it's getting hard to write his series. This fourth book took five years and was so long he split it in two, pushing the projected series to at least seven books. If each character remains this riveting, readers will be happy if the series never ends. Bring on *A Dance of Dragons*!

Wolfe, Gene
⇨ *Shadow & Claw.* <u>**Book of the New Sun**</u>. 1980. Orb, ISBN: 0312890176, 416p. `AW`.

Wolfe requires (and justifies) rereading. In <u>New Sun</u>, a casual reader will catch that Severian begins as an assistant torturer and becomes Autarch of all Urth. It takes additional readings to understand the events that unfold, to figure out that Severian is not a trustworthy narrator (despite his photographic memory), and to identify clues that show Urth is far-future Earth. I've given you some hints to get started; enjoy the puzzle!

Wright, John C.
The Last Guardians of Everness. <u>**Everness series**</u>. 2004. Tor, ISBN: 0812579879, 336p.

Wright's complexity comes not from many plot lines but from the mélange of mythology he weaves into a labyrinthine dreamland. Only four characters—a husband and wife and a father and son, all imperfect—stand against the forces of the Dark. In Wright's funny, fast-paced, but philosophical duology, fighting for the Light has its own challenges.

Zelazny, Roger
The Lord of Light. 1967. Eos, ISBN: 0060567236, 304p.

In Zelazny's science fantasy, Hindu gods rule a distant planet. When one leads a revolt, it becomes clear that the "gods" are Earth colonists who extend their lives and subjugate the natives with technology. Those who know Eastern philosophy will find many allusions, particularly that renegade Sam's tale is an allegory for the story of Buddha.

Frothy Fun: Lighter-than-Air, Easy-Reading Fantasy

Some may think that light fantasy is as easy to create as it is to read. But in practice it's like shaving with a two-handed sword: smoothness and butchery are separated by only a slip of the wrist. In an era of big, bloated epics and writers determined to test the limits of reader intelligence and the strength of paperback bindings, special appreciation is due to writers who keep up the tradition of fantasy with a light touch.

Asprin, Robert
Another Fine Myth/Myth Conceptions. <u>Myth series</u>. 1978–1980. Ace, ISBN: 044100931X, 400p.

Apprentice magician Skeeve falls under the tutelage of demon Aahz in the first two <u>Myth</u> books. Aahz can't wield power but can teach Skeeve. His ambition gets the two in trouble, but friendship wins the day in upbeat stories full of jokes and funny characters.

Brust, Steven
The Phoenix Guards. <u>Khaavren Romances</u>. 1991. Tor, ISBN: 0812506898, 512p.

Modeling his writing after the swashbuckling of Sabatini and Dumas, Brust's specialty is snappy dialogue. His humor comes from the exuberance of his leads, four swordsmen who aspire to become Imperial Guards, and his pompous narrator Paarfi, who is like a friend who talks too much but is so entertaining that you like him anyway.

Green, Simon R.
Drinking Midnight Wine. 2001. Roc, ISBN: 0451459350, 352p.

Green throws a boisterous party of a fantasy in this tale of a shy bookseller who follows a beautiful woman into a fantasy world. She doesn't want wimpy Toby but does tell him that he is a "focal point" in a battle against the evil Serpent in the Sun. Populated by a host of characters, charmingly updated from mythical roots, this is cute, zippy fun.

Huff, Tanya
⇨ *Summon the Keeper*. <u>Keeper's Chronicles</u>. 1998. DAW, ISBN: 0886777844, 336p.

In a blend of Buffy the Vampire Slayer, cozy mysteries, and chick lit, Claire, a Keeper, defends the universe from evil. She's summoned to a bed and breakfast to close a hole to Hell. The inn comes with a hunky caretaker, a randy ghost, and an evil counterpart in room 6. Claire's sarcastic cat Austin trades quips with his owner in a sexy, silly fantasy.

Swendson, Shanna
Enchanted, Inc. 2005. Ballantine, ISBN: 0345481259, 320p.
When fantasy blends with other genres, the results are often light fun. In this tale, a small-town girl wants to make it in New York City. Wholesome, magically immune Katie is hired by Magic, Spells, and Illusions, Inc. to update their image and combat dark enemies. Mayhem and fun ensue in a tale as sweet and finespun as cotton candy.

Watt-Evans, Lawrence
With a Single Spell. Ethshar series. 1987. Wildside, ISBN: 1587152851, 206p.
In this entry in the dependably amusing Ethshar series, smooth-talking Tobas convinces a wizard to take him on as an apprentice. Unfortunately, the wizard dies after teaching him just one spell. Left homeless, Tobas wanders the world in a series of adventures, hoping that quick wits and the magical ability to start fires can keep him out of trouble.

Weis, Margaret, and Hickman, Tracy
The Dragons of Autumn Twilight. Dragonlance Chronicles. 1984. Wizards of the Coast, ISBN: 0786915749, 448p.
Most books of this ilk are quick reading but forgettable, but occasionally, as in this opener to the Chronicles, the results are enthralling. A description of the plot would sound like any other company-of-heroes-on-a-quest story, but the results are transcendent. Three books in this series and many related series follow.

Repartee Animals: Dialogue-Driven Fantasy

"Beelzebub's bumbling uncle! What's hard about believable dialogue?" she queried viciously.

"Well, there are all kinds of dangers that a writer can fall into like a Malaysian tiger trap with sharpened bamboo stakes on the bottom," he riposted.

"I d'na ken yerrrr meaning, laddie." She lapsed into a thick Scottish burr under stress.

"You know, naughty minx: shizzle like inappropriate slang, or flowery expressions that don't ring as true as the bells of St. Mary's. And there's a risk of recording formal sentences when denizens of the real world converse in a patois of verbal shorthand," he sermonized.

"But I luv fantasy dialogue. Fast reading. Character developing. FUNNY!" she barked.

"Oh I know what you like," he leered, raising one eyebrow into a triumphal arch. "Daddy's got some sugar for you."

Anthony, Piers
Ogre, Ogre. <u>Xanth</u>. 1982. Del Rey, ISBN: 0345354923, 320p.

> <u>Xanth</u> has been a hit through 30 books and 30 years, thanks partly to screwball banter between oddly matched characters. Sarcasm, sass, and double entendre make readers feel they've met clever new friends. Try this entry, in which Smash, a half ogre who speaks in rhyme, loses witty exchanges with Tandy the nymph and six other damsels "in distress."

Baker, Kage
The Anvil of the World. 2003. ISBN: 0765349078, 352p.

> Baker breaks from her time-travel series for this rollicking fantasy about an ex-assassin who leads a caravan of eccentrics over waste and water. A childish demon, a matronly chef, and a boatload of other charming weirdoes and dim bulbs natter on hilariously through many adventures. Don't miss the duel of Fatally Verbal Abuse.

Beagle, Peter S.
A Fine and Private Place. 1960. Tachyon, ISBN: 1892391465, 296p.

> Beagle's first novel tells the story of Mr. Rebeck, who enters a cemetery and stays for 18 years. He visits graves, particularly of the newly dead, whose ghosts stay and converse with him at length until they forget life and move on. This is a philosophical book, but the best bits come from a wisecracking raven with more to say than "Nevermore."

Brust, Steven
Five Hundred Years After. <u>Phoenix Guards</u>. 1994. Tor, ISBN: 0812515226, 576p.

> This is the second of Brust's Three-Musketeers-channeling <u>Phoenix Guard</u> adventures. Khaavren, Aerich, Tazendra, and Pel are even quicker with their tongues than they are with their swords. Picture the jaunty arrogance of Errol Flynn or Cary Grant and you'll have the right idea. Brust obviously has a great deal of fun writing these novels.

Eddings, David
The Belgariad, Vol. 1. 1982. Del Rey, ISBN: 0345456327, 656p.

> In <u>The Belgariad</u>, young Garion plays straight boy for the verbal antics of crotchety Aunt Pol, wily and wolfish grandfather Belgarath, nimble-tongued "merchant" Silk, and gruff Barak. Oh sure, there's a plot and action and other distractions, but the best thing about this series is interplay between characters. This omnibus contains the first three novels.

Hamilton, Laurell K.
The Lunatic Café. __Anita Blake, Vampire Hunter__. 1996. Jove, ISBN: 051513452X, 384p.

> The cadre of supporting players surrounding tough, sexy Anita creates the perfect atmosphere for zippy dialogue in the middle books of Hamilton's series. This entry features Anita's love triangle with Richard, a werewolf in a battle to lead his pack, and Jean-Claude, a vampire whose interest earns Anita enmity from jealous Gretchen.

Elevated Muses: High-Tone, Genteel Fantasy

Readers either love or hate the courtly, high-tone, archaic patterns of genteel speech. The current fashion is a backlash against this style in fantasy; many authors deliberately put modern words in their characters' mouths, even in medieval settings. But when it's done well, without calling attention to itself, mannered speech helps create an atmosphere of years gone by. Here are novels, past and present, that use genteel language to pull the reader into the fantastic.

Carey, Jacqueline
Kushiel's Chosen. __Kushiel series__. 2002. Tor, ISBN: 0765345048, 704p.

> Courtly manners in Terre d'Ange are so impeccable that one almost forgets that heroine Phèdre is a courtesan and *anguisette* (i.e., a prostitute and a masochist). Emphasis here is on epic fantasy first, kinky eroticism second, so it's appropriate that Carey uses gentility to soften X-rated content to a soft-focus R. This is the middle book of the trilogy.

Croggon, Alison
The Naming. __Pellinor series__. 2001. Candlewick, ISBN: 0763631620, 528p. **YA**.

> Croggon is a poet as well as a young-adult author. That background shows in the lyricism of this quartet opener. Maerad, an orphan, becomes the student of a bard named Cadvan, who teaches her both his magical craft and her own heritage. The genteel language is graceful enough to remind one of Tolkien, as do the invented languages and history.

Dickinson, John
The Cup of the World. 2004. Laurel Leaf, ISBN: 0553494899, 432p. **YA**.

> Phaedra has dreamed of a mysterious knight since childhood. When he finally appears in real life, she marries him, spurning the noble suitors her family prefers. It turns out that her new husband is in rebellion against the King, and carries some other secrets as well. Dickinson's subtle use of medieval language gives this work real depth.

Dunsany, Lord
The King of Elfland's Daughter. 1924. Del Rey, ISBN: 034543191X, 256p.

Dunsany helped create the fantasy genre. His rich, poetic language may take some getting used to for modern readers, but once you've acclimated, the language makes it easy to fall under the enchantment of fantasy. In particular, his descriptions of light and landscapes prove that sometimes a few words can be worth a thousand pictures.

Eddison, E. R.
The Worm Ouroboros. 1922. Dover, ISBN: 0486447405, 464p.

Here's a classic from the misty age of Fantasy Before Tolkien. Eddison's fervent heroic prose will either send you into Elizabethan ecstasy or make you long for less flowery language. If you feel silly climbing this majestic mountain of purple prose, let yourself go. Be unabashedly romantic for a few hours and enjoy a beautiful bit of fantasy's past.

Kay, Guy Gavriel
A Song for Arbonne. 1992. Roc, ISBN: 0451458974, 512p.

The troubadours of medieval Provence inspired the tale of Arbonne, a matriarchal culture steeped in artistry. When Kay depicts it, his language has a fitting musicality. In other scenes, he switches to the perspective of militaristic northerners in Gorhaut, changing tense and style subtly, creating a different mood entirely. Masterful.

⇨ Tolkien, J. R. R.
The Return of the King. <u>The Lord of the Rings</u>. 1955. Houghton Mifflin, ISBN: 0618002243, 464p.

As Middle Earth darkens, as brave deeds reach their peak and sacrifices are made, Tolkien's glorious language reaches a grandiloquent peak. No other writer conveys such a sense of war's cost, even for the victorious. Tolkien considered himself a linguistics professor first and foremost; his love of language shows in every sentence.

Wrede, Patricia C., and Stevermer, Caroline
Sorcery and Cecelia. <u>Cecelia and Kate</u>. 1988. Magic Carpet, ISBN: 015205300X, 336p.

Austen fans love this Regency fantasy. Sharing witty, passionate letters, two cousins exchange tales of Kate's first London social season and Cecelia's country summer. Both young women find beaux, participate in mysterious events, nose into other's affairs, and dabble in magic, but each has a distinct voice. Two sequels follow.

Wurts, Janny
To Ride Hell's Chasm. 2002. Meisha Merlin, ISBN: 159222024X, 672p.

Some like Wurts's formal language, others find it tedious. This one-volume work is a good place to test how you feel. Princess Anja disappears on the day of her betrothal, and Mykkael, a mercenary, is sent to find and protect her. To do so, he must face demons loose in the kingdom and demons of his past, culminating with a ride into Hell's Chasm.

The Slangs and Argots of Misfortune: Gritty, Low-Tone Fantasy

Fans of low fantasy want violence to be messy. They want cynical characters who swear and screw up and get dirt on their faces. These readers can't empathize with characters who talk and behave like biblical prophets. This gritty style has existed since the days of pulp magazines but has become more prevalent in recent years. Hide these books from the optimistic and tenderhearted. So ugly they're pretty, here are some books to squat down in the mud and try.

Cook, Glen
The Tyranny of the Night. <u>Instrumentalities of the Night</u>. 2005. Tor, ISBN: 076534596X, 512p.

Cook was one of the first fantasists to go grubby with his <u>Black Company</u> series. He's back, with a new series about a world in which corrupt religion and dark magic collide and common folk fret more about an impending ice age. Cook introduces a slew of frail and angry characters trying to keep their heads above the rising tide of danger.

Graham, Ian
Monument. 2002. Ace, ISBN: 0441011357, 384p.

When a kind priest saves him from another beating, drunken Ballas shows his gratitude by robbing him and running away. The jewels he steals have magical powers that he accidentally unlocks. Chased by the corrupt church and its wardens, he lies, cheats, and kills his way forward, resisting an impressive number of chances to do the right thing.

Keck, David
In the Eye of Heaven. 2006. Tor, ISBN: 0765351692, 464p.

Squire Durand is set to inherit his village because its overlord has lost his son. When the son suddenly returns, Durand must go on the run. He's reduced to the role of sell-sword, struggling among dirty road folk and fighting in bloody tourneys for food to stay alive. With help from a tourney knight named Lamoric, Durand eventually makes a heroic turn.

Kemp, Paul S.
Twilight Falling. <u>Erevis Cale</u>. 2003. Wizards of the Coast, ISBN: 0786929987, 320p.

Every so often, an exciting book rises from the morass of guilty pleasure called Forgotten Realms. Kemp's trilogy about a contemplative assassin whose master has died is a dark gem. With two companions he doesn't trust, Cale is on the run from shape-changers. He doesn't know what they want, but it's obvious they don't wish him well.

Lynch, Scott
The Lies of Locke Lamora. <u>The Gentleman Bastards</u>. 2006. Bantam Spectra, ISBN: 055358894X, 672p.

First of a seven-part series, this superb debut is a gritty fantasy about a resourceful young gang leader. In this book about gang wars, characters speak and act like the street thugs they are. Locke and his friends pull off several clever capers but discover that they may have unintentionally become the tools of the Grey King, a new force in Camorra.

Micklem, Sarah
⇨ *Firethorn.* 2004. Bantam Spectra, ISBN: 055338340X, 400p.

Micklem shows the dark side of falling in love with a knight. Firethorn, a girl of rugged origins, is a minor conjuror and healer. She discovers too late that she is Sire Galan's "sheath," at risk of being shared by every man in his command. She struggles to stay in Galan's favor and survive a harsh, bloody war camp. The leads are drawn fantastically.

Stemple, Adam
Singer of Souls. 2005. Tor, ISBN: 0765350270, 240p.

We've seen urban fantasy about street musicians, but the streets are especially mean in this tale of sex, drugs, and rock and roll. Busker Doc, a recovering junkie, can't resist a vial left by a young woman, but this isn't heroin. Doc's eyes open to the fey world, where he is caught between two warring factions: the People of Peace and the Good Neighbors.

Details of Sound and Fury: High-Description Fantasy Signifies Everything

High description is a double-edged sword. Used well, it enhances the believability of imaginary worlds, enriching characters and enthralling readers. But if used poorly, it slows the progress of a novel to a crawl. If you prefer a lean, mean style, even good descriptive fantasy probably isn't for you. But if you were the kid who wished for more colors in your Crayola box, if you enjoy sensory details, then here are works you can see, smell, taste, and feel.

Dart-Thornton, Cecelia
The Lady of the Sorrows. <u>Bitterbynde trilogy</u>. 2002. Aspect, ISBN: 0446611344, 576p.

As this second book opens, Imrhien is healing, but her memory can be mended only by exposure to the world. In disguise, she goes to court, and a sumptuous court it is. Dart-Thornton's eye for scenery, clothing, and lavish feasts makes her Erith more vivid than most medieval worlds. The puzzle deepens as Imrhien becomes the target of evildoers.

Hobb, Robin
Golden Fool. <u>Tawny Man trilogy</u>. 2002. Bantam Spectra, ISBN: 0553582453, 736p.

Fitz returns in disguise to serve as skill-master for Prince Dutiful in this middle book. In Hobb's thick trilogies, action is infrequent, but tension is built through descriptions of daily castle life, including minor interactions that develop her characters better than most. Some find Hobb's pace glacial, but most enjoy the tease of her slow build.

McKillip, Patricia A.
Ombria in Shadow. 2002. Ace, ISBN: 0441010164, 304p. **AW**.

Atmosphere is everything in Ombria, a haunting city that sits atop layers of its own past (becoming an extended metaphor for history). The creepy city above and below ground casts its shadow on every detail as a dead prince's mistress, his artistic bastard nephew, and a sorceress's assistant each work to end an evil witch's regency for the boy prince.

Miéville, China
The Scar. <u>Bas-Lag</u>. 2001. Del Rey, ISBN: 0345460014, 608p. **AW**.

Although his people and creatures are intriguing, Miéville's most vivid characters are his settings, alive with details of rotting baroque splendor. It's easy to imagine yourself traveling in <u>Bas-Lag</u>, your gaze careening between the many attention-grabbing details. In *The Scar,* the setting is an enormous flotilla city made from lashed-together ships.

Pinto, Ricardo
The Chosen. <u>Stone Dance of the Chameleon</u>. 1998. Tor, ISBN: 081258435X, 640p.

After a succession crisis, Carnelian's family returns from exile to Osra-kum, the capital. As they progress toward the geographic and political center of their ritual-bound society (think medieval China or Japan), descriptions of increasingly ornate masks, elaborate metal robes, monstrous shoes, and barbaric protocol rites create a sense of power and impending danger.

Snyder, Midori
Hannah's Garden. 2002. Puffin, ISBN: 0142401358, 256p.

Cassie and her immature mother must put disagreements aside when they learn Grandpa Daniel is in the hospital. Returning to the family farm, they find two faerie factions battling for great-grandmother Hannah's magic garden, trashing the farm in the process. Charming descriptions of farm and garden bring nature magic to life in this family drama.

Williams, Tad
⇨ *The Stone of Farewell.* <u>Memory, Sorrow, and Thorn</u>. 1990. DAW, ISBN: 0886774802, 768p.

In the series' second book, Simon quests for Thorn, the sword King Josua needs to fight his corrupt brother. Critics contend that Williams's books could cover the plot in half the length, but that would ruin his style. He spends pages bringing nuances of behavior to life or detailing the landscape, creating the depth that many readers crave.

It's All about Me: Fantasy in the First Person

For those weaned on Tolkien and other epics that scatter plot lines across an enormous landscape, first-person point of view can be a bit of a shock. Because plot is limited to the scope of the narrator's experience, novels in this format are more intimate. How much you like a book may depend on your empathy for the narrator. This list is your fantasy fitting room. Try on these novels. If you don't like a narrator, shed their skin and try another until you find a perfect fit.

Butcher, Jim
Grave Peril. <u>Dresden Files</u>. 2001. Roc, ISBN: 0451458443, 378p.

The narration of wizard detective Harry Dresden echoes noir classics like Chandler or Hammett, placing them in a fantasy realm. And it's fun to walk in Harry's shoes. He has a fascinating job, with quirky friends and enemies. He's not perfect, but he gets the job done. In this third entry, violent ghosts stalk Harry and his friends.

Gardner, John
Grendel. 1971. Vintage, ISBN: 0679723100, 192p.

Retelling *Beowulf* from the monster's viewpoint, Gardner makes us feel for the creature. Grendel, a mama's boy, attempts to contact Hrothgar and his Danes but is rejected. Full of self-hatred, his internal dialogue leaps from philosophy to poetry to a nihilistic rage that drives him to kill. Whether you love this, hate it, or get lost, you won't forget it soon.

Hobb, Robin
⇨ *Shaman's Crossing.* <u>Soldier Son</u>. 2005. Eos, ISBN: 0060757620, 592p.

Hobb delights in burying her narrators up to the neck in troubles but gives them enough determination to dig themselves out. This new trilogy tackles big issues: class, race, and ecology. Her narrator is Nevare, a noble sent to officer's school. He's never been one to question, but mystical experiences open his eyes to injustice against himself and others.

Jones, Diana Wynne
Homeward Bounders. 1981. HarperTrophy, ISBN: 0064473538, 272p. YA.
  In this Jones classic, it's just as you suspected in your most paranoid mood: *They* are playing a game, and we are the pieces. When 12-year-old narrator Jamie finds out, he's thrown out of bounds into other worlds and different cosmic games. It's a long way home—can Jamie get back?

Lee, Tanith
Wolf Tower. <u>Claidi Journals</u>. 1998. Puffin, ISBN: 0142300306, 240p.
  Claidi, a teen, yearns to escape her harsh homeland. When an imprisoned stranger suggests that sanctuary exists, and he can take her there, Claidi falls for him and breaks him out of prison. In this series opener, Lee exploits the mystery of the first person by making the reader figure out, with Claidi, who is worthy of her trust and who is not.

Roberson, Jennifer
<u>*The Novels of Tiger and Del, Vol. 1*</u>. 1986–1988. DAW, ISBN: 0756403197, 640p.
  This omnibus of *Sword-Dancer* and *Sword-Singer* combines two strong volumes in the he-said, she-said series about male and female sword-dancers from different lands. Tiger and Del move from antagonism to grudging respect, partnership, and then love, giving two different interpretations of the same events as Roberson alternates between narrators.

Wolfe, Gene
Latro in the Mist. <u>Soldier of the Mist</u>. 1986–1989. Orb, ISBN: 0765302942, 640p. AW.
  Wolfe is the jester of first-person fantasy, using limited point of view to trick readers. In this omnibus, a Roman soldier's head wound limits his short-term memory to 12 hours. He keeps journals to remind him of key facts as he sojourns through Greece. Watch Latro's companions; some take advantage of him, reintroducing themselves with new names. In 2006, a new book, *Soldier of Sidon,* returned to Latro's story.

When Groan Men Scry: Puns as a Fantasy Tradition

Mundane folk may warn you, if called by a *Xanth*-er don't anther, but fantasy readers are required to like puns. It's in the contract. If puns make your head ache, too bad. Take two Asprin and read them. You're supposed to groan, but enjoy the pain. Apropos of Nothing, the humor of puns has been Callahan-ded down through generations of fantasy writers. Don't make a Myth-take: Piers the pompousness of epic trilogies. Pratchett your laughs up a notch with these books.

Anthony, Piers
A Spell for Chameleon. <u>Xanth</u>. 1977. Del Rey, ISBN: 0345347536, 352p.
> <u>Xanth</u> is a litmus test for how much you really like puns. Read the series in a hospital, where groans won't be out of the ordinary and doctors are standing by if you overdose. Pun-ishment begins with this first book. If you feel compelled to participate (and what punster doesn't?), Anthony includes hundreds of reader-suggested puns in the later books.

Asprin, Robert
Myth Directions/Hit or Myth. <u>Myth series</u>. 1982–1983. Ace, ISBN: 0441009433, 336p.
> Following *Another Fine Myth* and *Myth Conceptions,* this omnibus contains the third and fourth entries in the ultralight series about Skeeve the magical apprentice and his demon friend Aahz.

David, Peter
The Woad to Wuin. <u>Apropos of Nothing</u>. 2002. Pocket Star, ISBN: 0743448324, 512p.
> David pokes fun at fantasy conventions in his bawdy, darkly humorous, antiheroic series. This second book finds Apropos running Bugger Hall, a bar. When he steals a gem called the Eye of the Beholder, the enchanted gem transports him to the Tragic Waste where, painted in blue woad (think *Braveheart*), he leads a band of ruthless warriors.

Fforde, Jasper
The Big Over Easy. <u>Nursery Crimes</u>. 2005. Penguin, ISBN: 0143037234, 400p.
> The cases of Inspector Jack Spratt and Sgt. Mary Mary of the Nursery Crimes Division involve wordplay and the parody of folktales and mystery fiction. In this first entry, they crack the case of the downfall of Humpty Dumpty, a bad egg with many enemies. Up next is *The Fourth Bear.*

Noon, Jeff
Automated Alice. 1996. Black Swan, ISBN: 0552999059, 256p.
> Noon places Lewis Carroll's Alice in a dark, edgy future. She goes through a grandfather clock to an alternate Manchester, England of 1998, where she becomes the suspect in a murder. But forget the plot, read this for Noon's wordplay and trippy sensibilities.

Pratchett, Terry
Soul Music. <u>Discworld, Death series</u>. 1994. HarperTorch, ISBN: 0061054895, 384p.
> Pratchett doesn't use as many "punes" as many people think, but he does have plenty of wordplay and comic allusions. *Soul Music,* about "music with rocks in," has the most puns, particularly of band names. To see just how many of Pratchett's allusions you're not catching, look up the "Annotated Pratchett File" on the Internet some time.

Robinson, Spider
The Callahan Chronicals. 1977–1986. Tor, ISBN: 0812539370, 416p.

The perfect bar, Callahan's is speculative fiction's answer to _Cheers_. Although classified as science fiction, it's low on science and will appeal to fantasy fans. The specialties of the house are sympathy for the downfallen and long, shaggy dog stories ending in truly egregious puns. This omnibus collects stories from the first three books in the series.

Rogers, Mark E.
Samurai Cat Goes to Hell. **Samurai Cat**. 1998. Tor, ISBN: 0312866429, 320p.

Gory martial arts battles, talking cats, and endless gags (interpret _gags_ as you wish) are hallmarks of Rogers's series about Samurai Miaowara Tomo-kato. This sixth installment closes the series, sending him, appropriately, to hell to fight all of his former foes.

Reading Aloud Allowed

Fantasy fiction is wonderful for those who like to read aloud. To find a perfect bedtime story, start with a book that appeals to all ages: readers and listeners alike. Make sure it's full of great characters and dialogue so you can try all your funny voices. Pick a book with a breathtaking plot loaded with exciting action scenes, preferably with great cliff-hangers that will leave listeners longing for the arrival of tomorrow night. Here are some read-alouds that are guaranteed to please.

Black, Holly, and DiTerlizzi, Tony (illus.)
The Field Guide. **Spiderwick Chronicles**. 2003. Simon & Schuster, ISBN: 0689859368, 128p. (hbk.) YA.

With three endangered siblings and warnings to stop reading, the Chronicles resemble another read-aloud winner, Lemony Snicket's Series of Unfortunate Events. But Black's writing is less satirical, and mom is around for Jared, Simon, and Mallory. In this opener, they move to a spooky house, where Jared finds a handwritten book he can't put down.

Brust, Steven
The Book of Taltos. **Vlad Taltos series**. 1988–1990. Ace, ISBN: 0441008941, 400p.

Anything by Brust is a good read-aloud choice, but save it for your significant other: This is too rough for little ones. Try this two-book omnibus from the Vlad Taltos series. Full of witty banter and other irreverence, the series chronicles the life of a cynical assassin and minor mobster living on a world ruled by powerful magic wielders.

Dahl, Roald
Charlie and the Chocolate Factory. 1964. Puffin, ISBN: 0141301155, 176p. YA.
The Best of Roald Dahl. 1983. Vintage, ISBN: 0679729917, 528p.

Roald Dahl offers pleasures for a lifetime. Kids can start with the classic *Charlie,* in which a reader can unleash the inner Wonka during madcap adventures in the chocolate factory (just saying "Oompa Loompa" or "Augustus Gloop" is enough fun for me). Adults should sample his bizarre, wryly humorous, surprising, and often-grotesque short stories.

Funke, Cornelia
Inkheart. 2003. Scholastic, ISBN: 0439709105, 560p. YA.

In *Inkheart,* a father and daughter can read characters out of books and into the real world (and vice versa). That's something for rowdy little ones to think about as you read them to sleep. Make sure they know that you have the same power and that if they interrupt, you can't make any guarantees about where they will end up. Followed by *Inkspell.*

Juster, Norton
The Phantom Tollbooth. 1961. Yearling, ISBN: 0394820371, 272p. YA.

The language of Juster's classic rolls off your tongue as bored Milo visits with the Whether Man, Tock, the Humbug, Faintly Macabre, and the Princesses Rhyme and Reason. Just don't get stuck in the Doldrums or the Mountains of Ignorance.

Moers, Walter
The 13 1/2 Lives of Captain Bluebear. 2005. Overlook, ISBN: 1585678449, 704p.

Adults catch laughs that children miss in this story of a blue bear found afloat on the sea and raised by Minipirates. He swashes, buckles, and embellishes his way through screwball satirical adventures in the land of Zamonia. Moers's line drawings enhance the whimsy and give the reader something to show the listening audience.

Pratchett, Terry
Thud! Discworld, The Watch. 2005. HarperTorch, ISBN: 0060815310, 416p.
Where's My Cow? HarperCollins, ISBN: 0060872675, 32p. (hbk.)

The main plot of *Thud!* concerns the Watch's attempts to integrate a vampire while preventing a repeat of the Koom Valley battle between trolls and dwarves. The read-aloud highlight will be your re-creation of Sam Vimes's nightly read to his son, Sam Jr. For even more fun, obtain a copy of the very book he reads, *Where's My Cow?*

Wrede, Patricia C.
Searching for Dragons. Enchanted Forest Chronicles. 1991. Magic Carpet, ISBN: 0152045651, 272p. YA.

In *Dealing with Dragons,* tomboy Princess Cimorene sacrifices herself to a dragon to avoid a boring life of etiquette. In the follow-up, she searches with

King Mendenbar for Kazul, her missing King of Dragons. Wizard Telemain's long-winded jargon will twist a reader's tongue to funny results. This four-book series turns fantasy clichés inside out.

Slow Build to a Big Finish: Fantasy for 4:00 A.M. Finales

If you've read fantasy for a while, you'll know that in the 1990s the average book got heavier. Popular epic sagas drove a trend that still continues. Readers who enjoy such long books prefer a style that slowly introduces characters and subplots until critical mass is reached and the plot lines come together. If you regularly find yourself slowly pushing through pages before a dash through three hundred pages in a day or two to reach the big finish, this category is for you.

Carey, Jacqueline
⇨ *Kushiel's Dart*. **Kushiel trilogy**. 2001. Tor, ISBN: 0765342987, 816p.
   This book starts slowly, as the politics and mythos of Terre d'Ange are introduced and the character of Phèdre, a courtesan, is developed. But Carey sets the stage well: The preliminaries leave you deeply invested. Once the characters take to the road, the plot builds furiously to a powerful finish that leaves you breathless and emotionally moved.

Clemens, James
Shadowfall. **Godslayer series**. 2005. Roc, ISBN: 0451459946, 480p. (hbk.)
   Much of Clemens's series starter is wrapped in mystery as a disgraced knight works to discover who is behind the goddess murder of which he is accused. Backstories of many characters, the history of Myrillia, and the answer to the mystery play out slowly until a final flurry of action sends you *Shadow-fall*ing out of your seat.

Douglass, Sara
Enchanter. **The Wayfarer Redemption series**. 1996. Tor, ISBN: 0765341964, 688p.
   Middle books are prone to slow-burning buildup. Consider *Enchanter,* in which the reader must become reacquainted with characters from *Wayfarer Redemption,* then take in new developments that send this book twisting in its own direction. Douglass's complex romantic relationships and exciting finish avoid the trap of some middle books, in which every subplot remains unresolved and the book only sets the stage for the final volume.

Jordan, Robert
The Dragon Reborn. **The Wheel of Time**. 1991. Tor, ISBN: 0812513711, 704p.
   Jordan's books epitomize the slow build. The third volume of *Wheel* is typical: A dozen characters scatter across the world making small discoveries,

feeling great angst, and expanding their skills. Just when you think there aren't enough pages left to reach resolution, they gather at the Stone of Tear and have an exciting showdown with various baddies. Early in his series, Jordan still pulls plot lines together for an exciting finish.

West, Michelle
Sea of Sorrows. <u>Sun Sword series</u>. 2001. DAW, ISBN: 0886779782, 832p.

As it came out, readers compared West's series to <u>Wheel of Time</u>. It sprawled and spread farther with each book. West is ultimately more successful at pulling it all together. After three books of deliberate story building, West gets over the hump in this fourth volume. The momentum carries her to a strong finish in six books. It's worth the work. Start with *The Broken Crown* or the prequels, *Hunter's Oath* and *Hunter's Death.*

Wurts, Janny
The Curse of the Mistwraith. <u>Wars of Light and Shadow</u>. 1993. HarperCollins, ISBN: 0586210695, 841p.

In this tale of half brothers who grow up in very different ways, intricate description combines with complex characters to make a dense, heavy start. But as the story rises to the confrontation with the title wraith, the pace accelerates. Wurts finishes with great twists that set up the rest of the *Wars of Light and Shadow* series.

Fast-Paced, Can't-Put-'Em-Down Fantasies

Tired of books that take weeks to read? Sick of character lists that make *War and Peace* look like an intimate get-together? Unable to reach the summit of another Himalayan story arc? Never fear, there are plenty of fantasy frontrunners that dash out of the gate and sprint all the way to the finish. Quickreading classics wait to be rediscovered. Though they aren't necessarily short, these books will go by quickly.

Butcher, Jim
⇨ *Storm Front.* <u>Dresden Files</u>. 2000. Roc, ISBN: 0451457811, 352p.

Start with a gumshoe wizard with a strong code of justice but a stronger tendency to screw up. Pit him against powerful supernatural crooks on the mean streets of Chicago. Finish every book with fast-flying action. That's the essence of the <u>Dresden Files</u>, which *Storm Front* launches.

De Lint, Charles
Jack of Kinrowan. 1990. Tor, ISBN: 0312869592, 384p.

A young woman discovers her role (as the Jack of the title) in a fantasy world that coexists with our own. Some of de Lint's novels are more complex, featuring large casts of characters. This compilation of two short novels is quick and quirky: a delightful introduction to his basic approach to fantasy.

Freeman, Lorna
Covenants. **Borderlands**. 2004. Roc, ISBN: 0451459806, 560p.

It could be Rabbit, the likable soldier narrator, or the short chapters. Perhaps it's the interesting parade of secondary characters or refreshing freedom from soul-wrenching, labored introspection. However she did it, Freeman crafted a fast-reading gem in this first novel about an attempt to stop a border war between humans and the magical Faena.

Golden, Christopher
The Myth Hunters. **The Veil**. 2006. Bantam Spectra, ISBN: 0553383264, 384p.

Golden is becoming a favorite of readers who like fast-paced, pulpy tales. Both his Menagerie series (beginning with *The Nimble Man*) and this first course make clever use of pastiche, combining familiar characters from other sources. Here, a nervous groom travels into the Borderlands to stop a hunter of mythic beings (his guide is Jack Frost). Meanwhile, the Sandman crosses into our reality and begins a killing spree of his own.

Keyes, Greg
The Charnel Prince. **Kingdoms of Thorn and Bone**. 2004. Del Rey, ISBN: 0345440714, 512p.

Like its predecessor *The Briar King,* this book never lags, keeping a fast pace from start to finish. With action in every chapter, your attention isn't likely to flag either. It's a good sign for an epic when readers can't decide which of the host of characters they like to read about the most.

Lisle, Holly
Memory of Fire. **World Gates trilogy**. 2002. Eos, ISBN: 038081837X, 384p.

Two women follow different paths—Lauren through a mirror and Molly as a kidnap victim—from little Cat Creek, North Carolina, to a world of magic. They face challenges that have strong repercussions for life on our world. Lisle gets the pacing just right in a series start that motors along.

Salvatore, R. A.
Icewind Dale Trilogy. 1988–1990. Wizards of the Coast, ISBN: 078691811X, 1056p.

Reading Salvatore may result in lost brain cells, but you won't feel pain as dark elf Drizzt Do'Urden and company hack and slash through enough nasty creatures to fill a big ugly zoo. Yes, the characters survive too many impossible situations; yes, they speak in one-liners; yes, it's immature and clichéd; and yes, you'll have fun reading it.

Never-Ending Stories: Lots of Pages but Worth the Weight

All epic fantasy is not created equal. Some big books have enough padding to fill all the shoulder pads of the 1980s and cover Marlon Brando in *Last Tango in Paris,* with plenty of confetti left over for the celebration when you finish the book (or quit reading it). But others have good stuff on every page, leaving the reader wishing for more after hundreds of pages. Here, in order by size, are some big, beautiful fantasies that prove that fat is where it's at.

Cherryh, C. J.
  A Fortress in the Eye of Time. <u>Fortress series</u>. 1995. Eos, ISBN: 0061056898, 784p.
    Tristen is a shaping, an innocent in an adult body who was created by a dying wizard trying to fight the forces of evil. In this first of four <u>Fortress</u> novels, Tristen tries to understand his world even as he becomes involved in political intrigues. Strong characterization and a gift for imagery make Cherryh a writer to treasure.

Jones, J. V.
  A Cavern of Black Ice. <u>Sword of Shadows</u>. 1999. Tor, ISBN: 076534551X, 792p.
    This trilogy starter is about the struggle of northern hunters, particularly a young hunter with a magical gift and a city girl who has fled her father, to maintain autonomy in the face of growing evil. With fewer characters than most long fantasies, a visceral sense of setting, and a muscular plot, Jones leaves readers ready for the rest of the trilogy.

Rowling, J. K.
  ⇨ *Harry Potter and the Order of the Phoenix.* <u>Harry Potter series</u>. 2003. Arthur A. Levine, ISBN: 0439358078, 870p. `YA`.
    Here's the biggest doorstop (so far) of the series. Yes, Rowling probably could benefit from tighter editing, but the charm of this series comes from magical details and character interactions, not plotting. The pages go by so quickly that you won't notice how many you are reading.

Hobb, Robin
  Fool's Fate. <u>The Tawny Man</u>. 2003. Bantam Spectra, ISBN: 0553582461, 928p.
    This is the longest and the last of Hobb's six books about FitzChivalry Farseer. What a journey she puts him and his friends through! Hobb gets deep inside her characters. She gets readers emotionally invested, and that's the best trick of all to make pages fly by quickly.

Lackey, Mercedes, Flint, Eric, and Freer, Dave
The Shadow of the Lion. <u>Heirs of Alexandria</u>. 2002. Baen, ISBN: 0743471474, 944p.

Collaborations often fall flat, but this big brew of Renaissance history, fantasy, and romance succeeds, and in a style more complex than that typically used by any of the authors alone. This story of two ducal heirs turned into orphaned street urchins has a sequel, *This Rough Magic.*

Martin, George R. R.
A Storm of Swords. <u>A Song of Ice and Fire</u>. 2000. Bantam Spectra, ISBN: 0553381709, 992p. AW.

Our ladder of largeness continues with the third book of *Ice and Fire.* After this tome, Martin had so much going on that he had to split the fourth book into two parts. Normally, when a novel is told from multiple viewpoints, some of the narrators are less interesting than others, but with Martin, every voice is unique, every plot line works.

Williams, Tad
To Green Angel Tower. <u>Memory, Sorrow, and Thorn</u>. 1993. DAW, ISBN: 0756402980, 1104p.

Mirror, mirror on the wall, who's the fattest of them all? Of *good* books, my vote goes to the slab that caps Williams's series. It's so big that the paperback was originally published in two parts so the binding would hold together. It seems silly to summarize this much book in a few sentences, so I'll just say that Williams finishes his trilogy on a high point.

Never Toss a Dwarf: Fantastic Fantasies with a Low Page Count

You don't have to be a bodybuilder to enjoy fantasy fiction. There are still plenty of great books that you can fit in a pocket, sneak into a textbook to read in stealth, or finish before your next birthday. Let's have a small celebration of these sparkling little gems of fantasy.

Anthony, Piers
Castle Roogna. <u>Xanth</u>. 1979. Del Rey, ISBN: 0345350480, 329p.

Why do people keep reading Anthony's <u>Xanth</u>? Because it's sure to include silly fun that is fully resolved in one short volume. This zippy entry follows a boy magician and a giant spider on a quest to enable the love of a ghostly maid and a zombie.

Briggs, Patricia
Dragon Bones. <u>Hurog series</u>. 2002. Ace, ISBN: 0441009166, 304p.

When his abusive nobleman father dies, a boy who has played dumb all his life must convince others and himself that he deserves his inheritance.

Briggs specializes in something rare: short, self-contained, character-driven fantasies.

De Lint, Charles
Medicine Road. 2004. Subterranean, ISBN: 1931081964, 206p. (hbk.)

Irish twin sisters on the road to play rockabilly tangle with two wily Native American spirits in a Charles Vess-illustrated confection that could come only from the pen of Charles de Lint.

Ford, John M.
The Last Hot Time. 2000. Tor, ISBN: 0312875789, 208p.

In Ford's near-future fantasy, elves return to Earth after seeing what a mess humans have made, replacing much of our technology with magic. A Chicago ER doctor gets caught in the battle between elf gangs in a whimsical novel that is sure to send your mind reeling.

Kurtz, Katherine
Deryni Rising. **Deryni Saga.** 1970, rev. 2004. Ace, ISBN: 0441011683, 269p. (hbk.)

Here's a well-loved book written before fantasy sagas consistently spilled over 400 pages. Kicking off the epic Deryni Saga, this book features a young king trying to consolidate his political standing and magical powers. Kurtz builds an excellent medieval setting and fills it with political and religious intrigue of the first order.

Lackey, Mercedes
Arrows of the Queen. **Valdemar.** 1987. DAW, ISBN: 0886773784, 320p. **YA**.

Perhaps better for younger readers, this tale chronicles an emotional teenager who feels isolated from the world but finds her place through empathic magic. Curious fans might try this because it is the first of the *Valdemar* series or because it is the first of the prolific Lackey's 80+ novels.

Silverberg, Robert, ed.
⇨ *Legends.* 1998. Tor, ISBN: 0765300354, 608p.
Legends II: Shadows, Gods, and Demons. 1999. Del Rey, ISBN: 0345475771, 384p.
Legends II: Dragon, Sword and King. 1999. Del Rey, ISBN: 034547578X, 416p.

Sample the genre's best with *Legends,* in which fantasy writers set novellas in the same worlds as their best-known novels. Readers get a complete 100-page story and can preview the author's style before committing to long series. The genre's best writers (Pratchett, Feist, Martin, McCaffrey, Card, and Le Guin to name a few) are represented.

Appendix 1

Suggested Trilogies and Other Series

The Magic of Threes: Fantasy's Best Trilogies

Just as eggs come in dozens, world wonders come in sevens, and tangos are for two, fantasy books come in trilogies. Don't ask why, they just do. Maybe authors take that business about a story having a beginning, middle, and end too literally. Most likely it has something to do with that paragon of modern fantasy, *The Lord of the Rings* (which really isn't a trilogy at all, but a single book broken into three pieces for publication). For this list of fantasy's great trilogies, my criteria were that the series was outstanding, with no weak books, and that publication was complete as of this writing. Here is one writer's list of fantasy's best trilogies:

Tolkien, J.R.R.
   The Lord of the Rings. 1954–1955. Houghton Mifflin, ISBN: 0618517650, 1157p.
   This is the fancy 50th anniversary omnibus edition, but many versions are available.

Berg, Carol
   Rai-Kirah
      Transformation. 2000. Roc, ISBN: 0451457951, 448p.
      Revelation. 20001. Roc, ISBN: 0451458427, 485p.
      Restoration. 2002. Roc, ISBN: 0451458907, 480p.

185

Carey, Jacqueline
Kushiel's Legacy
    Kushiel's Dart. 2001. Tor, ISBN: 0765342987, 816p.
    Kushiel's Chosen. 2002. Tor, ISBN: 0765345048, 704p.
    Kushiel's Avatar. 2003. Tor, ISBN: 0765347539, 768p.

Donaldson, Stephen R.
The First Chronicles of Thomas Covenant
    Lord Foul's Bane. 1977. Del Rey, ISBN: 0345348656, 496p.
    The Illearth War. 1977. Del Rey, ISBN: 0345348664, 544p.
    The Power that Preserves. 1977. Del Rey, ISBN: 0345348672, 512p.

Hobb, Robin
Farseer
    Assassin's Apprentice. 1995. Bantam Spectra, ISBN: 055357339X, 464p.
    Royal Assassin. 1996. Bantam Spectra, ISBN: 0553573411, 673p.
    Assassin's Quest. 1997. Bantam Spectra, ISBN: 0553565699, 757p.
Liveship Traders
    Ship of Magic. 1998. Bantam Spectra, ISBN: 0553575635, 832p.
    Mad Ship. 1999. Bantam Spectra, ISBN: 0553575643, 864p.
    Ship of Destiny. 2000. Bantam Spectra, ISBN: 0553575651, 816p.
The Tawny Man
    Fool's Errand. 2001. Bantam Spectra, ISBN: 0553582445, 688p.
    Golden Fool. 2002. Bantam Spectra, ISBN: 0553582453, 736p.
    Fool's Fate. 2003. Bantam Spectra, ISBN: 0553582461, 928p.

Marillier, Juliet
    Sevenwaters
    Daughter of the Forest. 2000. Tor, ISBN: 0765343436, 560p.
    Son of the Shadows. 2001. Tor, ISBN: 0312875290, 464p.
    Child of the Prophecy. 2002. Tor, ISBN: 0765345013, 608p.

McKillip, Patricia A.
Riddle-Master: The Complete Trilogy. 1976–1979. Ace, ISBN: 0441005969,
    592p.

Moon, Elizabeth
The Deed of Paksenarrion. 1988. Baen, ISBN: 0671721046, 1040p.

Nix, Garth
Abhorsen
    Sabriel. 1995. Eos, ISBN: 0064471837, 496p.
    Lirael. 2001. Eos, ISBN: 0060005424, 720p.
    Abhorsen. 2003. Eos, ISBN: 0060528737, 528p.

Pullman, Philip
His Dark Materials
>*The Golden Compass.* 1995. Knopf, ISBN: 0679879242, 416p. (hbk.)
>*The Subtle Knife.* 1997. Knopf, ISBN: 0679879250, 352p. (hbk.)
>*The Amber Spyglass.* 1999. Knopf, ISBN: 0679879269, 544p. (hbk.)

Let's Make the Magic Last: Series that Hold Up from First Book to Finish

Well, OK, some fantasy series are longer than three books. Only a few of these avoid serious decline as writers run out of ideas and extend series to appease loyal fans and earn a steady paycheck. Here is a list of longer series that are of dependable quality. A recommended starter book is listed, along with the current length of the series and its collective title.

Brust, Steven
Vlad Taltos. Ten books in three omnibus editions, with one forthcoming.
>*The Book of Jhereg.* 1983–1987. Ace, ISBN: 0441006159, 480p.

De Lint, Charles
Newford. Seventeen books in a shared world with shared characters; books do not have to be read in a particular order.
>*Dreams Underfoot.* 1993. Orb, ISBN: 0765306794, 416p.

Gemmell, David
Drenai Tales. The 10 books in this series share a world and some characters but need not be read in order to be enjoyed.
>*Legend.* 1984. Del Rey, ISBN: 0345379063, 345p.

Howard, Robert E.
Conan. Many stories, currently in print in three omnibus editions.
>*The Coming of Conan the Cimmerian.* 1932–1936. Del Rey, ISBN: 0345461517, 496p.

Kurtz, Katherine
Deryni. Eighteen books in several subseries.
>*Camber of Culdi.* 1976. Del Rey, ISBN: 0345347676, 336p. (out of print.)

Lackey, Mercedes
Valdemar. 25 books in six sub-series.
>*Magic's Pawn.* 1989. DAW, ISBN: 0886773520, 352p.

Le Guin, Ursula K.
  Earthsea. Six books.
    A Wizard of Earthsea. 1968. Bantam Spectra, ISBN: 0553262505, 183p.

Lewis, C. S.
  The Chronicles of Narnia. Seven books in one omnibus edition.
    The Complete Chronicles of Narnia. 1950–1956. HarperCollins, ISBN: 0060281375, 528p. (hbk.)

Martin, George R. R.
  A Song of Ice and Fire. Four books so far, with at least three to follow. I'm going to give Martin the benefit of the doubt and put him on this list before he finishes.
    A Game of Thrones. 1996. Bantam Spectra, ISBN: 0553573403, 864p.

Pratchett, Terry
  Discworld. Thirty-three books and counting. These don't need to be read in order, although you might want to read some of the subseries in sequence.
    The Color of Magic. 1983. HarperTorch, ISBN: 0061020710, 240p.

Rowling, J. K.
  Harry Potter. Six books with one to come.
    Harry Potter and the Sorcerer's Stone. 1997. Arthur A. Levine, ISBN: 0590353403, 309p. (hbk.)

Zelazny, Roger
    Chronicles of Amber. Ten books in one omnibus.
    The Great Book of Amber. 1970–1991. Eos, ISBN: 0380809060, 1264p.

Appendix 2

Award-Winning Fantasies

World Fantasy Award for Best Novel

2006	Haruki Murakami	*Kafka on the Shore*
2005	Susanna Clarke	*Jonathan Strange & Mr. Norrell*
2004	Jo Walton	*Tooth & Claw*
2003 (tie)	Graham Joyce	*The Facts of Life*
	Patricia A. McKillip	*Ombria in Shadow*
2002	Ursula K. Le Guin	*The Other Wind*
2001 (tie)	Tim Powers	*Declare*
	Sean Stewart	*Galveston*
2000	Martin Scott	*Thraxas*
1999	Louise Erdrich	*The Antelope Wife*
1998	Jeffrey Ford	*The Physiognomy*
1997	Rachel Pollack	*Godmother Night*
1996	Christopher Priest	*The Prestige*
1995	James Morrow	*Towing Jehovah*
1994	Lewis Shiner	*Glimpses*
1993	Tim Powers	*Last Call*
1992	Robert R. McCammon	*Boy's Life*

1991 (tie)	Ellen Kushner	*Thomas the Rhymer*
	James Morrow	*Only Begotten Daughter*
1990	Jack Vance	*Lyonesse: Madouc*
1989	Peter Straub	*Koko*
1988	Ken Grimwood	*Replay*
1987	Patrick Süskind	*Perfume*
1986	Dan Simmons	*Song of Kali*
1985 (tie)	Barry Hughart	*Bridge of Birds*
	Robert Holdstock	*Mythago Wood*
1984	John M. Ford	*The Dragon Waiting*
1983	Michael Shea	*Nifft the Lean*
1982	John Crowley	*Little, Big*
1981	Gene Wolfe	*The Shadow of the Torturer*
1980	Elizabeth A. Lynn	*Watchtower*
1979	Michael Moorcock	*Gloriana*
1978	Fritz Leiber	*Our Lady of Darkness*
1977	William Kotzwinkle	*Doctor Rat*
1976	Richard Matheson	*Bid Time Return*
1975	Patricia A. McKillip	*The Forgotten Beasts of Eld*

Locus Award for Fantasy Novel

2006	Neil Gaiman	*Anansi Boys*
2005	China Miéville	*Iron Council*
2004	Lois McMaster Bujold	*Paladin of Souls*
2003	China Miéville	*The Scar*
2002	Neil Gaiman	*American Gods*
2001	George R. R. Martin	*A Storm of Swords*
2000	J. K. Rowling	*Harry Potter and the Prisoner of Azkaban*
1999	George R. R. Martin	*A Clash of Kings*
1998	Tim Powers	*Earthquake Weather*
1997	George R. R. Martin	*A Game of Thrones*
1996	Orson Scott Card	*Alvin Journeyman*

1995	Michael Bishop	*Brittle Innings*
1994	Peter S. Beagle	*The Innkeeper's Song*
1993	Tim Powers	*Last Call*
1992	Sheri S. Tepper	*Beauty*
1991	Ursula K. Le Guin	*Tehanu*
1990	Orson Scott Card	*Prentice Alvin*
1989	Orson Scott Card	*Red Prophet*
1988	Orson Scott Card	*Seventh Son*
1987	Gene Wolfe	*Soldier of the Miste*
1986	Roger Zelazny	*Trumps of Doom*
1985	Robert A. Heinlein	*Job: a Comedy of Justice*
1984	Marion Zimmer Bradley	*The Mists of Avalon*
1983	Gene Wolfe	*The Sword of the Lictor*
1982	Gene Wolfe	*The Claw of the Conciliator*
1981	Robert Silverberg	*Lord Valentine's Castle*
1980	Patricia A. McKillip	*Harpist in the Wind*
1979	J.R.R. Tolkien	*The Silmarillion*

Mythopoeic Award Winners—Adult Novel

2006	Neil Gaiman	*Anansi Boys*
2005	Susanna Clarke	*Jonathan Strange & Mr. Norrell*
2004	Robin McKinley	*Sunshine*
2003	Patricia A. McKillip	*Ombria in Shadow*
2002	Lois McMaster Bujold	*The Curse of Chalion*
2001	Midori Snyder	*The Innamorati*
2000	Peter S. Beagle	*Tamsin*
1999	Neil Gaiman and Charles Vess	*Stardust*
1998	A. S. Byatt	*The Djinn in the Nightingale's Eye*
1997	Terri Windling	*The Wood Wife*
1996	Elizabeth Hand	*Walking the Moon*
1995	Patricia A. McKillip	*Something Rich and Strange*

1994	Delia Sherman	*The Porcelain Dove*
1993	Jane Yolen	*Briar Rose*
1992	Eleanor Arnason	*A Woman of the Iron People*

Mythopoeic Award Winners—Children's Literature

2006	Jonathan Stroud	<u>The Bartimaeus Trilogy</u>
2005	Terry Pratchett	*A Hat Full of Sky*
2004	Clare B. Dunkle	*The Hollow Kingdom*
2003	Michael Chabon	*Summerland*
2002	Peter Dickinson	*The Ropemaker*
2001	Dia Calhoun	*Aria of the Sea*
2000	Franny Billingsley	*The Folk Keeper*
1999	Diana Wynne Jones	*Dark Lord of Derkholm*
1998	Jane Yolen	<u>Young Merlin trilogy</u>
1996	Diana Wynne Jones	*The Crown of Dalemark*
1995	Patrice Kindl	*Owl in Love*
1994	Suzy McKee Charnas	*The Kingdom of Kevin Malone*
1993	Debra Doyle and James D. Macdonald	*Knight's Wyrd*
1992	Salman Rushdie	*Haroun and the Sea of Stories*

Fantasy Novels that Won the Hugo Award

2005	Susanna Clarke	*Jonathan Strange & Mr. Norrell*
2004	Lois McMaster Bujold	*Paladin of Souls*
2002	Neil Gaiman	*American Gods*
2001	J. K. Rowling	*Harry Potter and the Goblet of Fire*

Fantasy Novels that Won the Nebula Award

2005	Lois McMaster Bujold	*Paladin of Souls*
2003	Neil Gaiman	*American Gods*
1991	Ursula K. Le Guin	*Tehanu*
1988	Pat Murphy	*The Falling Woman*
1982	Gene Wolfe	*The Claw of the Conciliator*

Index